D1357152

* 000103106 *

Crime, the Media and the Law

Wiley Series in

The Psychology of Crime, Policing and Law

Series Editors

Graham Davies
University of Leicester, UK

and

Clive Hollin
University of Leicester, UK

The Psychology of Interrogations
Confessions and Testimony
Gisli Gudjonsson

Children as Witnesses
Edited by Helen Dent and Rhona Flin

Paedophiles and Sexual Offences against Children
Dennis Howitt

Psychology and Policing in a Changing World
Peter B. Ainsworth

Offender Profiling: Theory, Research and Practice
Edited by Janet L. Jackson and Debra A. Bekerian

Crime, the Media and the Law
Dennis Howitt

Crime, the Media and the Law

Dennis Howitt
Loughborough University, UK

JOHN WILEY & SONS

Chichester · New York · Weinheim · Brisbane · Singapore · Toronto

Other Wiley Editorial Offices

John Wiley & Sons, Inc., 605 Third Avenue,
New York, NY 10158-0012, USA

WILEY-VCH Verlag GmbH,
Pappelallee 3, D-69469 Weinheim, Germany

Jacaranda Wiley Ltd, 33 Park Road, Milton,
Queensland 4064, Australia

John Wiley & Sons (Asia) Pte Ltd, 2 Clementi Loop #02-01,
Jin Xing Distripark, Singapore 129809

John Wiley & Sons (Canada) Ltd, 22 Worcester Road,
Rexdale, Ontario M9W 1L1, Canada

Library of Congress Cataloging-in-Publication Data

Howitt, Dennis.
    Crime, the media, and the law/Dennis Howitt
        p.   cm.—(Wiley series in the psychology of crime, policing, and law)
    Includes bibliographical references (p.   ) and index.
    ISBN 0-471-96905-2—ISBN 0-471-97834-5 (pbk.)
    1. Mass media and crime.   2. Mass media and criminal justice.
    I. Title. II. Series: Wiley series in psychology of crime, policing, and law.
    P96.C74H68 1998
    364—DC21   CIP   97-38901

British Library Cataloguing in Publication Data

A catalogue record for this book is available from the British Library

ISBN 0-471-96905-2 (cased)
ISBN 0-471-97834-5 (paper)

Typeset in 10/12pt Century Schoolbook by Vision Typesetting, Manchester
Printed and bound in Great Britain by Bookcraft (Bath) Ltd, Midsomer Norton,
Somerset
This book is printed on acid-free paper responsibly manufactured from sustainable
forestry, for which at least two trees are planted for each one used for paper production.

Contents

About the Author

Dennis Howitt is Senior Lecturer at Loughborough University. His books include: *Mass Media Violence and Society* (Elek Science, 1975); *Mass Media and Social Problems* (Pergamon, 1982); *Social Psychology: Conflicts and Continuities* (Open University, 1989); *A Measure of Uncertainty* (John Libbey, 1989); *Concerning Psychology: Psychology Applied to Social Issues* (Open University, 1991); *Child Abuse Errors* (Rutgers/Harvester Wheatsheaf, 1992); *The Racism of Psychology: Time for Change* (Harvester Wheatsheaf, 1994); *Paedophiles and Sexual Offences Against Children* (Wiley, 1995); *A Guide to Computing Statistics with SPSS for Windows* (Prentice Hall, 1997); and *An Introduction to Statistics for Psychology: A Complete Guide for Students* (Prentice Hall, 1977). He wrote, with Guy Cumberbatch, the Home Office commissioned report *Pornography: Impacts and Influences* (1990). His research interests include violence, the media, psychology and the law, drugs, loneliness, and racism, amongst other work. He is a Fellow of the British Psychological Society and a Chartered Psychologist.

Series Preface

The Wiley Series on the Psychology of Crime, Policing and Law publishes concise and integrative reviews on important areas of contemporary research. However, the purpose of the Series is not just to present research findings and critiques in a clear and readable form, but also to bring out their implications for both policy and practice. In this way, it is hoped that the Series will be useful, not only to psychologists, but to all those concerned with crime detection and prevention, policing, and the judicial process.

This latest book in the Series is, in fact, the second contribution by Dennis Howitt. In his first book in the Series, Dr Howitt offered a searching discussion of the sensitive topic of sexual offences against children. One of Dr Howitt's strengths as both an author and an academic are that he is willing to ask difficult questions of complex areas, sometimes challenging the orthodox view. As might have been predicted, Dr Howitt's book received a range of reviews: some reviewers applauded its willingness to ask hard questions, other reviewers were clearly uncomfortable with the text.

In this book Dr Howitt moves to another area altogether, the interplay between crime and the media. In taking on this topic Dr Howitt is, indeed, returning to an area in which he previously made a significant contribution with a much cited report, written with Guy Cumberbatch, on the topic of mass media and violence.

In this book Dr Howitt explores a full range of crimes and their portrayal in the media, marshalling the research literature as the issues unfold. Across areas such as pornography, violent crime, racial motivated crime, and drugs, the text explores the complex interaction between the media, the crimes, and public understanding and reaction. If he remains true to form, this book will please some reviewers and, to put it mildly, irritate others. Whatever stance one takes, it will be difficult to deny that Dr Howitt will have asked the difficult questions. We believe that one of the functions of this Series should be about asking hard questions: for this reason alone, and there are many others, Dr Howitt's book is welcomed as an addition to the Wiley Series in the Psychology of Crime, Policing and Law.

Finally, this is my last editorial contribution to this Series. I wish my replacement well as I move on to new projects.

CLIVE HOLLIN
University of Leicester

Preface

A book on crime, media and the law may seem like a gimmick, frippery with little consequence. There are surely greater issues to be addressed concerning the criminal justice system. We are all aware that the mass media have been blamed for the woes of crime, violence and delinquency with greater intensity than substance. The point of this book is to test the extent to which the serious study of the media needs to be incorporated into our understanding of crime and the criminal justice system. It turns out that while the media may be researched as social institutions in their own right, the media are fully understood as part of a more complex interplay with government, police, courts, pressure group politics and public opinion, much as any mature appreciation of crime itself would entail. Whatever else, the media in modern society provide imagery and information about crime which constitute a key resource for public opinion. This is not a static matter but a complex process in which the media interact dynamically with the other major institutions to create the agenda of crime issues and help shape the public's understanding of crime. The audience for the media, similarly, do not simply learn crime messages, they create their own understanding of crime realities which are often distinctly different from those apparent in the media.

Part of the concern about the mass media is the fear that crime itself is influenced directly and adversely by the contents of the television, movies, newspapers and other media. Nowadays, researchers generally eschew the hope of finding simple, direct causes of crime. Nevertheless, research into the possible criminogenic effect of media has provided a focus for those who hope that crime problems can be solved by crackdowns on violent videos, movies and pornography. This stretches far beyond the issue of validity of such claims, into the network of interrelationships between the media, politicians and pressure groups, such that fear of media effects are fuelled by the media themselves. Research is implicated in this complex political process and cannot be ignored in any evaluation of the debate. Serious study of crime, media and the law cannot afford to ignore addressing to what extent this view can be sustained by the research on the direct effects of media on crime.

The origins of this book were in the desire to establish the study of media and criminal–legal processes as a serious and significant enterprise. There are numerous books and although the study of media and crime has a long history in psychological and social scientific research, it has often been trivialized by populist accounts and research which has only passing relevance for the serious issue of crime itself. For that reason, research on real crime, real criminals and real media forms the mainstay of this study of crime, media and the law. This does not lead to a dry and turgid focus but to a much more dynamic and integrated sub-discipline in which psychology plays a leading part, as it always has done in the study of media.

Acknowledgement

I am most grateful to Celia Kitzinger for her valued advice and suggestions.

Dennis Howitt

CHAPTER 1

Linking Media and Crime

'The Media. It sounds like a convention of spiritualists.' (Tom Stoppard, 1978, *Night and Day*)

Crime represents society as it wishes not to be, and so is crucial to our understanding of society. Not surprisingly, then, ever since improved transport and cheap newsprint in the nineteenth century led to truly *mass* media (Boyce et al., 1978; Schudson, 1978), crime has been an extensive feature of all mass media of entertainment. From then on, the influence of newspapers, cinema, radio, television, comic books, video and video-games has been decried (Petley, 1997), as had that of plays in even earlier times (Cumberbatch, 1994); moral bankruptcy or worse being among the more optimistic predictions. The media are held to chip away at honest, decent and traditional values, leaving many to the temptations of crime, itself evidence of a general drift into social decay. Whether or not there was ever a golden age, largely free from crime, is a moot point; nevertheless, the fervid alarmist consensus has seen society worsening under the impact of the media. Fear of the effects of the media has been endemic among those who fear social change; politicians, of all sorts, believe that the media influence the public powerfully, competing with moral entrepreneurs for the minds of people. The broking of ideas about the causes of crime is part of the stuff of such politics. Crime, politics, media and public opinion and research intertwine in a complex web of mutual influence. Unravelling the elements of this is a major task which calls for a careful appraisal of the media's social role.

ROOTS OF CONCERN

Each new medium of mass communication has been greeted with fresh concern (Cumberbatch, 1994). Popular entertainment (music, music hall and the like) has rarely been seen as a force for good (e.g. Friedlander, 1996). Books were and are persecuted, banned and burnt (Jackson, 1932) with a regularity which has nothing to do with the findings of media research. Nineteenth century 'penny dreadfuls' were associated with youthful thieving (Murdock, 1997). The cinema was scrutinized for the harm it was doing as soon as it was an established commercial success. Social workers, well-meaning amateurs during the nineteenth century, became increasingly organized and professional during the early part òf the twentieth century (Howitt, 1992). Cinema's popularity, especially among children and the working class, attracted the attention of these new professionals as early as 1909. The social effects of the cinema thus held potential for professionals who wished to improve the social condition of the poor—and their own professional status. Leading social workers visited movie houses, estimating audience sizes and other things, which resulted in familiar speculations about the influence of movies on the morals of young people. According to Jowett, Jarvie and Fuller (1996), such commentaries were 'the first important observations about the movies and their influence' (p. 25). A seminal work on delinquency, William Healy's *The Individual Delinquent* (1915), included case studies which purportedly showed the adverse influence of the movies on delinquency.

Psychology, sociology, criminology and cultural and media studies all contribute distinctive perspectives to the understanding of the media–crime relationship. Each discipline contributes its own unique set of values which influence the sorts of knowledge which are valued and what is dismissed as largely worthless (Howitt, 1991; Kimble, 1984). The professional values of psychology, for example, include the following features which have greatly affected the ways in which psychologists have studied crime and the mass media:

- By their training, psychologists are rendered 'objective' and minimally subject to values or ideology in their professional work. This may lead to a neglect of the ideological biases in interpretations of research findings, for example.
- The quantitative measures used by psychologists are 'real' rather than being social constructions. This leads to a failure to question the actual meaning of whatever is being measured.
- People are vulnerable to 'variables' which make them 'do' things. This leads to a disregard of some of the most interesting questions about the role of the media in relation to crime.

Most of the above have been regularly criticized by radical psychologists and others (Kline, 1988; Parker, 1989; Reason and Rowan, 1981; Sarason, 1981; Williams, 1988). Traditionally, psychologists have valued highly research examining cause-and-effect sequences, especially as far as they can be identified through the use of controlled laboratory experiments. In contrast, sociologists have generally found such psychological knowledge flawed because it decontextualizes complex social phenomena. From this viewpoint, much psychological research is a facile and crude analogue of how the media operates in modern society (Vine, 1997). Even a cursory study of mass media research reveals several tensions between such different disciplinary value systems. The media–crime question, because it forces disciplines closer together, encourages somewhat heated interdisciplinary debates and a rich diversity of approaches. The range of questions about crime and the media stressed by different disciplines have included:

- The nature of the media's coverage of both fictitious and real-life crime.
- Influences of media content on the public's conceptions of crime, fear of crime and beliefs about what should be done about crime.
- The role of the media in determining the activities of key personnel in the criminal justice system, such as the way in which crime news is managed by the police in order to create a positive image of their work.
- Prejudicial outcomes of media coverage of crime on justice for alleged offenders.
- The role of the media as a cause of crime.
- The part the media can play in crime prevention.

Just two topics dominate the field of crime and the media—sexual crimes and violent crimes. This is substantially due to external political influences on research (Canter and Strickland, 1975; Rowland, 1983). The economics of research are such that research monies tied to specific topics are very attractive to researchers. Government and media institutions both contribute funding for media research. Some research goes where the money is—that is the point of the system. In the USA, the major player in virtually all forms of research world-wide, several major political initiatives since the 1960s and earlier have addressed sex and violence in the media (e.g. Baker and Ball, 1969; Commission on Obscenity and Pornography, 1970; Surgeon General's Scientific Advisory Committee on Television and Social Behaviour, 1972; US Attorney General's Commission on Pornography, 1986). Few other psychological or social scientific research issues have attracted quite so much public attention, although sexual violence or violent sex are particularly heady and potent combinations.

Little relationship exists between the crimes which get researched and the relative numbers of victims they affect. Property crimes dwarf practically every other form of crime, according to police and government statistics (Office for National Statistics, 1997; US Department of Commerce, Economics and Statistics, Bureau of the Census, 1996); far more victims are involved than in any other type of crime. Research into the relationship between the mass media and property crimes such as theft, auto-theft and burglary is sparse; they also tend to be topics somewhat under-represented in complaints about the media, compared with sex and violence. Speculative explanations of this are possible. Crime against property is difficult to attribute to the media in market economies which, by their nature, are about consumption; the promotion of consumerism is a major function of the mass media. It is less problematic to voice concerns that violent and sexual imagery in the media encourage crime against people. Similarly, it is more convenient to blame individuals, parents and families for the break-down of social order; holding capitalism responsible would be a more intractable allegation. Whatever the explanation, an audit of media—crime research will reveal serious excesses and omissions. For example, middle-class property crimes such as fraud are also disregarded in the debate about media effects on crime.

Of course, any account of the media and crime has an excessively wide brief to consider. Crime ranges from computer hacking to cannibalism, with infanticide, espionage, extortion, illegal immigration, avoiding paying a bill in a restaurant, counterfeiting designer jeans and many others somewhere in between. The problem of unevenness of our knowledge about the media and crime is not eased by this.

THE SILENT DISCIPLINE

Until quite recently, media–crime links have been of rather restricted, and very occasional, concern among criminologists. This is superficially a curious state of affairs and difficult to understand. The mystery lessens when the main interests of modern criminology are considered; why individuals become criminal is not a prime interest of modern criminologists. Criminological research into the media's role in making criminals has been rare (Cumberbatch and Howitt, 1989; Howitt and Cumberbatch, 1975) and this situation has only changed slightly in recent years. Criminologists may be correct to take the view that the origins of crime are primarily in the social structure rather than in media images. One important criminologist argues that there are three major types of modern criminology (Hudson, 1993), which she lists as:

- *Administrative criminology*, which concentrates on issues associated with criminal justice policy. One of its most important aims is to contribute to the work of professionals involved in the administration of the criminal justice system. Issues and concerns raised by these professionals form the main impetus to research. Much of this sort of criminology is financed directly by government or offices of the criminal justice system. The causes of criminality are unimportant compared to issues like sentencing policy.

- *Radical criminology*, which seeks to demonstrate the 'true' nature of the crime problem. Within a capitalist social system, for example, crime issues can only be understood if social class is part of the perspective. The marginalization from the economy of swathes of people as a result of market forces is a typical concern of radical criminology.
- *Critical criminology*, which aims to identify the 'true' nature of the state and its exercise of power. While this approach shares a lot with radical criminology, it parts company in important ways. Hudson (1993) mentions 'black muggers' as a crucial example of an issue at the root of critical criminology. Essentially, the concept of 'black muggers' may be seen as an ideologically motivated construction. As such, it seems to reflect the needs of the state more than any objective wave of crime perpetrated by black people. The state may have an interest in promoting the image of 'black muggers'. For example, the fear of black crime might be used to justify all sorts of state actions against black people and may also homogenize the views of the vast majority of the population against immigration. From this perspective, crime is merely part of the wider political agenda.

Although a smattering of the radical and critical criminologists have actively researched and theorized about the media over the years, straightforward cause-and-effect influences have not featured in their writings. Criminals and crime are not taken as problems in their own right; they cannot be isolated from the larger social setting.

There is a fourth type of criminology, *mainstream criminology*, which Hudson (1993) suggests is a rather misleading term. The name should not be taken to imply that it is either the most influential or the most common sort of criminology. Instead, mainstream criminology is that which follows the mainstream of applied social science, which is and was dominated by a positivistic-empiricist orientation (Hagan, 1985). Mainstream criminology:

> '... can be identified primarily by an absence of concern with the role of the state in producing crime, an absence of concern with the part played by social reactions in producing criminal identities, an absence of any appreciation of crime and criminal justice as contingent outcomes of social-political configurations. In mainstream criminology there is no deconstruction of definitions of crime and no fundamental challenge to state punishment strategies of practices: its concern is to assist state correctional policies by providing information about criminals which will facilitate fine-tuning of penal practices.' (Hudson, 1993, p. 3)

These are much the same epithets that have been used against other research which explores the direct effects of the media on crime (Murdock, 1997; Rowland, 1997; Vine, 1997). The criticisms essentially question whether the causes of crime, violence and sexual assault can be identified through empirical methods which may involve little or no theoretical input. While it is easy to accept that much modern research into media–crime relationships harks back to the positivist traditions of pre-war psychology and social science, some good came out of this. Probably the most positivist of all criminological traditions is that of criminal statistics, such as those of crimes known to the police. Despite many critiques little short of damning, such data has been the bedrock of a sizeable amount of media research, especially in relation to violent and sexual crimes against the person (Chapters 5–8).

In the recent history of media research, some criminologists have begun to consider important aspects of the media–crime equation. There is a strong influence of sociology on their thinking, especially the perspective which views media as social organizations. This forces us to regard media as manufactured products rather than crystal-clear mirrors on society (Cohen and Young, 1973). Media organizations must be seen as part of a wider network of interrelating and interdependent organizations and institutions, such as the police, courts, pressure groups and government (Negrine, 1989). Construed in this way, it becomes easy to see that the roles of editors, journalists, producers and other media personnel are much more actively constructive than sometimes they themselves publicly allow. More than anything, research based on this perspective has amply demonstrated the social nature of news. In this sense, the media and the contents of the media are political. Crime and justice news have regularly featured in this perspective (e.g. Cohen and Young, 1973; Surrette, 1992). Barak (1994) coined the term 'newsmaking criminologists' to describe such researchers:

'. . . newsmaking criminologists distinguish themselves from those weakly founded condemnatory judgements of media pundits and others because they ground their analyses and critiques on scientific assessments. As students of the mass media, social construction and criminal history, newsmaking criminologists appreciate that some trends have changed in the election and presentation of newsworthy criminality over the past 150 years, such as the tendency to define criminals as outside the community. However, other trends have remained constant, such as the appeal of and to sensationalist crime coverage. Newsmaking criminologists ask questions about how the inherent selectivity, summation and simplification of news production influences the context of what becomes newsworthy crime and deviance. They ask questions about the relationship between changes in media biases and changes in the wider social order. They also ask questions about the various stereotypical profiles that are used to construct images of criminals and victims.' (Barak, 1994, pp. xi–xii)

MODELS OF THE MEDIA

While there are numerous theoretical and conceptual approaches to the understanding of the audience for the mass media (McQuail, 1987), three main models of the media are basic to the issue of media and crime; these are the *effects, uses-and-gratifications* and *cultural ratification* models. They have different intellectual and historical roots in mass media research (Ang, 1996). Each has a distinctive approach to how the relationship between the media and the audience is construed and, by implication, the issue of crime and the media. Moreover, the differences in emphasis of the various contributing disciplines become clearer when we discover that they went their separate ways several decades ago. The reintegration of these separate intellectual streams is an important task for a media criminologist.

The Effects Model

Systematic research into the effects of the mass media dates from the late 1920s and early 1930s (Howitt and Cumberbatch, 1975; Murdock, 1997). This coincides with the period of initial expansion of social research in general. Among the earliest research initiatives were the Payne Fund Studies into the role of the cinema in the social behaviour of young Americans. The Payne Fund acted as politically as any other such research bodies have done since then. Jowett, Jarvie and Fuller (1996) trace the internecine battles over the meaning of the research and attempts by the Committee, itself, to give the strongest anti-media spin possible on the data their researchers had collected on movie influence. This early research included contributions from distinguished psychologists, sociologists and specialists in criminology of the time (Blumer, 1933; Blumer and Hauser, 1933; Cressey and Thrasher, 1933; Shuttleworth and May, 1933; Thurstone, 1931; Thurstone and Chave, 1929). But this was a highly political and uncomfortable initiative. The bad lessons learnt about collaborative research led to the disciplines drifting apart, to concentrate eventually on their own distinctive concerns.

This period was of great historical importance to the field of media research. It was a time of great faith in the power of the media to produce change. Whether this faith is described as optimism or pessimism depends somewhat on what these powers are assumed to be. The media, nevertheless, were seen as forces for social change. One cannot overestimate the role of then-recent history in forming this view. The nineteenth century had been a period of social turmoil in which the industrial revolution had moved people from closely-knit agrarian communities into rapidly growing cities. Revolt against the established order was evident; it was easy to see things as consequent on the actions of uncontrolled, irrational and uncoordinated mobs. The French and, later, the Russian revolutions, the growth of mass trades unions and the like were clear exemplars. The Great War, while not the first war to involve the media, showed how advertising might be used to recruit and control the mob temporarily. The emergence of cinema and radio allowed even greater freedom to communicate with the masses. Mass society theory argued that society was becoming fragmented and individualized, breaking societal and family ties which held the masses in control (Howitt, 1982).

Some of the greatest social thinkers of the early part of the twentieth century had characterized society in ways which contributed to the view that weakening social structures were leading to a fragmentation of communities. The inevitable consequence of this was a rather alarmist theory about the nature of the relationship between the media and their audiences. This theory, the effects model, understood people to be uncontrolled, irrational and uncoordinated socially, easy prey for the powerful media. At its simplest and crudest, it can be caricatured as *the golden bullet* or the *hypodermic syringe model*; the implication of these phrases being that the media act directly on the individual audience member, who is helpless to resist the communicated message. So, if one knows the message generated by the media then one can expect the audience to respond accordingly. This approach to media effects struck a resonance with some psychologists of the period. The *behaviourist* school of psychology, which dominated the discipline academically for more than half of the twentieth century, claimed that valid knowledge can only come from studying that which is directly observable, not that which was hypothesized or inferred. It was, then, a theory of knowledge which was stripped of meaning and experience; the equation was merely between a stimulus input which led to a behavioural response. Furthermore, behaviourism was a product of modernism, in which science and technology were seen as solving all problems. From this perspective, it is appropriate to analyse human behaviour into small, component parts; thus, complex human behaviours were seen as reducible to stimulus–response (SR) links. This reductionist perspective further decontextualized the psychology of the time. The founder of behaviourist psychology, John Watson, had carried out probably the first media research when he was commissioned to study the effectiveness of an anti-venereal disease film (Lashley and Watson, 1922). Since behaviourism sought to identify universal and natural laws of human behaviour; this approach is described as *positivist*. As a theory of knowledge rather than of human psychology, it is quite fairly labelled as empiricist. Research into the effects of the mass media implicitly accepted many of these principles.

One of the effects model's most representative schools in media research was associated with Hovland at Yale University in the 1950s and 1960s (Hovland, 1954; Hovland and Janis, 1953). Hovland sought to establish the principles underlying when communications affect attitudes and beliefs. Numerous studies explored the characteristics of the 'media' stimulus which led to different sorts of attitude change. For example, did scary messages make the audience succumb more (Janis and Feshbach, 1953)? This led to lively academic debates for years, as did other issues like the primacy–recency effect—whether it is best for a message to come before or after a competing, antagonistic message (Janis, 1980). Although such approaches dominated the field for a long time, it became obvious that the mass media's audience could not be studied effectively in a psychologist's laboratory free from social interaction and competing messages (Hovland, 1954). Generally speaking, since the 1960s, laboratory work relevant to mass media has concentrated on the effects of media on sex and violence.

Psychologists working in their laboratories were rewarded with many 'hits', i.e. research findings demonstrating substantial effects of communications. Researchers coming from other traditions had no such success and grew rather sceptical about the possibility of draconian media influences in real life away from the research laboratory. During the 1940s and 1950s, field researchers became increasingly perplexed that their research was failing to demonstrate any other than relatively trivial influences of the mass media on the audience. It was emerging that the messages of the media might be accepted, rejected, ignored or even reversed by readers, listeners and viewers. This led to the dawning of *the age of pessimism* about media effects among media specialists, although psychologists working in laboratories remained convinced that there were effects. Wartime research on attempts to motivate American soldiers was part of the disillusionment; even Carl Hovland's earliest research into this demonstrated the difficulties (Hovland, Lumsdaine and Sheffield, 1949).

Early research into the effects of election campaigns was a crucial part of the pessimism. The media, as threats to democracy by dint of their influence on 'the mob', ought to be powerful determinants of election results. In the USA, since presidential elections are for fixed terms, election campaigns last for several months, with extensive media coverage. Lazarsfeld and Berelson, among others, carried out 'panel studies' of elections. A 'panel' is a representative group of the electorate; it differs from a sample in that each participant is interviewed at several different points in time. This allows researchers to assess how much opinions change over time. The effects on voting patterns of the

1940 presidential campaign were studied in this way (Lazarsfeld, Berelson and Gaudet, 1948). Residents of Erie County, Ohio, were asked their voting intentions in May, preceding national conventions and intense media coverage, and at later stages in the election campaign. The overwhelming majority did not waver at all in their voting intentions. Democrats at the previous election said that they intended to vote democrat again; Republicans remained staunchly republican. Only about 5% of the electorate changed political allegiance. A later study (Berelson, Lazarsfeld and McPhee, 1954) showed that the presidential campaign of 1948 converted merely 8% of the population. This pattern was reproduced elsewhere. For instance, Butler and Stokes (1969) found as few as 2–3% of voters switching parties. If anything, political campaigns spoke to the party faithful and succeeded in keeping them faithful. Persuasive communications can persuade—but not many. (Modern election research is even more sophisticated and is more inclined to see voters as being persuaded by the media, since voting has become increasingly volatile e.g. Cantor, 1975; Conley, 1994.)

Inherent to this pessimism about the effectiveness of the media to influence people is a view of the audience. Viewers, listeners and readers constitute an *obstinate audience* which resolutely remains substantially unaffected by the media.

The Uses-and-gratifications Model

The lack of dramatic effects of the media found in field studies led Joseph Klapper to publish his book *The Effects of Mass Communication* in 1960. In this he did not argue that the media have no effects, merely that any effects were very limited. Klapper claimed that what he called the 'phenomenistic' approach offered more hope for understanding the influence of the mass media on people. For phenomenistic, read 'functionalist' or *uses-and-gratifications*. The phrase points us towards replacing the question 'What do the media do to people?' with that of 'What do people do with the media?'. Rather than ignoring the active role which readers, viewers and listeners have in relationship to the mass media, it should become central to our understanding of the interplay between the user and the medium. People actively choose, select and interpret what they see or read in the media. Uses-and-gratifications has its origins in research first published in the 1940s, which laid down a basic methodology as well as the nature of the problem (Herzog, 1944, 1954; Warner and Henry, 1948). Underlying the uses-and-gratifications approach is the idea of *function*—the purposes that the media serve in people's lives. Of course, no single and simple set of functions of the media are likely to apply to all media for all people in all circumstances. The earliest research concentrated on the gratifications which were gained from listening to American day-time serials. These major functions are described by Klapper (1960) as *emotional release* (feeling better, for example, when one's troubles are shared by characters in the series) and *school of life* (such as when people claimed, for example, that they learned how to deal with their own lives from such programmes). A classic study in the uses-and-gratifications tradition was that of Berelson (1948), who studied the role of newspapers in the daily habits of the newspaper reader. The daily newspaper served a minor but useful function; its absence because of strikes caused some disruption to readers' daily routines.

Interest in uses-and-gratifications was never intense until the idea gained greater popularity in the 1970s under the influence of Elihu Katz. The new research featured studies of British soap operas such as *The Dales* and *Coronation Street* (Blumler, Brown and McQuail, 1970). Researchers sought to develop typologies of the needs satisfied by different sorts of programmes. One example of this (Blumler, Brown and McQuail, 1970), suggested a fourfold classification of functions as:

- Diversion (e.g. escape from routine, emotional problems).
- Personal relationships (companionship and social utility).
- Personal identity (as a result of favourite media or favourite types of programmes).
- Surveillance of what is happening in the world.

Others have offered longer or shorter lists, but this version of uses-and-gratifications has been eclipsed by a more flexible approach in which the search for general typologies has declined. The uses-and-gratifications model has been effective in understanding the individual audience member's personal response to the media—how the media fit in with the general features of his/her life including his/her past experience and other media experiences (Blumler and Katz, 1974; Rosengren, Wenner and Palmgreen, 1985).

The model of the audience which characterizes this approach is that of the *active viewer*. This goes some way to explaining why so many people are seemingly uninfluenced by the media (e.g. Messenger Davies, 1989; Silverstone, 1989). However, there is nothing new in the idea since it dates back to early criticisms of the 'effects model' of mass communication:

> '... it suggests that television "does something" to children. The connotation is that television is the actor; the children acted upon... Children are sitting victims; television bites them.' (Schramm, Lyle and Parker, 1961, p. 1)

There are various possible reasons for the lack of profound media effects, many of which have some implications for the view of the audience as active participants in the mass communication process:

- Market and other forces mean that the media cannot afford to stray too far from audience interests. Usually, the media reflect the beliefs, values and politics of much of the audience.
- Many of the concerns about television are centred on issues influenced by many other factors. Television's unique contribution is, therefore, difficult to assess when we consider problems so deeply embedded in our culture as racism and sexism.
- Beliefs and attitudes are perhaps so strongly grounded in other aspects of social structure that they are resistant to the influence of the media. Research evidence suggests that people are more vulnerable when they are removed from their regular social environment.
- Perhaps the messages of the media are neither so unequivocal or clear-cut as they are claimed to be by pundits.
- People see the media world as one with few lessons for their day-to-day lives.

The three concepts of *selective exposure*, *selective perception* and *selective retention and recall* all emerged as early attempts to explain the lack of media effects. *Selective exposure* simply refers to the tendency of people to choose what media they use. They do not have to read *The Times* if they choose not to. For a time it was argued that this form of selectivity included an element of people choosing to use the media which tended to support their own point of view. Thus, a political right-wing reader will choose a right-wing newspaper. So, in a sense, people's attitudes match the content of the media they choose but not because their chosen media affected their attitudes. While there is some evidence in favour of this, it is untrue that people find ideas which conflict with their own uncomfortable to read or hear. The research evidence suggests that although there is a tendency for people to be exposed to attitudes similar to their own, this is due to factors such as social class or occupation (Freedman and Sears, 1965; Sears and Freedman, 1967). *Selective perception* refers to the process by which people see in what they read, view, or hear just what they want to perceive, i.e. the person structures the perception, rather than the perception structuring that person's thinking. There is plenty of evidence available of this (e.g. Cooper and Jahoda, 1947). The final aspect of selectivity is *selective memory*, which is claimed to be the process by which we remember what is consistent with our own views. The evidence on this is inconsistent (e.g. Greenwald and Sakumura, 1967; Smith and Jamieson, 1972).

The Cultural Ratification Model

Howitt (1982) suggested that there exists a third model of the mass media process alongside the effects and uses-and-gratifications models. This he describes as the *cultural ratification model*, which is quite unlike the other two models in significant respects. In contrast to the effects model, it implies that the media function to stabilize society, not to cause change; in contrast to the uses-and-gratifications model, it de-emphasizes the extent to which people are seen as crucial influences in the process. The basic principle of the cultural ratification model is that the media, along with many other social institutions, act as agents of political control within society. That is, the media are so allied to the power structure of the state that inevitably they serve to support and maintain power structures and dominant ideologies. In particular, the media present a world view which continually and pervasively regenerates the ideological structures required for the maintenance of existing power hierarchies. A similar idea was advocated by researchers such as Gerbner, who argue that the media serve to reinforce ideologies rather than to undermine or change them:

> 'Television. . . is an agency to maintain, stabilize and reinforce—not subvert—conventional values, beliefs and behaviours.' (Gerbner et al., 1979, p. 180)

Carey (1989) discusses essentially the same model of the role of communications as *ritual* and holds it responsible for maintenance, reparation and transformation of social reality. The effects model of communication, in contrast, is described as *transmission* and primarily concerns change.

The *cultural and media studies* tradition in media research is related to this in certain respects. A central feature of this approach is its emphasis on appreciating media imagery as an important enterprise in its own right, irrespective of any influences of this imagery on changing the audience. When cultural and media studies researchers consider the effects of the mass media, their emphasis is on understanding the wide variety of responses to the material as part of more general cultural phenomena (e.g. Gauntlett, 1997; Hill, 1997). Single monolithic 'effects' are discounted. Generally speaking, the cultural and media studies approach has little affinity with the traditional 'effects' model, with its emphasis on the individual as an individual, empiricist methods such as surveys and laboratory experiments, and neglect of the breadth of media content. An important emphasis in the cultural and media studies approach has been on the normality of the media's role in people's lives, rather than on massive and socially dangerous effects. Media use is integral to all aspects of a person's life.

One basic fact is clear—the fascination with the media and crime has been anything but ephemeral. Why should this be so? Part of the answer illustrates ideas inherent in the cultural-ratification model. One of the more imaginative explanations of the interest in media and crime is to be found in Sparks's (1995) account of the media and 'social censures', a term first used by Sumner (1990). It describes the process by which ideological categories become objectified—such as when laws are being made and enforced. For Sparks, the issue is how certain ideologies come to dominate and to count more than others. There are two ways in which the media are involved in social censures:

- Television and the other media, in their narratives and accounts, construe things in terms of a set of categories: what is virtuous, what is a vice, and what is a threat. The media bifurcate the world into good and bad, using rigid categories (Howitt, 1982). In this way the media engage in a process of censuring social activities according to simple and relatively objective rules. For Sparks, this is censure *by* the media.
- The media's narratives and accounts are profoundly moralistic in their undertones. Despite this, when television, for example, presents imagery of violent crime, these representations are regarded as reprehensible. Consequently, the medium and its messages become construed as social problems which have to be solved. Calls then follow for the stricter regulation of the media. Alongside these, it is argued that the contents of the media indicate a crisis in law and order. 'To this extent television content can be called upon as evidence in support of a censorious outlook on more general aspects of modern life.' (Sparks, 1995, p. 52). That is, this is censure *of* the media.

Such a censorious and pessimistic vision of society, then, is older than the mass media. That it pre-dates television, video and other modern media, is irrelevant to its continuing influence. The age-old anxieties underlying censorious and pessimistic thought may merely be exacerbated by the modern media but this does not reduce their impact on social thinking. Television, with its emphasis on and attention to violence, provides the 'lexicon' by which television itself can be criticized and through which it can extend as a critique of modern society:

> The fear of mass society and the fear of television go hand in hand. A particular sense of desertion attaches to the fear that the master institutions of cultural continuity and identity have, as it were, gone over to the side of modernity, of scepticism, of the heterogeneity of belief and experience. The discourse of Protestant moral conviction, whose legitimizing principles include a certainty of centrality and orthodoxy, finds itself marginal and in dissent. (Sparks, 1995, p. 56)

Social permissiveness has become increasingly accepted by the state during and since the 1950s. This change was completely contemporaneous with television's growth in saturation of homes throughout the Western world (Hall et al., 1978). Consequently, television became a major target in the attack on permissiveness itself. In this way, television can be seen as a major 'demon' of modern populist conservative fundamentalism which dominates thinking and research about the media, albeit inadvertently. The media are not merely forces for evil, they symbolize modernity. In this way, the media provide a sharp contrast to the images of social order and stability harking back to an ill-defined and indefinite historical period—the 'good old days'. The implication of this is that the harsh and constant criticism of the media's coverage of crime is itself confirmation that the media are helping to ratify cultural values. The media constantly present us with warnings of how bad things could be.

At the core of the following chapters is the belief that all of these views of the media are important and that it is fundamentally unhelpful to disregard any of them prematurely in the exploration of media and crime. Unfortunately, most of the research into the media and crime post-dates the separation of the major lines of media research. A more comprehensive understanding of the role of the media in the criminal process comes from integration rather than separation.

CHAPTER 2

Theories of Crime and the Media

'Heroes are handsome and villains are ugly.' (Udry and Eckland, 1984, p. 47)

The media's role in crime goes far beyond direct cause-and-effect influences on criminal acts. Take social policy on crime, for example, which involves the media in a variety of ways. Politicians publicize their achievements on crime by appearing on television or issuing press releases; they excuse their failures by similar means. Crime is part of politics at all levels and the role of the media is vital as a consequence. Newspapers, radio and television may, themselves, focus on rising crime in order to pressure governments. In consequence, new crimes may be defined; stalking is a good example of this. The seizure of the profits of drugs dealers is an example of new punishments for an old crime. Members of the public may be mobilized by media publicity to do something about crime. The links are many and various—social institutions, news media, policy makers, pressure groups and the public all intertwine in a pattern of mutual influence. There is:

'... a trisected chamber of reverberating effects among the media, the public and policy makers. Effects are multidirectional, prompted by the media and impacting on the media, by the public and on the public, and by manipulating policy makers as well as on responsive policy makers.' (Doppelt and Manikas, 1990, p. 134)

Nevertheless, media research has concentrated more on the criminogenic power of the media—i.e. television, newspapers and cinema as causes of crime. Such criminogenic effects may involve either direct or indirect processes:

- *Direct influences.* These reflect a straightforward effect of crime in the media on the viewer or reader. If pornography causes sexually violent crimes, then this is an example of a direct influence.
- *Indirect influences.* The media might have their effects through indirect effects of media coverage of issues other than crime. For example, the ways in which the media deal with marriage, sex,

adultery, divorce, feminist issues and lone-parent families may undermine the traditional family. The media may play a rather circuitous role in causing crime, since there is an association between divorce, lone-parenthood and social problems including crime (Bradshaw and Millar, 1991; Goode, 1992; Holmes, 1993; Kissman and Allen, 1993; McMillen, 1992; Owusu-Bempah, 1995, 1997; Roll, 1992; Wallerstein and Kelly, 1974, 1980). Similarly, the media's emphasis on wealthy lifestyles and consumerism may induce a feeling of economic deprivation in viewers and readers (Hartmann and Husband, 1974). Potentially, this may encourage the adoption of deviant means of achieving such a lifestyle.

Indirect influences have rarely been studied, presumably because of the inherent complexity of doing so. Direct effects, themselves, are far from easily investigated to everyone's satisfaction.

THE MEDIA'S CRIMINOGENIC POTENTIAL

The media's involvement with crime may thus be either relatively narrowly or somewhat broadly conceived. The public's concern about media influences on violent crime, sexual crime and delinquency merely emphasizes matters of simple direct effects to the exclusion of other roles the media may play. Complexities are disregarded, whether they involve media content, media production, media organizations or the communities and families of audience members. This contrasts somewhat with the major theories of crime, relatively few of which make such direct connections between crime and its causes. Significantly, the media are rarely mentioned in these theories despite the vast range of different approaches; they range from biological theories involving genetic and constitutional determinants, through psychological theories emphasizing personality or some form of internal psychological conflict, to sociological theories holding that subcultures and social structure are the key to crime.

    Which, if any, of these theories has any bearing on the media–crime issue? What do they suggest is the role of the media in the crime process? Theories of crime have emerged from numerous perspectives. Nevertheless, broadly speaking there is a consensus about what the important theories and concepts are. One wide-ranging overview (Shoemaker, 1996) highlights the main theories of delinquency. As with most such reviews, the media are mentioned just in passing or not at all. In other words, the implications of these theories for the media need to be teased out even though most links have to be tentative and conjectural. Although Shoemaker is a criminologist, his list of theories is not materially affected by this; other specialists from this and other disciplines generate highly similar lists (e.g. Hawkins, 1996; Vold and Bernard, 1986). The psychologist Blackburn (1993) provides a rare example of a serious account of crime which discusses the influence of the media, if only in relation to violent crime. This is very much the exception which proves the rule of media neglect.

Biological and biosocial theories suggest either that crime is inherited genetically or that criminals are constitutionally different. Once criminologists sought the signs of crime in the physiognomy of criminals (Lombroso, 1911) or in their constitutions (Sheldon, 1949). Today, few take this seriously; criminality is not perceived as a mark of Cain in the faces of the criminal classes. Such views seem as archaic as Lombroso's explanation of why women tend to be less criminal than men—women have not evolved sufficiently to throw forth degenerates of the sort which characterize male criminals! Television may make us couch-potato-shaped but Sheldon and Lombroso were not referring to that.

Such criminological sign-reading was abandoned long ago as futile, although occasionally psychologists have dipped into the same murky pool. Revisionist constitutionalists such as Eysenck (1977) are essentially biosocial in the sense that any biological propensity to crime can only manifest itself through socialization processes. Eysenck has suggested that some criminals tend to become socialized only slowly because they condition (learn) poorly; so one might speculate that extra socialization by the media might be beneficial. If viewers merely learn how to be criminal from television then the reverse would apply. Television, however, promotes overwhelmingly prosocial rather than antisocial messages (Greenberg, 1980). It is interesting to note that in his book on the antisocial effects of sex and violence in the media, Eysenck essentially abandoned his biosocial account of crime (Eysenck and Nias, 1978).

Nevertheless, there has been sporadic evidence of the effects of the media on physiology. For example, it has been claimed that the media have a direct physiological effect on the audience which leads to an increased likelihood of violence (e.g. Bryant and Zillmann, 1986; Zillmann, 1979, 1982; Zillmann and Bryant, 1986; Zillmann and Johnson, 1973). Emery and Emery (1976) suggested that television blunts the higher mental or cognitive functions. Television, then, is a dissociative medium which reduces the viewer's involvement in life. Krugman (1970) found evidence that alpha brain-wave rhythms, signs of dissociation, occur very readily when television is watched. Alpha rhythms usually occur in the absence of visual processing by the brain, that is, when one's eyes are shut and visual imagery is absent. Working through a process of habituation, television is 'a simple, constant, repetitive, and ambiguous visual stimulus which gradually closes down the nervous system' (Emery and Emery, 1976, p. 82). This produces symptoms analogous to those caused by physical damage to parts of the brain. Whether or not this is related to crime is open to speculation; it might imply that the viewer is in no state to resist the television's antisocial messages.

Certain sorts of *psychological approaches* also lack obvious relevance to the media. Psychoanalytic theories of crime, which stress the role of internal conflict in crime, are not very pertinent to the media. Just how could the media generate psychodynamic conflict? Although it is possible that crime is the consequence of acting-out internal conflict, the media have no obvious role in generating that psychic turbulence. Similarly, the sorts of personality characteristics that may lead to crime are not obviously media-related. Emotional instability and immaturity, for example, have not generally been blamed on the media, although they have been linked to crime. Television's precocious acceleration of the social development of youngsters has been regarded as a greater problem than any effect on retarding maturation processes (Noble, 1975). Equally, it is difficult to see the role of the media in promoting another relevant psychological characteristic—egocentricity (Bromberg, 1953). Egocentricity is the lack of ability to see the world from the point of view of anyone but oneself. Most of the concern about television and the other media centres on their role as a 'window on the world', which is not easily equated with egocentrism. On the other hand, one might have some sympathy with the comments of Snyder (1995) who believes that personality and intellectual limitations make youngsters more responsive to any media influence:

'Children and adolescents with limited ability to think in the abstract may come away with the wrong message. Thus, in sum, when the media become the message, movies may indeed play an important role in shaping the future of our youth.' (p. 336)

In contrast, some theories of crime have much more resonance with what is known from media research and theory. *Rational choice theory* (Jeffery, 1976) assumes that crime is a rational process in which the likely gains and losses from illegal activities are evaluated. The media, in this context, provide a great deal of information about the gains and costs associated with crime. This may be flawed and misinformative, nevertheless it could be incorporated into any rational decision. Thus, there is information to be gleaned from the media about, for example, the likelihood of arrest for a crime, the sentences given and the social status which can be gained from having wealth or expensive cars. Before assuming that the media have an adverse influence on this, note that the media actually over-emphasize the chances of being caught for a crime (see Chapter 3). In this sense, the media present crime as a bad option.

Social disorganization and anomie theories regard crime as the result of a breakdown of community controls and ties. The media may have a role in this. For example, the media are clearly an essential part of the modernization process. They disseminate information about changes in social values and promote modern, individualistic value systems. This is clearly antagonistic to the traditional sense of community. Crime news may encourage fear and suspicion within the community, which isolates people socially (see Chapter 4). Furthermore, the media portray individuality as a virtue, as when the lone gunslinger rides away from town to pursue his lonely and isolated quest for individual justice. At the same time, the media may actively promote a sense of community, as in community broadcasting. *Control theories* assume that attachment to conventional social beliefs and social institutions insulate individuals from crime. Researchers hold that often the media serve to reinforce conventional beliefs and, indeed, may be at least as effective at promoting positive and good behaviour as teaching violence and aggression (Chapter 14).

Social class subcultures are involved in some crime (Miller, 1958). Certain youngsters, primarily identified by their class background in such theories, may identify themselves and others as a distinctive subculture, possibly associated with particular patterns of media use or a distinctive style of music. The famous 'Mods' and 'Rockers' of 1960s media-criminology each had very different musical styles associated with them (Cohen, 1972, 1980). 1950s Rock 'n' Roll was blamed for delinquency; more recent styles of music have been held reponsible for drug use and related crime. It has been suggested that cinemas serve as a focus for some youth subcultures—sometimes they may simply be a meeting place for disaffected youngsters. In this context, *interpersonal and situational explanations* of crime impinge on such a subcultural view; the concept of differential association with criminals is particularly relevant (Cloward and Ohlin, 1961). Underlying this is the view that criminality is learnt and encouraged by mixing with bad apples. The more a youngster, for example, is attracted to popular cultural styles which are also attractive to delinquents, the more likely he/she will associate with crime-prone individuals. This may be further exacerbated by processes identified by *labelling theory*—labelling people as deviant increases the likelihood that they will be forced into more deviant behaviour, possibly through a process of identity development (Lemert, 1967). There is plenty of evidence that the media create dichotomies of good and evil. This applies to a range of criminal activities which, without media reinforcement, might not have resulted in such a negative response from the public. Drug-takers of all sorts, for instance, are labelled as sick or addicts by the media, which may help determine the response of the police to them, for example (see Chapter 12).

THEORIES OF CRIMINAL VIOLENCE

Media research tends to be empirically rather than theoretically based. This is especially so when the effects of the research are considered, although some media researchers speculate about why the media may affect violent crime. Characteristically, most writers on the effects of media violence neglect general theories of violent crime although they may incorporate rather specific theoretical speculations into their writings. So it is relatively unusual to find general theories of violence being discussed by media violence researchers. One exception to this is Lefkowitz et al. (1977), who provide a slightly different list of relevant theories from those of Shoemaker, Blackburn and others, partly because they restrict themselves more in scope. As will be seen in Chapter 5, Lefkowitz et al. have contributed numerous books and research papers to the research literature on media influences on violence in society. Their research has been a dominant feature of the debate during four different decades so far. Few are as well placed to identify the key theoretical concepts. Once again, it is difficult to see the pertinence of the media to some of the theories of violence but it is important to look for any possible implications there may be. Lefkowitz et al.'s list was:

- *Cerebral mechanisms.* We have already seen some faltering attempts by researchers to show that television, in particular, has effects on the brain. However, attention to the issue has been scant, partly because of the difficulties of relating such effects to complex social behaviours such as crime and violence. Although it is a banal assumption that the media affect the brain, the problem is identifying distinctive influences of the media in relation to crime.
- *Genetic explanations.* Lynn, Hampson and Agahi (1989) is a rare recent example of researchers employing genetic considerations in research on the effects of media violence. However, Lefkowitz et al. mentioned the once popular but now defunct XYY theory of violent crime. This is based on the idea is that the Y-chromosome determines maleness, which has conventionally been associated with aggression and violence. If a man has a XYY-chromosome pattern, then he possesses 'two doses' of the chromosome that leads to aggression. However, it is not actually related to criminality. In short,

Lefkowitz et al.'s example has nothing obviously relevant to the media.

- *Hormones and aggression.* While it is known that levels of male hormones may be linked to aggressiveness in male animals, this is far from clear for human males. There is very little research on the effects of the media which affect hormone production, so we may ignore such explanations. Furthermore, the evidence that the media affect both females and males undermines even a more complex explanation, which would suggest that those with high levels of hormones are more susceptible to media influences.

- *Frustration and aggression.* This is the classic, if somewhat discredited, psychological theory of aggression. It suggests that aggression is the direct consequence of psychological frustration (Dollard et al., 1939). Indeed, the earliest versions of the theory suggested that frustration is always the precursor of aggression! Now it is accepted that frustration is just one among many potential causes. It is difficult to see that, in general, the media lead to frustration rather than to its reduction. To the extent that the media have been construed as 'opium'-like in their effects, they might be construed as soothing frustration rather than increasing it. The rare exception to this, which mentions frustration as a part of media effects, deals with the consequences of intervening artificially in viewing, purely a methodological artefact (Feshbach and Singer, 1971).

- *Social learning theory and aggression.* This is probably the major theoretical input into the psychology of media effects. It suggests that people learn about the social world through the same mechanisms as any other learning process. So rewards and punishments can be crucial (Bandura, 1973; 1983; Bandura and Huston, 1961; Bandura, Ross and Ross, 1961, 1963a, 1963b). The concept of imitation (or modelling) was a major contribution to laboratory-based laboratory studies of media effects. Imitation is simply the ability of people to copy complex social behaviours by observing others doing things. This learning may be extremely rapid and does not depend on numerous opportunities to observe the behaviour being modelled. If the media portray crime, then the viewer may learn criminal behaviours through such observation, it is argued.

- *The cultural envelope.* Some cultures are characteristically violent which increases the likelihood that individuals will act aggressively. In some cultures, sanctions against violence are weak. Since the media are essential to modern cultures, they may contribute to the general ambience of violence; for example, they may emphasize violent solutions to problems.

Lefkowitz et al.'s list of theories of aggression is not recent. Despite that, it is significant that few fundamentally new theories of aggression have been incorporated into the writings of researchers in the field. Huesmann (1986) adds *script theory* to the list. The idea underlying script theory is that aggression is not merely a set of random responses to events but something much more organized and sequenced. Thus, we all have at our disposal a repertoire of ways to deal with situations which may or may not involve violence. For example, imagine a drink has been spilled on someone in a bar, seemingly accidentally. For some people an appropriate scenario would be to accept graciously the apology and perhaps decline an offer to pay for the cleaning of the stain; other people may have a different 'script' to deal with the situation. They may regard the incident as socially embarrassing and threaten the other person with violence or throw a drink over them. Of course, such differences in 'scripts' are likely to be socially learnt, implying that the media may be one source of this learning.

It is notable that criminologists and sociologists, when considering violent crime, employ much the same set of theories that were used to account for crime in general earlier in this chapter—such as violent delinquent subcultures and social control theory (Tedeschi and Felson, 1994).

SETTING THE CRIME AGENDA

The theories of crime discussed so far in this chapter are somewhat restricted in their foci. They overlook the political processes involved in crime and our understanding of crime. Although crime may be seen as the result of social disadvantage, for example, the processes by which crimes are defined, disregarded or denounced are ignored by these theories. This is somewhat curious, since a brief study of the media will reveal numerous interest groups pressing their views about crime. Government officials may create alarm about illicit drugs, for example; feminists have altered our understanding of crimes such as rape. Irrespective of the direct role of the media in causing crime, they are vital to the politics of crime (Downes and Morgan, 1994). Media researchers have stressed the contribution of the media to issue-creation and their role in defining the nature and extent of crime in society.

McCombs and Shaw (1972) suggested that although the media are relatively unsuccessful in making us think about issues in a certain way, they are much more effective in defining what issues we should be thinking about. The media set the agenda for public opinion by highlighting things to be considered, discussed and debated. The media may not persuade us what to think about, say, welfare fraud but they do force us to consider the issue. This elegantly simple idea of the *agenda-*

setting function of the media pushed research in new directions. It makes intuitive sense—why do we talk about paedophile registers when once marital rape was on our lips? These are controversial issues over which we may only agree to disagree.

The difficulty with the concept of agenda-setting lies in defining the media's role precisely. Is the agenda created by the media, or is it the result of press conferences, press releases, lobbying, discrete telephone calls and lunchtime meetings? The relationships involved may be complex. Take, for example, Wanta and Foote's (1994) study of the role of the media in the US President's policy agenda. The influences of George Bush's presidential statements and media coverage of his chosen issues were examined. There are several conceivable pathways:

- The media may cover the President's statements contemporaneously as news.
- The media may highlight the topics raised by the President for a period of several weeks following his pronouncement.
- The President may adopt themes being promoted by the media and present them as his policy priorities.

Media coverage of specific themes in the periods prior to, at the time of, and after the President's statements provided the basic data. Generally speaking, it was very clear that the media picked up the issues raised as priorities by the President and incorporated them into their coverage over the following few weeks. The presidential statements were not simply being reported as news as such and then immediately abandoned. This was the case with many issues but it was not so for crime. There was no lag between the presidential statements on crime and the media's response; this, as it stands, may imply that the media merely reported the president's concerns and did not take on board his agenda. Yet the media had covered crime intensely *prior* to the President putting crime on his personal agenda. Wanta and Foote suggest that this may be an example of the President responding to media concerns rather than *vice versa*. (It would be equally reasonable to suggest that the media anticipated the President's concerns; for example, they could have been deliberately leaked to the media. Alternatively, both the President and the media may have been responding to the lobbying of anti-crime pressure groups.) Later chapters contain more positive evidence of the influence of the media on setting the crime agenda.

There are other examples of the media being ineffective at setting the crime agenda. A historical example of this involves newspapers' coverage of lynching in the USA in the late 1880s–1920s (Wasserman and Stack, 1994). Just how was the crime covered by national newspapers and did this set the political agenda? The correlates of inclusion in the national media are strikingly similar to those which determine modern crime coverage. Lynchings were more likely to be reported if: (a) they were in areas with easy communications; (b) they involved rape or sexual assault or murder; and (c) there were several victims. Lynchings peaked around 1892 but then slowly declined to the 1920s. Much like modern crime stories, there was no direct relationship between the number of lynchings and their newspaper coverage, since news coverage of lynchings increased as the crime declined. Southern politicians had considerable national influence and did not favour action against lynching:

> 'While the national press in this time period did not significantly alter the southern political system by changing social conditions that might prevent such atrocities, it did sensitize the American public and political elites to the social pathology of the southern political system and its use of extra-legal means to maintain racial control. When the more dramatic social and political changes occurred in the southern political system in the 1950s and 1960s, the national political elites were more sensitized to the social pathologies of this subregion of the nation.' (Wasserman and Stack, 1994, p. 87.)

Another instance of the apparent failure of the media to lead the agenda on crime comes from a study of child abuse reporting (McDevitt, 1996). According to her, the numbers of child abuse and maltreatment stories reported in daily newspapers showed much the same pattern of change as did reports of abuse made to mandated agencies. For the 25 years studies, there was no trend for increased numbers of child abuse reports to follow news stories concerning abuse; news stories did not lead reporting by the public. McDevitt claims that changes in national policy led to both increases in news stories and child abuse reporting to agencies. While this interpretation may be correct, some caution is always appropriate regarding aggregate statistics. The lack of a statistical relationship in this case may reflect the possibility that the public are more influenced by particular spectacular news stories than aggregates of numerous news stories. For example, several authors have identified newspaper reporting of the death of the child Maria Colwell in 1973 as the beginnings of child abuse as a major social issue in Britain (Howitt, 1992: Parton, 1985).

MORAL PANICS

The way in which issues are placed on the agenda can be construed in another way. This is the idea that the media can be part of a process by which 'moral panics' are created. Care needs to be taken with the concept, since it risks being a description rather than an explanation. It refers to those circumstances in which society becomes alarmed at events occurring within its midst. Cohen (1972, 1980) studied the youth groups known as 'Mods' and 'Rockers' in Britain in the 1960s. These were warring factions, each of which had its distinctive modes of dress, music and even modes of transport. From time to time, these groups would descend upon seaside towns and cause havoc, according to the media. The media, Cohen claimed, defined the nature of the events and cast the two groups into the role of social deviants. Eventually, the argument goes, such 'deviants' begin to live up more and more to their image:

> 'An initial act of deviance, or normative diversity (for example, in dress) is defined as being worthy of attention and is responded to punitively. The deviant or group of deviants is segregated or isolated and this operates to alienate them from conventional society. They perceive themselves as more deviant, group themselves with others in a similar position, and this leads to more deviance. This, in turn, exposes the group to further punitive sanctions and other forceful action by the conformists—and the system starts going around again.' (Cohen, 1980, p. 14)

As a consequence, the press and public began to perceive hooliganism even in the most trivial of episodes, which began to become part of an inventory of charges which could be laid against the Mods and the Rockers. The court system responded to this media-inspired panic by increasing punishments for members of these groups. The public itself became more anxious as a consequence and concerns about the threat posed by Mods and Rockers heightened. The media blamed Mods and Rockers for the low numbers of visitors to these seaside towns, apparently ignoring the fact that the weather was very bad that year. The media and public response was simply out of all proportion to the facts.

There may indeed, have been more fuss and fume than truth in these episodes, although a sudden and uncontrollable sense of alarm does seem to be involved. That may merely be a consequence of the way things appear to those of us dependent upon the media for our knowledge of such youth groups. It should not be forgotten that the 1960s was a period of national concern about young people and violent crime in particular. The Mods and Rockers may have merely epitomized the emerging youth cultures of the time when money, transport and independence began to identify a new generation of youngsters; the 'teenager' was a relatively new phenomenon. The ways in which youngsters could be framed ideologically had changed. The panic, therefore, may have been more about the shifting ideologies of the time than about specific, possibly criminal, events. There is a case for considering 'moral panics' as signalling a shift in dominant ideologies (Hall et al, 1978). If this is the case, then such panics need to be explained by reference to these ideologies, rather than left as a descriptive phrase.

There is also a danger of using the term selectively and in a value-ridden way:

> '... the way in which the term "moral panic" is used to describe official and media concern about specific crime problems suggests that it is a polemical rather than an analytic concept. It seems virtually inconceivable that concern expressed about racial attacks, rape, or police misconduct would be described as a "moral panic". This is because the term has derogatory connotations: it implies that official and media concern is *merely* a "moral panic" without substance or justification.' (Waddington, 1986, p. 258)

MEDIA AND CRIME THEORY

Although the media extensively feature fictional and non-fictional crime, the nature of the involvement of the media is not entirely predictable from theories of crime. The obvious processes by which the media might influence individuals into criminal acts seem to involve imitation or similar forms of observational learning, although the effect may be a deterrent one depending on circumstances. This notwithstanding, it seems inappropriate to disregard a multitude of possible other media influences on the public and those responsible for crime policy or its implementation. There are important issues about what gets put on the crime agendas of all of these parties. The mass media do not simply communicate criminogenic messages, they tell us about the worlds of crime, law enforcement and criminal justice. As such, they are part of creation of certain crimes as social issues, political platforms concerning crime, and the definition of who and what is deviant.

CHAPTER 3

Constructing the Image of Crime

'At the moment you begin reading this, some poor bastard three years out of journalism school is sitting at a video-display terminal in a newspaper office somewhere . . . fingers darting on a key-board. No doubt a cursor flashes through line after line of the same simple, tired equation: "A 17-year-old West Baltimore youth was shot to death yesterday in a murder that police say is related to drugs . . ." Or, perhaps: "The battered body of a 25-year-old Queens resident was found by police along the shoulder of a Long Island express-way. . ."'. (Simon, 1995, p. 35)

'Factual' crime in newspapers and on radio and television is the result of a value-ridden news selection process. Partly, the emphasis of news on drama which sensationalizes and personalizes events determines what is included. Nevertheless, what is read, heard and seen as news is something other than 'just the facts'. The media tell us about crime and then what to think about crime. News about crime is not an accumulation of individual acts, it is selected, represented and politicized in ways which extend beyond any simple conception of 'fact'. Institutional processes and journalistic practices also contribute to news-gathering and selection in ways which leave us with *partial* crime news in both senses of the word. Just what is on the agenda and who does it influence?

There is reason to believe that much non-fictional coverage of crime shares some of the production values of fictional programmes. For example, a great deal of crime coverage emphasizes the 'human interest' aspect of crime rather than its criminal-justice implications. While the thousandth burglary this year may be profoundly important in terms of the priorities of the police and criminal-justice systems in general, such an anonymous crime may not even deserve a passing reference in the media:

'Stories about individual crimes—with their characteristic portrayals of villains and victims—also have dramatic value. The dramatic potential is heightened when the victim or offender is a celebrity, when the incident is of a very serious nature, or when the circumstances of the offense are atypical. In addition, the routine crime story is a rather uncomplicated matter, and it is unnecessary for news workers to assume that readers or viewers require an extensive background in order to appreciate the story. The lack of factual complexity associated with the ordinary individual crime story generally means that it can be easily written and edited by news workers whose professional activities are consistently regulated by rigid deadlines.' (Sacco, 1995, p. 144)

Just like the horror movie, with its characteristic theme of the random victimization of hapless individuals, great dramatic value is attached to news stories involving random crime. Stranger killings attract a great deal of interest as a consequence. But as they are atypical of violent crime, such emphases can seen as misinformation—at least for those who might interpret the media literally as a window onto the real world.

REPORTING TRENDS

Worldwide, newspaper crime reporting shows remarkably consistent trends (Marsh, 1991). Countries across several continents—Europe, North America and Australasia—demonstrate striking similarities. Disproportionate emphasis is placed on rape and murder, and violent crimes against the person in general. Detailed analyses of media in specific countries also reinforce this impression. Sacco and Fair (1988) studied crime stories appearing in a Vancouver newspaper, revealing clear and recognizable trends. Of the crime stories, 80% could be classified as 'hard' news stories about specific crime incidents. Generally these stories were new; only one-third of them were follow-ups of previous reports. 'Soft' crime news, such as features, letters and editorials, made up about 20% of crime news. Crime news presented a very limited range of perspectives; those of court officials and the police dominated. Partly as a consequence of these limited sources, news stories paint a falsely optimistic picture of the rates of arrest and punishment of offenders.

'Newspapers in the United States and elsewhere provided very little, if any, information regarding the causes of crime or how to avoid victimization. This can result in increased levels of fear of victimization on the part of certain segments of society.' (Marsh, 1991, p. 76)

Given that the sources of crime news reside primarily in the criminal justice system, it is not surprising to find that news emphasizes the prosecution case and casts suspects in a bad light, although this may not be so true of crimes against women (see Chapter 9). Since numerous studies have demonstrated distortions in news media's portrayals of crime, it might be wondered whether this image is generally accepted by the public as an accurate picture of crime in the community. However, in line with a great deal of evidence to suggest that public opinion and media content are often only tentatively linked, studies of the audience show that crime news in the media and public perceptions of crime are not intimately related. In fact, the public's perceptions of crime is a bigger distortion of reality even than that of the media (Graber, 1980). Possibly, the public view the distortions of the media through yet another distorting lens. Graber, accepting that crime news is a fiction, suggested that:

> 'The public lives in a world of unreality when it comes to criminals, victims, and the criminal justice system.' (p. vii)

Her claims are based on an intensive study of *The Tribune* newspaper in Chicago and its readers. A sample of the general public was repeatedly interviewed by researchers over a period of time; questioning mainly concerned their knowledge and awareness of crime. Content analysis of the newspaper revealed that about half of news items concerned street crimes, one-sixth terrorism and one-fifth each for corruption and drug offences. Business crimes made up just about one-twentieth of crime news items. (Similar trends were found for British newspapers by Schlesinger, Tumber and Murdock, 1991).

The newspaper was not the prime source of crime information for everyone except for certain issues or topics. For example, nearly 60% of the public claimed the newspaper as the source of information about which geographical locations are dangerous because of crime; the rest mentioned word-of-mouth as their source. Less than a quarter said that they obtained their ideas about crime-fighting activities from the newspaper. It is also wrong to assume that the media coverage of crime is important to all of the public; many people have very little interest in crime news. Half of Graber's sample claimed that they gave crime news only a minimum of attention. Even where someone had read the newspaper, typically two-thirds of the crime stories within it were ignored. The average reader read only 18% of crime stories completely; much the same proportion were partially read. Some of the public have only the sparsest awareness of crime; over one-third of Graber's sample were unable to spontaneously recall even one crime incident without prompting.

Comparisons of the newspaper crime rates with rates of crimes known to the police revealed marked discrepancies for certain crimes:

1 *Over-represented crimes*: Perhaps the greatest contrast was between newspaper murder rates and real-life murder:
   - Of news stories, 26% were about murder, whereas the real-life crime figures suggested that only 0.2% were murder.

- Of newspaper crimes, 3% were rape, whereas these amounted to only 0.4% of crimes known to the police.
- Robbery was 11% of newspaper crime coverage but only 6% of police records.
- Assault was 6% of newspaper coverage but only 4% of police records.

2 *Under-represented crimes*:   Among the most under-represented were:
  - Burglary was reported in only 2% of crime news stories but made up 12% of crimes known to the police.
  - Theft was just 3% of crime news crime but 36% of crimes known to the police.
  - Car theft was 0.7% of crime news crimes but 11% of crimes known to the police.

That is, news media crime reports over-represented violent street crime, especially murder, rape and assault. Acquisitive crimes such as robbery, burglary and theft were grossly under-represented.

The image of criminals aggregated from crime stories in the newspaper showed a marked disparity with the public's beliefs about real-life criminals. The public suggested that criminals are most likely to be unemployed (53%), poor (28%) or uneducated (12%). News media criminals were more likely to be bureaucrats (30%), professionals (17%), managers (15%) or unemployed (11%). The public disagreed with newspaper perspectives which portray rich victims being preyed upon by the poor; two-thirds of victims came from the middle- and upper-income groups in the newspaper reports. The public were more likely to see the poor as engaged in a self-destructive battle with other poor people.

The profound contrast between the newspaper and its readers extended into explanations of crime. When asked to identify the major cause of crime, the public seemed to have a rather social view: 35% nominated poverty or unemployment, 15% alcohol or drugs or instability, 14% group pressure or boredom, and 13% deficiencies in home life. In contrast, explanations of crime given in the newspaper were dominated by the deficiencies of the criminal justice system (37%) which had only been mentioned by 11% of the public. Political system deficiencies amounted to 20% of newspaper explanations but were virtually disregarded by the public. Media violence was infrequently mentioned by both the newspaper (2%) and the public (3%) as a cause of crime.

Graber provides a model of the crime audience which is far removed from the passive recipient of aggregate messages from the mass media. The audience quite clearly does not act actuarially on aggregate themes extracted from the media:

'In the final analysis, the most important actors in determining the
impact of crime and justice news are the millions of individual news
recipients. While they depend on the media for the bulk of their informa-
tional raw material about current happenings, they are free to pick and
choose among news offerings. They can, and often do, ignore them in
whole or in part. They can also transform the contents to complement
their preconceived notions or to assuage their existing hopes or fears.
When it comes to image formation, they are not puppets whose strings are
pulled by the media or by the pronouncements of public officials. Rather,
they are the puppeteers who work with available resources in ways suited
to their own experiences, needs, and expectations.' (Graber, 1980, p. 115)

In a similar vein, Roberts and Grossman (1990) claim that the image of
the public as being extremely tough on crime and tough on criminals
does not correspond very well with reality as expressed through public
opinion surveys. They note what they call 'the myth of the neo-
conservative public'. So, for example, the public, when asked to give the
single, most effective way of controlling crime, generally failed to mention hanging and flogging and similar harsh retributions despite the
toughening of political attitudes towards crime of the time. Just over a
quarter mentioned harsher sentences, while under 5% wanted increases in police strength. In contrast to the 'tough on crime' rhetoric,
over 40% of the public mentioned action against unemployment as the
most important thing that could be done in the fight against crime. It is
particularly significant in this context to note a study of public perceptions of sentencing (Roberts and Doob, 1990). In this, participants read
either newspaper accounts of crimes or a summary of actual trial
documents. Of those reading the newspaper story, 63% believed that
the sentence given was too lenient, whereas only 19% of those reading
the court documents thought this. In other words, news items dealing
with the trial created the very public anxieties about sentencing which
are then used by the media to demand firmer sentencing.

The general lack of correspondence between the news media's coverage and the public's perceptions of crime has a long pedigree. In the
USA, Davies (1952) examined the consistencies between changes in
crime rates, changes in the relative amounts of coverage that newspapers gave to different types of crime, and changes in public perceptions of crime rates. Generally there was no correspondence between
public perceptions and newspaper coverage. Similarly, in Britain,
Roshier (1971, 1973) examined the relationship between the newspapers read by people to their perceptions of crime and crime rates. No
relationships were found except for the familiar belief that more crimes
are solved than actually are. Another British study found that estimates of crime rates given by readers of local newspapers were *lower* for
readers of local newspapers which gave the *most* space to crime (Croll,

1974). If this relationship is to be interpreted, the public is in a process of actively discounting media messages!

Of course, this should not cause us to reject entirely the possibility that the media shape public views of crime. What it does mean is that 'actuarial' or 'statistical' models of audience information processing work badly (Howitt, 1982). What is meant by this? The theory is that people do *not* form accurate judgements as to the amounts of different types of crime they see in the media. These judgements are not equated with real-life crime rates either; the media are not used as a window on the world of crime. Roshier (1969) showed that the public could not even accurately *estimate* the coverage given to different types of crime story by newspapers. Given this, it is hardly surprising that they are seemingly uninfluenced by these aspects of crime news content.

Another, more recent, major study of crime news found similar trends to most other studies (Chermak, 1995):

> 'The news media present a limited portrait of crime, victims, and defendants. The production of news eliminates the vast majority of crimes that occur from consideration, and those that remain are presented as they are defined by criminal justice sources and are used to entertain consumers rather than enlighten them. What gets presented about crime does benefit society in some ways. The public rarely gets media exposure to less violent crimes, even though these are the crimes people are most likely to experience. Other types of crime are less newsworthy because they lack an easily identifiable individual. Corporations charged with committing environmental crimes, for example, are rarely in the news ... The selection of certain events over others illustrates the hegemonic model of public communication, in which news organizations are spokespersons for dominant groups and their ideology ...' (p. 176)

Information about crime incidents came from the police (29%), courts (25%) and defendants (9%). Other categories of potential informants about crime were rather uncommon—victims and their acquaintances, for example. There was an asymmetry in the aspects of crime which are covered. Thus, discovery of a crime was a feature of 19% of crime news stories, arrest 15%, charge 13%, impact on victim's family 13%, verdicts 4% and sentences 7%. Different, but nevertheless significant, aspects of the criminal justice system received little or no coverage. Among matters 'ignored' were probation and release from prison. About 11% of all news stories dealt with crime; the overwhelming majority of crime was about specified crime incidents (74%). Stories about other aspects of crime were far less common. So stories about crime policy amounted to 21% of items; editorials about crime made up about 3% of items. Stories reflecting public opinion about crime were rare, as were reports of aggregate statistical data such as crime statistics. Violent crimes against the person were fairly commonly reported—far in excess of their true incidence—as other studies have found. Thus, nearly a quarter of stories concerned murder. Drugs stories comprised one in ten items. Common crimes such as robbery and burglary were little reported.

Very little was reported about the characteristics of victims other than their gender which was routinely mentioned. Information concerning their race, age, occupational and marital status was fragmentary:

> 'Serious crimes are generally more newsworthy than less serious crimes. Both young and elderly victims raise the importance of crime stories, although young and elderly defendants have a less consistent effect on newsworthiness. All elements of a crime can interact to increase how newsworthy a crime becomes; the level of newsworthiness, in turn, affects the way a particular crime story is produced.' (Chermak, 1995, p. 82)

TELEVISION IMAGERY

Much of our discussion of real-crime and the media has to dwell on newspaper coverage. The best studies, in general, have confined themselves to newspapers. Even if newspaper coverage were typical of all crime news coverage, it would not follow that all media are processed in the same way by the audience. For example, radio news tends to be regular and rolling. The same news item is repeated, with or without change, on several occasions before it is replaced. Consequently, it may be hard for a regular listener, say, casually tuned-in while getting on with other tasks, to avoid radio crime news stories. Furthermore, the lack of a single identifiable 'market' for all media, carries with it the assumption that different media are aimed at different sectors of the audience. This brings with it differences in the coverage of and emphasis on crime.

In their study of news media around Toronto, Canada, Ericson, Baranek and Chan (1991) investigated several different media. They studied radio stations, newspapers and televisions in some depth; the media were also stratified to include popular *and* quality media. Both type of medium and quality had a bearing on the crime news coverage. Television and radio gave more emphasis to violent crime as a proportion of crime news items. Violent robbery was a common feature of violence in the popular media, but largely ignored by the quality news media. Economic crimes (theft, fraud, burglary, bribery and breaches of contract) were reported more by the newspapers than by radio or television. Generally speaking, economic crime was rarely reported unless there was another newsworthy feature associated with it.

Interim data from an intensive audit of British news coverage—television, radio and newspapers—reveals that established trends in media crime coverage remain (Golding, Edwards, Howitt, Mclaughlin and MacMillan, 1997 unpublished). For all the media combined, 68% of crime stories involved crimes against the person, whereas only 9% involved property crime. Although there were some differences between the media in terms of the ratio of crimes against the person vs property crimes, the trend was not great. There were proportionately more crimes against property reported in newspapers and the least reported on radio. Given that crime is a political issue (Downes and Morgan, 1994), one might note the extent of politicians' involvement in crime news stories. Of stories concerning crime against persons, 8% mentioned politicians in some way (although not as criminals), and politicians were mentioned in 5% of crimes against property. This perhaps suggests that crimes against people have more political resonance than property crimes.

The concentration of researchers on newspaper crime is understandable given that they are the prime location for extensive news coverage of all types—newspapers are capable of handling many more stories than routine television or radio news bulletins. Violence dominates studies of television. Although there are numerous content analyses of television violence, these tend to dwell on fictional programming (Chapter 5). An exception to this trend is a study of American television 'reality shows', which investigated the extent of both visual depictions of violence and talk about violence (Whitney et al., 1997). Of course, talk about most things is a feature of much low-budget programming and so should not be ignored when seeking the widest possible picture of media coverage of crime. Whitney et al. define a reality programme as a non-fictional presentation which gives the appearance to giving a realistic account of current or historical matters. All of the police shows analysed (e.g. *America's Most Wanted* and *Real Stories of the Highway Patrol*) contained visual violence, as did 75% of documentaries and 85% of tabloid news programmes. Talk about violence without visual depictions of that violence was most frequent, not surprisingly, in talk shows such as *Oprah Winfrey, Montel Williams* and *Ricki Lake* (30%), and news and public affairs programmes (22%). Most types of reality programmes contained some talk only about violence without accompanying graphic video, with the exception of police shows.

In general, reality programmes present males as both the main perpetrators and victims of violence—just as with most forms of crime coverage. This trend was clearest for violence presented visually—90% featured men as perpetrators and 58% men as victims. Turning to talk about violence, the figures fall. Men were involved as the perpetrators in nearly 70% of instances and victims in 54% of cases. Care should be taken to distinguish overall trends from what happened in specific types of programme. Talk shows diverged greatly from the overall pattern. The *visual* perpetrators of violence in talk shows were mainly female (70%), as were 42% of victims. Furthermore, although *talk* about violence in talk shows described 42% of perpetrators as being female, over 50% of the victims talked about were female.

In reality programming, 81% of the perpetrators of violence were in the 21–44 year-old range. Their victims were also overwhelmingly in that age range (72%). Children of 12 years or younger and people of 65 years or older were rarely or never the perpetrators of violence. The 65s and over were infrequently victims of violence but children of 12 years or under were quite commonly victims (11%). Thus, reality-television may not reflect an identical image of crime-news reporting throughout each sub-genre. This is important given that we know little of the sources of people's perceptions of crimes. Cavender and Bond-Maupin (1993) suggest that reality programmes such as *America's Most Wanted* and *Unsolved Mysteries* present much the same image of crime as has been established in television crime drama. Like other media, such programmes distort the realities of crime greatly. For example, over half of the 'cases' presented in these programmes concern murder, which is a small fraction of real crime. The programmes use cinematographic techniques to present the dangers of modern urban living as graphically as possible while at the same time using conventions from regular news programmes to enhance their claims of reality:

'... crime is used to symbolize the uncertainties of modern life, that criminals are evil, abnormal people, and victims are portrayed as being vulnerable. Such tales nurture the very fears that produce urban legends.' (p. 315)

Little, if anything, is known about their impact on their audience.

THE IMAGE OF POLICING

'There is a clear disjunction between public images of the police and the reality of police work conveyed by social scientists and shared by the police. The image of *Starsky and Hutch*, *Kojak* and *Baretta* patrolling freeways and slums, outsmarting, outfighting, and outmugging dangerous criminals stands in sharp contrast to the reality of police work ... Even the investigative division of police departments is engaged in little crime-related activity. Most time is spent in routine administrative or clerical work or in attempts to locate and interviews on cases that experience has shown will never be solved.' (Christensen, Schmidt and Henderson, 1982, p. 227)

Graber (1980) noted in her Chicago study that the public rate the performance of the police very favourably compared with the rest of the criminal justice system, such as the courts and prisons. This is inexplicable in terms of the realities of police success. For Christensen, Schmidt and Henderson (1982), the favourable view of policing is partly a consequence of the police's public relations strategy. They studied a putative police sweep which was well-publicized as part of a crack-down on crime. Such sweeps employ proactive policing, which actively seeks out crime, rather than the reactive approach used to deal with routine crime complaints. Despite a great deal of publicity, the police succeeded only in arresting drunks, narcotics violators, perpetrators of lewd acts, prostitutes and felons. Although the police lauded this as a great success, virtually no mention was made of achievements in relation to 'index' offences, the eight serious crimes in American police parlance (homicide, forcible rape, robbery, aggravated assault, burglary, larceny-theft, motor vehicle theft, and arson (Clifford, 1996)). Reporting of such proactive police activity creates an image of the police as dynamic, effective and efficient investigators of crime. Such a view is not supported by the low detection rates confirmed by the crime statistics. Furthermore, there is reason to believe that there is no single overall evaluation of policing which pervades public opinion. For example, Skogan (1996) reviews evidence to suggest that trust in the police and satisfaction with their work varies over time somewhat unpredictably. Only certain aspects of policing are consensually regarded as satisfactory—'responding to accidents and medical emergencies', 'crowd control', and 'dealing with serious motoring offences'. Less satisfaction is expressed in terms of 'detection and arrest for violent crime' and 'dealing with white-collar crime'. At the very bottom of the satisfaction table was 'detecting and arresting burglars'.

Image creation in modern policing is considered by Sacco and Fair (1988) in terms of Altheide and Johnson's (1980) concept of *bureacratic propaganda*. This refers to the way organizations survive by creating an aura or appearance of legitimacy—which includes the need to show that the organization is doing the job it was created to do and that disaster would befall society but for that organization. This is not merely a policing characteristic, it has been found in a range of other organizations (Howitt, 1992), but:

> 'In the case of the police, for instance, the high level of public visibility emerges from the belief on the part of agency managers that a high public profile facilitates the accomplishments of organizational goals.' (Sacco and Fair, 1988, p. 115)

In order to demonstrate the relationship between newspaper crime and real-life crime, Sacco and Fair (1988) developed what they describe as a 'frequency ratio'. This essentially involved the ratio of a particular type of crime's occurrence in newspapers to its frequency in uniform crime reports (the criminal statistics). Thus, if murder is disproportionately emphasized in a newspaper, it obtains a large frequency ratio; if it is under-represented, then its frequency ratio dips to less than one. Homicide, rape, robbery, gambling and drug offences were over-represented, while non-violent but common offences, such as breaking-and-entering and theft, are disproportionately ignored. Irrespective of the offence involved, the press portrayed policing as a successful and effective enterprise by reporting crimes for which arrests had been made. Rape, drug offences, gambling offences and assaults all tended to be represented in the media in association with a successful arrest. The tendency was especially strong for theft and breaking-and-entering, despite their relative infrequency in newspaper crime reports. According to the researchers, this explains why the public believe that the police do a good job:

'... press imagery tends to reflect more favourably upon the police than upon other agencies of social control ... These patterns ... are the logical outcome of the particular linkages that join the institutional activities of legal control to the institutional activities of news production.' (p. 121)

Nevertheless, not everyone sees the media as so sympathetic to the police. In Britain, one psychologist, an ex-serving police officer, presents the police service very much as victims of journalism, not the managers of journalists (Ainsworth, 1995). There is doubtless truth in both points of view.

Crime news emphasis on police perspectives has wider consequences than merely portraying the police in a good light (Sacco, 1995). The police-slant dwelling on policing success reaffirms traditional approaches to law and order. Unlike, say, social workers, the police tend not regard the causes of crime in social terms; instead they attach blame to the individual offender and his/her family. More police and policing is the ideal solution to crime offered by the false media image of successful policing.

MENTAL ILLNESS AND CRIME

A dominant image of the mentally ill is that of unpredictable and bizarre violence. This seems true of both the public's views of mental illness and that portrayed by the mass media. Whether the similarity is due to media influence or because the media merely represent general social beliefs is not clear.

There is evidence that the belief that the mentally ill are violent was firmly established during the nineteenth century (Torrey, 1994). This was partly under the influence of the medical profession, which was responsible for creating concern about numerous other moral issues during that time (Howitt, 1992). For example, Dr John Gray in 1857 described 49 cases of attempted or achieved homicide among patients he had treated for serious mental illness. As reproducers of culture, not surprisingly the mass media began to associate mental illness with violence until it became a media cliché. Early movies were not immune, since the stereotype of the mentally ill as homicidal maniacs featured in *The Maniac Cook* of 1909. Modern movies such as *Psycho, Repulsion, Friday the 13th, Halloween, Nightmare on Elm Street, Silence of the Lambs* and *Single White Female* continue this tradition. Such stereotypes are not inconsequential, since they may contribute to the problems faced by mental patients when they seek housing and jobs, for example.

Traits such as dangerousness and unpredictability are common features of the representation of the mentally ill in newspapers (Day and Page, 1986) and television (Wahl and Roth, 1982). The association appears to be highly newsworthy—stories linking mental illness to crime seem to have a good likelihood of being front page news. A study of television drama showed that over two-thirds of mentally ill characters were violent. According to Levey and Howells (1994), a substantial minority of the public regard mentally ill people, especially schizophrenics, as violent and dangerous.

Mental health professionals have revised their beliefs about violence and mental illness in recent years. Changes in the care of mentally ill people, following advances in drug treatments among other things, have led to de-institutionalization. Instead of being confined to secure psychiatric hospitals, the mentally ill have increasingly received community-based care. Early studies of criminal violence in the mentally ill have to be considered in this light, as there is less of a risk to the public when mentally ill people are isolated from the community in institutions. Thus, early studies of violence in the mentally ill suggested that they had no particular propensity to violence, but this may be regarded as an artefact of their institutionalization (Torrey, 1994). More recent evidence affects the earlier view:

> 'The studies ... verify the fact that the vast majority of individuals with serious mental illness are not violent and are not more dangerous than individuals in the general population. A subgroup of such individuals, however, are more dangerous, and the data suggest that this problem is increasing.' (Torrey, 1994, p. 658)

Similar points are made in Levey and Howells' (1994) review. They conclude that people suffering from schizophrenia are relatively more likely to be violent than the average person, but that relatively few people are schizophrenic. So people are at much greater risk of violence perpetrated by substance abusers and working-class males, since these groups are much more common in the community. Beck (1994) claims that the links between schizophrenia and violence are particularly well-established irrespective of gender. Nevertheless, he agrees with other reviewers who suggest that mental illness is rarely associated with criminal violence in absolute terms. Most violence is perpetrated by those without psychiatric diagnoses.

Despite its historic roots, it is not easy to explain the public's widely-held beliefs about people with schizophrenia. One possibility is that they may be over-represented in the more extreme and bizarre forms of violence, as in matricide. Some widely publicized cases in which the mental state of the offender is in question may reinforce this view. Little media coverage of schizophrenia fails to support public perceptions. Levey and Howells (1994) see this as being largely a matter of the media serving to reinforce public opinion rather than forming public opinion in the first place, although they add:

'Media portrayals of violence and mental illness are likely to promote a perceived correlation between schizophrenia and violence because the media considerably over-report instances of violent crime relative to its true incidence in the criminal statistics . . .' (p. 319)

A number of studies have demonstrated that media documentaries can have a positive impact on beliefs about mental illness (e.g. Belson, 1967). In contrast, Domino (1983) suggested that the motion picture *One Flew Over the Cuckoo's Nest* led to less positive attitudes compared to a control group which had not seen the film. Wahl and Lefkowitz (1989) chose a TV-movie *Murder: By Reason of Insanity* for study. This was based on a real-life incident in which a man on day-release from a psychiatric hospital killed his wife. The film pressed home the message that greater care needs to be taken to prevent dangerous patients being allowed back into the community. The network in question tried to avoid any possible stigmatizing effect of the film by broadcasting a warning that the film should not be taken as a reflection of mental illness, since relatively few actually commit acts of violence. Under-graduate psychology students watched either the film, or the film plus the warning trailer, or a control film (*Murder on the Orient Express*) and then completed the Community Attitudes Toward the Mentally Ill questionnaire which measures:

- *Authoritarianism*, which includes beliefs that the mentally ill are different from other people and need hospitalization.
- *Benevolence*, which involves the responsibility of the public to help and be sympathetic towards the mentally ill.

- *Social restrictiveness*, which stresses the belief that mentally ill people need to be avoided and restricted by virtue of their dangerousness.
- *Community mental health ideology*, which reflects acceptance of mental health services and the mentally ill into the community.

Seeing the film about the psychiatric patient made viewers more authoritarian, less benevolent, more socially restrictive and less inclined to community mental health ideology. However, the warning trailer seemed to make absolutely no difference to viewer attitudes.

Others have approached the question slightly differently and found evidence that the media can be of help in destigmatizing mental illness. Mayer and Barry (1992) describe how a coalition of mental health organizations effectively promoted an anti-stereotypical view of mental illness through the media. In particular, they were concerned about the presentation of a particular news story concerning a man who killed his grandparents and two neighbours in a small town in South Carolina. Included with this was a story about a client of the coalition and his family:

'The newscaster prefaced the interview by stating, "Another segment of our community that has been hard hit by this story is the families of those who are schizophrenic. Many are worried that it can foster misunderstanding about the disease, a disease that can make behaviour unpredictable, but not always violent . . ." When asked to comment on the murders, the client said, "I hope nothing like that ever happens to me". The reporter asked, "Do you think you could ever do anything like that?" The client answered, "No, ma'am!" The interviewer concluded that the client "knows he has to take his medication every day. Without it, he's not violent, but he doesn't feel right. With his shots and tablets, he feels better". The interview added balance to what would have been a damaging story.' (Mayer and Barry, 1992, p.78)

Coronation Street, one of the world's all-time most successful soap operas, once adopted a story-line very much like that of Hollywood's *Fatal Attraction* concerning 'erotomania'—that is, an obsessive, sexual fixation on someone which seems immune to rejection or spurning. While erotomania is not known to be a major concern among mental-health professionals, its dramatic potential is manifest. Furthermore, the story-line was just another variant of the theme associating mental illness with violence. Gail and Martin, a long-term couple in the soap-opera, were subjected to the attentions of Carmel, a young nurse, crazy for Martin. There was violence between Gail and Carmel, who eventually tried to abduct Gail and Martin's baby from the home of their child-minder. Philo (1993), asked groups of viewers to say, 'How would you have reacted in the situation with Carmel, if you had been Gail?'

Two-thirds of the replies concerned aggression or violence of some sort or another: 'killed her', 'battered her bloody mouth in', 'kicked hell out of her', 'scratched her eyes out', 'I would have killed the cow', 'slapped her and called police', 'hit her one' (p. 19). Some replies were more sympathetic to the character: 'got a doctor for her', 'sent Carmel to see a psychiatrist'.

Despite all of this, some of the viewers rejected the media imagery and denied its validity on a variety of grounds:

> 'Some members of the groups expressed a profound distrust of the media, especially of news reporting, which they saw as focusing on extreme cases. A middle aged man ... questioned the link between mental illness and violence simply on these grounds. He was so distrustful of the media that he in effect believed the opposite of the main trends in reporting. He wrote that his views "largely reflect media influences", but only in the sense that he did not believe what was being said.' (p. 27)

There is no easy path from media content to media influence.

MEDIA CRIME AS IDEOLOGY

Barlow, Barlow and Chiricos (1995) argue that crime news is essentially ideological and construes crime and criminal justice in ways which serve the needs of the powerful. Consequently, they predicted that economic cycles should be associated with changes in the amount and nature of crime news. A content analysis was conducted of crime news reported in *Time* magazine in the post-war period. Economic stagnation as measured by unemployment was a key feature of the period from the late 1960s onward. At other periods, the American economy was in a far better state, with low unemployment in the 1950s. The researchers were concerned with whether the contents of crime stories differed in their ideological structures with changes in the economy—especially the types of crime (violent or non-violent) and the characterization of the criminal:

> '... it is an inversion of the social reality of crime in capitalist society to portray the classes and races most victimized with the capitalist social structure (in terms of alienation, inequality, unemployment, poverty, and crime) as predators on society, whereas the classes that reap a larger share of society's benefits are portrayed as victims.' (Barlow, Barlow and Chiricos 1995, p. 6)

A number of hypotheses were generated. These included the suggestion that crimes of violence will receive more attention in areas of economic stagnation; the evidence did not support this hypothesis. Nevertheless, the image of criminals during periods of economic stagnation tended to be much more negative than in periods of lower unemployment:

> 'If ideologies of crime are the critical link between conditions in the political economy and crime control policy, the news media are a particularly important site for exploring these linkages. Crime news may well be vital to securing popular consent for new criminal justice policies that are implemented in hopes of creating conditions conducive to a stable political economy, but that continually fail to have a significant impact on crime.' (Barlow, Barlow and Chiricos 1995, p. 16)

Further hypotheses about the characteristics of the offender—greater proportions of non-white offenders, for example—were considered. Compared to statistics on arrested persons, where race was mentioned in a crime report it was disproportionately more likely to be a black or non-white person. When social class was referred to, it was usually in the context of white-collar employment; unemployment was seldom mentioned. Barlow, Barlow and Chiricos (1995) accept that there is a relationship between unemployment and crime and so found this particularly striking. They interpret this as evidence that working-class crime is regarded as so common that it is not newsworthy.

CRIME NEWS FIT TO PRINT

Probably only the detail of this chapter contains surprises, since the broad trends of the research findings could be anticipated by anyone thoughtfully considering their daily newspapers or television. It is obvious that the news is a selective process and that the selection owes as much to the values of theatre and drama as much as it does to 'objective' facts about crime. What is not obvious is the audience's response to this material. The evidence suggests that the public have their own beliefs and priorities concerning crime, which may depart from the composite view of crime expressed through the media. For these reasons, there may be reason to doubt that:

> 'Media constructions of crime problems address both the frequency and the substance of private trouble with crime. Rhetoric regarding both of these dimensions serves to impress on readers and viewers the gravity of particular crime problems and the need to confront them in particular ways.' (Sacco, 1995, p. 147)

Here we seem to have some grains of truth, not the entire picture.

CHAPTER 4

Cultivating the Fear of Crime

'Not to worry, though, for as the naked city rages outside, you're sitting in front of the set watching your favorite crime show. A can of beer in one hand, a can of mace in the other.' (Rosenberg, 1995, p. 110)

Millions of people become victims of crime each year; the rates of victimization vary by age, sex and geographical location, among other factors. Studies in *urban* America show that over a quarter of households include at least one individual who has been victimized each year (Miethe, 1995); 1 in 20 of urban households experience violent crime each year. Although murder rates have been relatively stable, nevertheless violent crime in general, including assault and rape, doubled during the 1980s and 1990s. Property crime, with the exception of burglary, increased greatly; larceny-theft, for example, multiplied two-and-a-half times. Victimization is damaging; such 'primary victimization' may lead to secondary consequences which severely reduce an individual's quality of life. Areas of town may become personal 'no-go' areas at night, intruder alarms and spray-weapons may be purchased, neighbourhood anti-crime initiatives organized, victim support groups joined, new transport methods adopted, young people and strangers become distrusted, the victim may move home, and therapy or counselling sessions are attended (Miethe, 1995). Some victims merely withdraw from participation in life. Others appear largely unaffected by either their own victimization or the risk of victimization in their neighbourhood. Not all anti-victimization strategies increase. For example, despite media claims that educated middle-class women were seeking the power of the gun and buying guns at high rates, the proportion of women owning guns was more or less constant over the years in the USA (Sheley et al., 1994).

CRIME FEARS

Crime is a major source of concern among the public in Europe and the USA (Cumberbatch, 1989; Watkins and Worcester, 1986); only unemployment bothers them more. It is also an issue which the public wants the government to tackle. Despite the situation in urban America, some argue that actual experience of victimization is not common, even for minor crimes, in some communities in some countries (see Hough and Mayhew, 1985; Office for National Statistics, 1997; US Department of Commerce, Economics and Statistics, Bureau of the Census, 1996; Walmsley, 1986). However, it is difficult to judge what levels of crime the public are expected to tolerate. Cumberbatch contrasts life in what he regards as relatively crime-free zones with exposure to crime through the mass media; as many as 7000 crimes annually may impinge on the individual in the UK through these indirect media sources. Ito (1993) suggests that there is an asymmetry between the actual risk of victimization and the fear of victimization. So, in a Japanese survey, over 50% of participants expressed a fear of burglary, even though the actual risk was less than 1%. Similarly, a 1988 survey (Kiyonaga, Inoue and Oda, 1990) found that 54% of respondents expressed fear of burglary, whereas the risk of victimization in reality was only 0.9%. Many more people expressed fear of assault despite there being little objective risk of them being victimized in this way.

As we saw in Chapter 1, much early psychologically-based media research assumed that movies and television have instant and direct effects on violence and other antisocial behaviour. This, among some researchers, was replaced by a view that the media are quintessentially integral aspects of modern society and that social factors attenuate any direct influence of the media. In other words, the media are part of our culture capable of informing us about key aspects of this culture. As such, media influences are likely to be long-term and cumulative. In this view, the media are not set firmly in opposition to society destroying its fabric; instead, from cradle to grave, the media constantly reaffirm the need for a stable society. Social stability is the message of the media; society is held together by the images the media present, the media encourage us to share one world view. Television, newspapers, cinema and radio teach us to fear things alien—crime, drugs, violence—which our culture normatively rejects. Crime threatens our culture and ways of living, so the media ought to encourage our fear of crime.

The view that the media cause fear of crime had its origins in several massive content analyses of the media which dwelt, especially, on crime and violence (Gerbner, 1972; Gerbner et al., 1977; Signorielli and Gerbner, 1988). Gerbner and his colleagues argued that crime portrayed in television drama departed in many significant ways from real-world crime. Crime on television is the work of strangers and madmen who, at any moment, select one of us at random to be their victim. This is a gross distortion of crime realities, since most of us are in greatest physical danger closer to home from those close to us or other acquaintances. In the world of television, the family is equated with safety and nurturance; in reality, the family is dangerous. Thus, the family and community, cornerstones of society, are buttressed by media crime imagery to appear to be what they are not.

The first step in understanding media cultivation of the fear of crime is to identify television's message. Through content analysis, according to Gerbner, television's messages can be identified by counting the characteristics of crime and violence on television. He called this *message system analysis*. So, for example, if young people are disproportionately represented as criminals on television, the message is that young people are criminals and, consequently, we should fear them. The greater this differential between the messages of television and real life, the greater the cultivation potential of television. For Gerbner, the process by which these symbolic messages are learnt boils down to a simple equation: people who watch the most television are the most likely to absorb television's symbolic messages; those who watch the least television will be the least influenced. Of course, appropriate statistical allowance has to be made for any social and demographic characteristics which might be related to both the amount of television watched by an individual and that individual's beliefs so producing spurious relationships. The extent to which heavy and light viewers differ in terms of how much they accept television's message is known as the *cultivation differential*. According to Gunter (1987):

> 'Several steps are required to prove empirically that this empirical relationship exists. First, do individuals perceive television to be violent? Second, do viewers generalize television percepts to the real world? Third, do individuals who perceive the real world as violent also have greater fear of crime? Gerbner and his colleagues provide no evidence on these questions, but nevertheless assume that they have sufficient information from their content analyses of prime-time television to be able to define one kind of response concerning fear of crime as the "television answer" ... fear of crime is a highly subjective reaction and may not be easily predicted on the basis of purely objective measures of the rate of occurrence of criminal activity on television.' (p. 10)

Some confusion exists over how cultivation effects occur; the mechanisms involved have not been fully explicated. Furthermore, the situation has been confounded by Gerbner's chosen style of analysis—in particular, his use of global measures of television viewing rather than viewing of specific programme types. If a process of social learning is involved, then watching crime programmes should be primarily responsible for the fear of crime. Anxiety follows from the details of the programmes.

The process of cultivation effects could be very different from that envisaged by Gerbner. One suggestion is that high levels of television consumption may encourage viewers to be passive and generally uninvolved in real ife. Consequently, heavy viewers will be ill-prepared to fight off victimization and may be very afraid of crime as a consequence. This process is absolutely nothing to do with television teaching viewers that the world is a mean, vicious and evil place; it is a consequence of viewers' media-induced passivity. According to Gunter (1987), there is a sort of vicious cycle whereby those who fear crime are encouraged to stay at home and watch more television, which tells them things which reinforces their anxieties about the outside world.

Nevertheless, and whatever the truth of this, the initial research by Gerbner found an association between heavy viewing of television and what might be termed 'fear of victimization' (Gerbner et al., 1977, 1978). Great caution is warranted, though, about the nature and extent of the cultivation effects of television. Even Gerbner's own research found rather unimpressive relationships between the amount of television viewing and fear of crime measures. Since his research was based on large samples, even tiny relationships in magnitude can nevertheless reach statistical significance (Howitt and Cramer, 1997). Gerbner et al. (1980) reported a correlation of 0.12 between television viewing and scores on a measure of how mean and violent the world is perceived to be. Even this small relationship declined further when demographic factors which relate to both viewing and attitudes are taken into account. After these statistical controls the correlation reduced to only 0.04, which means that only about two-thousandths of the variation in attitudes in seeing the world as mean and violent is accounted for by the Gerbner hypothesis. This is evidence of extremely small media effects.

A number of early replication studies confirmed the broad trends of Gerbner's data (e.g. Bryant, Carveth and Brown, 1981; Hawkins and Pingree, 1980; Morgan, 1983; Williams, Zabrack and Joy, 1982), although they were subject to very serious challenge by some critics (Hirsh, 1980, 1981a, 1981b; Hughes, 1980). Weak theory and weak methods may be partially responsible for this. The fear-of-crime hypothesis has some intuitive appeal but, in order to take it further, the simplicity of Gerbner's early position has to be replaced by more sophisticated views.

RECONSTRUCTING THE FEAR OF CRIME QUESTION

Reservations have been expressed about the cultivation concept. For example, is it reasonable to assume that those who watch the most television are also watching the most crime? Are there any personality variables which might explain any relationships found. *Locus of control* is one such variable and refers to the extent that the individual feels in control of his/her own destiny rather than pushed and pulled by other forces, for example. British research has shown that this variable is crucial in the relationship between viewing and being afraid of being victimized. When it is controlled for statistically, then the relationship between viewing and being afraid of victimization disappears (Gunter, 1987; Wober and Gunter, 1988). Cumberbatch (1989) points out that there have been a number of failures to replicate these fear-of-crime findings (Killias, 1983; Piepe, Crouch and Emerson, 1977; Stroman and Settger, 1985; Wober and Gunter, 1982; 1988).

Beliefs about the extent of crime may not be related to fears of victimization. Although young men are the most likely to be the victims of violence, fear of such violence may be greatest in the elderly. There may be even a cultural perspective to this. In Japan, for example, Kiyonaga and Takasugi (1990) found that fear of victimization declined with age, in contrast with Western research. In Japan the level of fear is more comparable with the actual risk of victimization. Nevertheless, Hoshino (1976–1977) remarked on the lack of correspondence between the fear of crime and the actual levels of crime in the immediate locality. So although farming areas have relatively little crime, the fear of crime in such areas was high.

It is all too easy to confuse quite distinct concepts in this area of media cultivation effects. So, for example, one should take care to differentiate (a) an individual's beliefs about the likelihood or probability of being victimized, from (b) the fear of being a victim. This may be why young men seem less afraid of violence than might be implied by their risk of victimization. Much of the research on media cultivation stresses the risks and ignores fears as such. An individual's ability to cope with victimization rather than the risk of victimization may be crucial in determining fear (Sparks and Ogles, 1990). Thus, an infirm, elderly person may be afraid of violent attack, despite knowing that it is unlikely that he/she will be victimized. Sparks and Ogles carried out a telephone survey of people in high- and low-crime-rate cities. Fairly standard cultivation research measures were used, as well as a measure of fear of violence. Many aspects of the fear of crime were totally unrelated to media exposure. These included the likelihood of being victimized, fear of walking out at night, believing that one's own neighbourhood is safe at night and believing that one's own neighbourhood is dangerous. The amount of television viewed did predict, however, things like being afraid of being murdered, being threatened with a knife, being beaten by someone you know, and being beaten by a stranger. As is common in this research, statistical controls were made for factors such as real-life experience of victimization, sex, age and crime levels of the city, but these implied no change to the interpretation of the findings in this instance.

One would not expect people to have a simple, undifferentiated fear of crime which is constant irrespective of who they are, the nature of the crime and where they are at the time, among other things. It follows that the determinants of the fear of crime are complex and require very careful research to tease them out. So, for example, Bazargan (1994) looked at the role of demographic factors in creating the fear of crime among low-income elderly black people in New Orleans. Holding a number of other variables constant, fear of crime *at home* was associated with lower educational achievement, loneliness, feeling neighbours to be relatively untrustworthy and not vigilant against crime, and personal experience of victimization. The media did not seem important. Greater fear of crime *outside the home but in the neighbourhood* was expressed by people who were lonely, knew of crime victims, lived in high-rise accommodation, and watched television news often. Thus, there was evidence that media influences may be different for inside-the-home vs outside-the-home fears of crime.

The neglect of the location of the crime is one reason why the outcomes of media cultivation research have been superficially inconsistent. If the media portray crime in distant, far-off places, then they are unlikely to be communicating messages pertinent to the individual's own situation; there may be better sources of information about local crime. Take research on the public's anxieties about youth crime, for example (Pryor and McGarrell, 1993). People were sampled in different parts of Indianapolis, one with a youth gang problem and the other with few youth gangs. Participants were asked, 'During the past 12 months, how serious a problem do you think youth gang crime has been in your neighbourhood?" as well as a similar question but about other parts of Indianapolis. Generally, people regard youth gangs as quite serious in *other* parts of Indianapolis. The best predictor of this was recall of exposure to stories about youth gang crime on the television news. Recalling such a story was associated with over 70% regarding the gang situation as quite serious compared with about 50% with no such media recollections. Other interpersonal factors were also associated with perceptions of youth crime. Knowing a victim and being able to recollect talking to others about youth gang crime were also associated with the perception that youth gang crime was increasing in other areas. The main factor which led people to believe that there had been an increase in youth gang crime in their neighbourhood was being young themselves.

Studies of the fear of crime in the respondent's *immediate neighbourhood* tend to find no evidence that the media cultivate a fear of crime in the reader, listener or viewer (Heath and Petraitis, 1987). In marked contrast, fears of crime in *society at large* are consistently associated with higher levels of media use. Heath and Petraitis tested this in a number of medium-sized cities. They measured total weekly television viewing but also assessed the amount of viewing of different types of programmes. Fear of crime in *distant* settings was based on questions measuring expectations of being victimized in New York. Beliefs about the likelihood of a typical New Yorker being victimized were also measured. The more people viewed television, the more they feared crime in such a distant setting. Fear of theft in New York was highest for men if they watched a lot of television. The trends were not so clear when viewing crime drama is considered—but men who watched a lot of crime drama were the most likely to think that the risks of New Yorkers getting mugged were high. Although the findings are not completely consistent, there was some evidence in favour of the expectation that higher media consumption produces fears about crime in distant settings.

The researchers' expectations of *no* media effects on fear of *local* crime were not supported. Local crime fears were based on estimates that the average person in the local city would be victimized by thieves and muggers. Against the researchers' expectations, fear of crime in the local city was also related to watching crime drama. However, answers to the classic media cultivation question, "How safe do you feel out on the streets in your neighbourhood alone at night?" seemed to suggest that for the local neighbourhood, the predicted lack of cultivation effects was correct. Local crime may be much more local than the researchers had originally expected. In people's cognitive world of crime, the local city was essentially a distant setting.

Heath and Petraitis carried out a second, more refined study. The improvements included obtaining information about viewing of a number of prime-time crime shows. A sophisticated statistical procedure (factor analysis) established that there were two separate dimensions of fear of crime—urban and neighbourhood fear of crime:

- *Urban fear.* This is measured by such questions as, 'How likely is it that the average person in New York City would be mugged or seriously assaulted in a year's time?' and 'How safe do you think a teenage girl would be in New York City alone out on the streets at night?'. In accordance with expectations, higher levels of urban fear was related to watching more television and also watching more crime drama.
- *Neighbourhood fear.* This is measured by questions such as, 'How safe do you think a teenage girl would be in your neighbourhood alone out on the streets at night?' and 'How likely do you think it is that you would be the victim of a mugging or serious assault in your neigh-

bourhood in a year?'. Again in support of the researchers' expectations, fear of neighbourhood crime was unrelated to the amount of television viewing.

There were trends which were incompatible with any version of the fear-of-crime hypothesis—women who watched a lot of television and lived in high-crime neighbourhoods tended to be low on fear of crime! Similarly, crime drama viewing tended not to be associated with neighbourhood fear. People living in high-crime neighbourhoods were more afraid of crime in the neighbourhood *if* they watched a lot of crime shows. Based on the pattern of findings, the researchers argued that these very limited neighbourhood cultivation effects only occur in circumstances in which their neighbourhood matches the television world of crime:

> '... "out there" *does* include immediate neighbourhoods if those neighbourhoods look like the crime-ridden neighbourhoods depicted on TV. Although frequent TV viewers come to believe in the "mean" world, most of them do not live in it. Rather, frequent viewers tend to see their own worlds as havens in the midst of the violence "out there".' (Heath and Petraitis, 1987, p. 122)

In her study, Heath (1984) investigated the relationship between local newspaper crime coverage and fear of crime in many areas of the USA. Each newspaper was coded to give the percentages of local, sensational, and random crime stories. Randomness was defined as circumstances in which there was no evidence that the victim had engaged in some action which increased his/her vulnerability by, for example, going to a bar in a rough area of town. Sensationalism referred to the nature of the crime rather than the treatment of the crime as a stylistic matter; thus, extremely violent or bizarre crimes typified sensationalism. Although there might be some doubt as to whether sensationalism is the correct word to describe this, where the newspaper contained a great deal of local crime news which was either random or sensational then the public's fear of crime was higher.

In an analysis of a large sample of US cities surveyed in the mid-1970s, Liska and Baccaglini (1990) asked 10 000 respondents of sixteen or more years of age variants of the usual fear of crime issue—how safe do you feel in your local neighbourhood in the day? at night? The newspapers in those cities were coded in terms of the amount of local versus non-local crime news they contained for a variety of types of crime—homicide, rape, assault and the like. High fear of crime was predictable from high coverage of local crime:

> For very violent crimes (homicide) our findings clearly show that the effect of coverage on fear simply depends on whether the crime is local or

non local. Local homicide stories increased fear, and non-local homicide stories decreased fear. (p. 367)

This might suggest that local media might be more pertinent to the enhancement of the fear of crime.

WHAT SORT OF MEDIA EXPOSURE?

The doubts expressed about Gerbner's assumption of the value of the total viewing as an indicator of cultivation effects have been systematically tested. Are there any better indexes of the cultivation effects of viewing? Potter and Chang (1990) examined several *media exposure* measures:

- Total exposure.
- Programme-type exposure.
- Programme-type exposure controlling for total exposure.
- Proportional exposure for show types—i.e. dividing time devoted to a particular programme type by the total devoted to all programme types.
- Weighted proportion—this is the simple proportion of each viewing type multiplied by the total number of hours of weekly television viewed.

Twelve different programme types were used—situation comedies, action adventure, prime-time soap operas, daytime soap operas, news and so forth. Beliefs about the real world were measured using questionnaires involving:

- *The Crime Measure Index*: estimates of the numbers of people involved in law enforcement, the percentage of violent crimes in all crimes and the percentage of people who have committed a serious crime.
- *The Victim Index*: estimates of the chances of being in a car accident, fist fight or murder in the current year.
- *The Index of Violent Death*: estimates of the percentages of people who will die from murders, accidents or suicide in the current year.
- *The Divorce/Affair Index*: estimates of the percentages of marriages which will end in divorce and the percentage of married people who have extra-marital affairs.

These exposure and beliefs questionnaires were administered to teenagers as part of a media-cultivation study.

The well-established scepticism expressed by critiques of Gerbner's approach was warranted. Simply comparing heavy and light viewers when seeking cultivation effects was not very satisfactory. Total viewing was at best a poor predictor of any of the cultivation indexes. Furthermore, there was evidence that some of the more refined cultivation indexes proposed by Potter and Chang worked rather better. Media cultivation effects measured using the proportion measure were the clearest and most consistent predictors, although any of the media measures, with the exception of total viewing worked fairly well:

> '... exposure to particular kinds of programs is predictive of cultivation measures over and above the predictive power of total viewing alone. Furthermore, the cultivation measures are related in a differential manner to the types of exposure. With the ... crime measure, higher estimates are related to more exposure to cartoons and less exposure to news.' (Potter and Chang, 1990, p. 329).

It should be stressed that, once again, demographic variables such as age, sex, race, household income and parents' educational and occupational status were relatively highly correlated with the cultivation measures. Indeed, they were rather better predictors of differences in perceptions of the world than were any of the media exposure measures. So television exposure was a relatively weak predictor of cultivation effects, compared to other factors.

SOCIAL AND PSYCHOLOGICAL VARIABLES AND THE FEAR OF CRIME

What is the nature of the psychological processes involved in cultivation? Just why do heavy viewers respond differently from light viewers to crime issues? Shrum (1996) suggests that one possible mechanism may be what he describes as the 'availability heuristic'. This means that human memory can access certain information more readily than other information; the most accessible information is that which is most readily available to help form social judgements. Thus, if the media create a pool of powerful imagery related to crime in the minds of viewers and readers, then this will be more readily accessed and more influential than other crime information when making judgements about crime. Shrum obtained information from students about their viewing of three different soap operas over a two-week period. He concentrated on the 'critical portrayals' in these soap operas—that is, dominant events in the programmes. In this way the researcher hoped to capture some of the vividness of the key events shown. Crime-related problems, especially rape, were among the major themes of the soaps. One would expect, therefore, that viewers of soaps during that period would have rape imagery more accessible in memory than non-viewers.

So when asked, 'What percentage of women are raped in their lifetime?' or 'What percentage of police draw their guns in an average day' or 'What percentage of Americans have been the victims of violent crime', those with relevant imagery accessible in memory will be able to reply more quickly. The reaction times to the questions seemed to support the researcher's hypothesis about the effects of viewing on the availability of imagery for making social judgements. Overall, television viewing showed no such relationship, suggesting that viewing of the specific episodes was responsible for these cultivation effects.

Viewers differ in terms of their sophistication about television. Those who doubt the reality of television portrayals of the world may not be so susceptible to the cultivation effects of the medium. Potentially, several distinct dimensions of the perceived reality of television might be important in encouraging or discouraging cultivation effects. These were measured using distinct scales (Potter, 1986):

- *Magic window*.   This is the extent to which the viewer believes that television is an accurate representation of actual life and that it shows the world as it really is.
- *Instruction*.   This is the belief that television is a good instructional aid for all types of learning, as opposed to a valueless distortion of the world.
- *Identity*.   This is the perceived similarity between events and characters on television and people and events in real life. 'Those who seek information from television probably feel a sense of identity with certain characters and believe that the television world is fairly realistic.' (p. 163).

Potter carried out a cultivation study in which he measured the amount of television viewed each week (including action/adventure, situation comedies, drama, news, sports and cartoons). According to the sample in question, these replies were compared with either a questionnaire concerning the likelihood of being victimized or one about specific causes of death. Several samples of participants were studied (both university students and adolescents at school).

A complex statistical analysis (stepwise multiple regression) was carried out on the data. Television exposure (irrespective of the measure in question) showed only weak cultivation effects. These became virtually zero when demographic factors were controlled. The perceived reality of television was the best predictor of cultivation effects:

'When college subjects were partitioned according to their scores on the Magic Window dimension, the high group exhibited the cultivation effect, while the low group exhibited a reverse effect, so that higher amounts of viewing were associated with lower estimates of victimization. When subjects were grouped according to their scores on the instruction and identity dimensions, the cultivation effect was generally among subjects only in the low groups.' (Potter, 1986, p. 168)

Media cultivation effects are only one aspect of the fear of crime. Television may interact with a range of psychological and social factors which are difficult to extricate from media cultivation effects. Vitelli and Endler (1993) examined the role of several variables in the fear of crime:

- *Availability index.* People vary somewhat in the number of times they are victimized by crime and, indeed, in terms of the amount of crime they witness against others. They also differ in terms of how much information about crime they obtain from other people. The availability index is based on all of these things, together with the number of crimes they have heard about through the media.
- *Vividness of recall.* This was based on the respondents identifying a memorable crime and the amount of direct references to the detail of the crime.
- *Perceived competence index.* This was a measure of the individual's ability to cope with a variety of victimization situations.
- *Trait anxiety.* A measure of the individual's enduring levels of anxiety, as opposed to situationally produced anxiety.
- *Fear of being victimized.*

Availability of images from the media and personal perceived competence were the only predictors of fear of crime in males. The influence of the media was important for females but their general level of anxiety was also a predictor of fear of crime. Much the same procedure was employed for a follow-up study. This time, emotional arousal to specific crime risk situations and a different measure of general emotion arousal were employed. For males, the study found that none of the variables effectively predicted situation-specific fear of crime. For females, the availability of direct crime experiences and high vividness of images of crimes predicted fear of crime.

FUTURE CULTIVATION

What changes will the future bring with the introduction of newer technologies and new variants of older technologies? Newspapers are not produced like they used to be and they do not look like they used to. Television viewing 50 years ago provided little or no choice of programmes for many. In order to switch from channel to channel, where a choice existed, the viewer had to leave the armchair. One of the rare attempts to study the effects of the new media environments like cable and video is that of Perse, Ferguson and McCleod (1994). They argue that the role of the new technologies is to move people away from the broadcast media mainstream by providing them with alternative sources of programming which do not so relentlessly promulgate messages which promote the fear of crime. If they are correct, then it suggests that users of the newer media environment, to the extent that they use the technology to get away from the mainstream of media output, will be *less* prone to cultivation effects. So the use of electronic remote control devices (RCDs) allows the switching of channels, and hence a wider variety of programming. On the other hand, if the newer media environment is merely used to obtain more of the same, then cultivation effects will remain and perhaps become enhanced. So, for example, the use of video cassette recorders (VCRs) to time-shift mainstream programming results in more viewing of the same sorts of programmes which should do nothing to reduce the cultivation effect. In two studies, Perse, Ferguson and McCleod found some, but limited, support for their hypotheses about the influence of newer technologies on reductions in the fear of crime. So cable subscribers and those who watched more specialized cable channels showed lower levels of fear of crime and interpersonal mistrust. However, the use of VCRs and RCDs failed to demonstrate the hypothesized relationships:

> 'The widespread adoption of and use of newer television technologies require that mass communications researchers re-evaluate traditional media effects. With cable, VCR and RCDs, television content is less likely to be uniform and viewing is less likely to be habitual. Cable television, VCRs and RCDs allow people to construct their own media environment and lead to greater audience fragmentation and polarization. Television's traditional impact via enculturation and mainstreaming, and other traditional media effects, may be slowly but dramatically altered.' (Perse, Ferguson and McCleod, 1994, p. 100)

In support of this, Morgan and Shanahan (1991) found that higher consumers of television tended to have beliefs which reflected media 'enculturation' if they also used video a lot. In contrast, those who watched little broadcast television but used video quite substantially tended to have rather fewer media-'enculturated' beliefs.

HOW MUCH IS FEAR OF CRIME IS CULTIVATED?

While there is evidence in favour of the view that the media cultivate a fear of crime, the consensus seems to be that these are generally minor and very limited effects. Indeed, obtaining any sort of relationship between media use and perspectives on crime is a rather uncertain matter. Sacco (1982) surveyed people in Alberta in Canada to see if their media consumption was related to their ideas about crime. There was no such relationship for three crime variables—feeling safe walking alone in one's neighbourhood; perceptions of the safety of the city in which one lives; and the attention paid by individuals to the issue of crime. Perhaps this experience was something of a salutary lesson, since Sacco (1995) argues that issues like beliefs about personal safety may not be powerfully affected by the news media. He suggests that the effects of the news media may be much more broad than that and reflect ideological matters. For example, by presenting crime as an individual matter, the blame is directed away from social structure variables. One might add that this could include greater willingness to believe that violence in the media influences youngsters directly or that crime and structural unemployment are unrelated. This is to regard responses to crime as political in nature—determined by broad ideological concerns. If this is the case, then it should come as little surprise to find that such ideologies are resistant to the influence of the mass media, just as any other political ideology tends to be.

Over all, it is difficult not to believe that the media do have a limited effect much as Heath and Gordon (1996) argue:

> 'The message is clear. Media messages do not affect all of the people all of the time, but some of the messages affect some of the people some of the time. As we move into an age of ever-expanding technological options in the mass media, we need to recognize that the process is as complex on the human side as it is on the technological side.' (Heath and Gordon, 1996, p. 385).

This seems a moderate and largely accurate summary of what is known of cultivation effects on crime—especially local crime which might affect the individual. Whether or not this is good enough depends a little on one's perspective. The lack of impressive cultivation effects so far found in the research may simply indicate that our theories and empirical methods for establishing relationships leave a lot to be desired (Potter, 1993). Cultivation effects may, in reality, be rather stronger than research has been able to demonstrate. There are significant problems in defining what sorts of television and other media content are likely to be influential on the audience. After all, content analysis provides no guarantees that the reader or viewer perceives the contents of the media in the same way.

CHAPTER 5

School for Violence?

'The first man I ever saw shot was a petrol bomber, shot during the internment riots on August 9th, 1971. He was hit in the spine, the shock of the 7.62 full-jacketed round, travelling at nearly twice the speed of sound, lifting his entire body into the air. It was an incredible thing to see, I can still replay the scene in my mind all these years later. One minute the youth was running at full stretch, the next it was as if a giant invisible hand had suddenly whipped away his legs. He hit the ground rolling, over and over, screaming in a high-pitched, almost childlike voice. I would never look at a John Wayne movie in the same way again.' (McCallion, 1996, p. 206)

Violence among young people is part of the drama against which media effects are debated. The relative risk of violence is high. The main cause of death in children in America, for example, is injury; one-third of these deaths by injury are the result of interpersonal violence (Lowry et al., 1995). For homicides involving just one perpetrator, killers and their child victims are most likely to be the same age group. There is a 60% probability that a person between 10 and 24 years, if killed, is killed by another young person of the same age group. According to Lowry et al., the media contribute greatly to these violent trends. Many commentators on American society share his belief. Indeed, astonishment has been expressed that decades of research on television and children's social behaviour has left media policy and child-rearing practices largely unaffected. Although television is held to blame, it is also held to be potentially part of the solution to violence:

'... it is wrong to assume that the antisocial messages propagated by television are necessarily more potent than the prosocial ones. In fact, potentially, it all may be the other way round.' (Friedlander, 1993, p. 80)

In contrast to the lack of influence of media violence research, research on domestic violence has been effective. Friedlander suggests that seminal research work during the 1970s led to profound changes (Gelles, 1979; Gelles and Cornell, 1985; Straus, 1992). Not only has public policy been influenced by research into the nature and extent of violence within the home, there is evidence that the risk of violence has been reduced there as a consequence. Spanking and other forms of physical punishment have declined following the first publication of these research findings.

Superficially, Friedlander is right to point to the lack of consensus over what should be done about media violence. Few issues have attracted more public outcry and greater research attention than the question of the effects of violence in the mass media. Interest has peaked in waves following the introduction of new media of mass communication. Popular newspapers, the cinema, radio, comic books, television, home video and satellite have all attracted their critics (Howitt and Cumberbatch, 1975; Wartella and Reeves, 1985). There is nothing new about research into the effects of the media on the violence of young people. As we have seen, such studies began in earnest with research into the role of the cinema and delinquency commissioned in the late 1920s, collectively known as the *Payne Fund Studies* (e.g. Cressey and Thrasher, 1933; Shuttleworth and May, 1933). Today, despite a great deal of published research, the media violence debate has reached no consensual conclusion. Furthermore, research in the field continues (Bushman, 1995; Reid and Finchilescu, 1995).

So why has the golden question 'Is real-life violence caused by the media?' failed to generate a consensus among researchers? At first sight, it does not seem to be an especially difficult question for researchers to deal with. It is, however, a political matter in virtually every sense of the word:

- It is political since it has ramifications to the cornerstones of the political agenda: the nature of childhood, the nature of the family, traditional values vs modern values, the role of education, and the need to control all-powerful media.
- It is political because politicians want an answer—albeit their preferred answer.
- It is political because it edges towards the issue of the political control of the mass media and thus the notion of an independent press.
- It is political because attitudes have been differentiated to some extent along left–right political dimensions.

It is also a political question in terms of the politics of research. While media violence research dates back to the beginnings of modern social scientific research (Howitt, 1982), it allows researchers from a variety of disciplines to quarrel over the 'best' ways of studying the media. It would be a gross misrepresentation to suggest that psychologists and psychiatrists have preferred the media effects position, whereas sociologists and media studies researchers have argued that this is simplistic and naive beyond measure. Despite the crudity of this division, there is more than a grain of truth in it, although the disciplines do not line up quite so neatly in reality. The bulk of research into the effects of media violence has concentrated on the visual media, such as motion pictures, television and video. The penetration of television throughout the vast majority of homes in the Western world and elsewhere, and its appeal to children, inevitably make it a prime target for the interest of media researchers.

THE WEIGHT OF EVIDENCE

None of this amounts to the sort of situation in which public policy and research are likely to gel. This is hardly an exceptional situation for research into sensitive issues; school class sizes, unemployment and crime, drugs policy and the like also attract similar disagreement and dissension. There have been numerous policy initiatives on media violence, but these have been guided far more by intangible notions of 'common-sense' than by research (Barker, 1997). Possibly more crucial than disagreements among researchers is the difficulty in fine-tuning programming in the light of research findings. Very little research has addressed the day-to-day practicalities of the presentation of violence in television programmes (Cumberbatch and Howitt, 1989). Instead, researchers have preferred to ask very general questions concerning the overall effect of media violence or, at best, the effects of particular types of programme. It is simply not good enough to argue, say, that violence in the media makes kids more violent in real life. Does it matter who does the violence, hero or villain? Does it matter if people are bloodied and visibly injured? Does media violence just make kids more unruly or does it lead to violent crimes?

Numerous studies of the media have shown how common violence is as a feature of programming (Cumberbatch, Hardy and Lee, 1987; Mustonen and Pulkkinen, 1991). Nevertheless, the ubiquity of violence in the media, in itself, is not evidence of an adverse effect. Common sense may suggest that the more violence, the greater the effect, but this is to assume that media effects are the result of a cumulative drip, drip, drip. It makes no allowance for the possibility that particular representations of violence in the mass media have a disproportionate effect compared to their frequency. A particular movie or television programme may have more influence on a particular child than the rest. Claims have been made about the considerable number of research studies and publications into media violence. For example, it was suggested long ago that media violence research includes in the region of a thousand research studies, spanning psychology, psychiatry, sociology and media studies (NIMH, 1982). An up-to-date estimate would probably at least double that figure.

The consensus of research opinion accepts that media violence does cause violence in society, although a number of critical reviews have challenged this consensus (e.g. Barker and Petley, 1997; Belson, 1996; Coughlin, 1985; Duhs and Guntan, 1988; Freedman, 1984, 1986, 1988; McGuire, 1986). On the basis of a straightforward tally of the conclusions drawn by researchers based on their studies, the verdict is fairly clear-cut. The old estimate, that nearly 80% of studies claim that media violence causes violence in real life (Andison, 1977), is possibly still more or less true (e.g. Cumberbatch, 1989; Hearold, 1986; Huesmann and Malamuth, 1986; Liebert and Sprafkin, 1988). The question is whether or not one should be prepared to accept the weight of this evidence. Why should we ignore the studies which disagree with the majority? At face value, this seems a rather silly question. However, it is a vital one since it is doubtful that all research is of equal value and some research may be better than the rest. This would not matter if the best research always pointed to one conclusion, irrespective of its style or broad methodology. Unfortunately this consistency is lacking, at least superficially.

THE CASE FOR CRIMINOLOGICAL RELEVANCE

One major difficulty with the consensus view is its disproportionate faith in numerous rather contrived and artificial laboratory studies. These usually show a brief snippet of television, film or video violence which is treated as being analogous to the variety of violence experienced in regular television or movie viewing. In real life, media violence is rarely presented as a decontextualized fragment; normally it is placed in a thematic context and in the context of other programming. According to Stipp and Milavasky (1988), research which has involved real-life programmes as opposed to snippets has demonstrably failed to reveal significant effects of media violence. Furthermore, studies which have decontextualized media violence have generally also resorted to using similarly decontextualized measures of its effects. These measures have tended to be highly stylized, only distantly related to the violent crimes which have caused public outcry. Some studies, for example, involve such 'violent' activities as hitting a blow-up clown-doll which squeaks if its nose is hit (Bandura and Huston, 1961; Bandura, Ross and Ross, 1961; Kniveton and Stephenson, 1970, 1972). This is difficult to equate with, say, the street muggings which cause public alarm. Similarly, other studies use electric shocks administered in the safety of the psychological laboratory, the participants having been encouraged to do so to an experimenter who had been somewhat malicious to them earlier (Berkowitz and Rawlings, 1963; Berkowitz,

Corwin and Heironimus; 1963). A modern variation on this theme is the putative administration of a 'painfully' intense white-noise signal (Bushman, 1995). Proof that these have any bearing on unprovoked attacks on defenceless elderly people in their own homes by young offenders has long been awaited. These attacks, rather than white noise, outrage the public and media alike.

Different research methodologies have different strengths and weaknesses, so it is perhaps pointless to strike at the Achilles heel of a particular method. Anyway, the difficulty is that studies employing different methodologies tend to yield different conclusions. This leads to the problem of specifying the sorts of research which can be relied on as valid when drawing conclusions. The following are some of the main criteria which enables the elimination of the most trivial research from consideration:

- *Criminological pertinence.* Not all research relates to demonstrably serious anti-social acts. The more the research demonstrates this criminological validity, the greater the weight we ought to place on it. In this context, obviously it is better to study real-life crimes rather than how rude, cheeky or sassy youngsters who watch a lot of television are to their teachers in school.
- *Control of extraneous factors.* Within research it is often possible to examine competing explanations of relationships between media violence and aggression by using methodological and statistical controls. More faith should be placed in research which attempts this.
- *Real-life media representativeness.* In order to draw conclusions about the mass media, the materials used in research ought to be as close to those which are broadcast as possible and shown in a context as similar to the viewer's normal viewing as can be achieved. Scenes from a cartoon or a single violent scene from a movie patently do not meet these requirements; they represent everyday media consumption poorly.

While these may appear to be reasonable criteria, they have not received universal acceptance. Of course, the selection of which criteria to apply cannot be a fully objective act. Those who do not wish children to play aggressively with toys might be happy to rely on research using a squeaky-nosed clown. Others may choose to adopt what they see as a cautious stance in which any evidence of adverse effects is given priority over more neutral findings. Who is to say that these decisions are not reasonable? Depending on what research meets one's particular criteria, it is possible to argue the case that media violence leads to violence or quite the reverse argument. These are value-laden matters. However, to the extent that we are interested in media influences on violent crime, it is possible to focus on the research which is most obviously criminologically pertinent.

It may not be too hyperbolic, then, to suggest that media violence research in its totality is beyond synthesis. Apart from arguing that the research is confusing, no conclusions can be reached without disregarding swathes of contradictory research in the process. Partisan reviews have little appeal unless their criteria are accepted. Research based on laboratory experimentation most consistently supports the position that viewing violence makes one more violent. Although the earliest laboratory research on media violence (Feshbach 1955; 1963) appeared to support the catharsis position, later research quickly reversed this. Catharsis means that viewing media violence leads to the 'safe' discharge of aggression. The implication of this is that once a viewer has been 'made safe' in this way, he/she is much less likely to act aggressively in real life. Catharsis theory has generally received little or no support from research, although there are exceptions (Feshbach, 1961; Feshbach and Singer, 1971). In other words, contradiction is present even in laboratory studies. Partly for that reason, it has become increasingly common to employ statistics to analyse patterns over many studies of media violence in order to identify possible trends; this is known as meta-analysis. In meta-analysis the objective is to collect together all pertinent research studies in order to examine the trends over all of the research. In other words, meta-analysis is a statistical technique which identifies the trends in an array of studies. One advantage of meta-analysis is that it is possible to assess whether a particular type of research, a particular type of violence, a particular type of measure of violence or a particular type of individual, for example, is more likely to show particularly strong responses to media violence.

Does the claim that laboratory-based research has demonstrated adverse media influences within the laboratory setting stand up to such an analysis? Hearold (1986) found that by far the greatest and clearest effects of media violence are obtained in laboratory experiments. Furthermore, a similar meta-analysis but on a more restricted set of studies also found much the same substantial effects for experimental studies (Wood, Wong and Chachete, 1991) as did the meta-analysis by Paik and Comstock (1994). Physical violence against an object or with aggressive toys was found to be the most influenced type of effect in experiments (Paik and Comstock, 1994). Meta-analysis, in general, tends to find the least effects in surveys.

So it is beyond doubt that laboratory studies implicate the media in violence. Nevertheless, to concede this is not to accept that violence in real life results from viewing media violence. Since laboratory research with children tends to dwell on boisterous play and similar activities, the extent to which such play behaviours relate to adult criminal violence remains to be decided. Of course, play violence may be the precursor of future criminal violence—but there is no direct evidence of this link from media-violence research. Meta-analytic studies of have shown that research involving criminal violence has only the weakest of links with media violence (Paik and Comstock, 1994).

Pushing a pea with one's nose gives a very poor view of the pea. Similarly, laboratory studies of media violence risk adopting a too-narrow perspective. Let us ask what initially seems to be a very stupid question. What, for example, if studies using non-violent programmes produce exactly the same sorts of effects which have led laboratory researchers to conclude that media violence leads to real-life violence? Surely we would have doubts about the worth of the evidence if, say, humorous films produced the same aggressive consequences as violent films? Would we want to ban funny films on the grounds that they make children aggressive? If this seems more than a little bizarre then take note that serious experimenters into the effects of media violence have both raised this as an issue and carried out research which supports it. They have shown that humorous films compared with control films do produce more aggression; similarly, aggressive films are quite effective in producing humourous responses to humorous material (Tannen-baum, 1971; Tannenbaum and Zillmann, 1975). To further confound the issue, it has even been shown that there is a major increase in *prosocial* behaviour following exposure to film *violence* (Mueller, Donnerstein and Hallam, 1983)! Even pre-school educational pro-grammes such as *Sesame Street* led to substantial increases in aggres-sion in laboratory studies (Coates, Pusser and Goodman, 1976). In this study, children with low levels of aggression generally had a threefold increase in their aggression following seeing such 'prosocial' pro-grammes! In another study, it was found that children's attention to high action cartoons was as great as it was to violent cartoons (Huston-Stein et al., 1981). Either cartoon led to heightened aggression in a free-play situation. This seems to confirm the curious contention that the thematic content of the cartoons was immaterial to determining its effects (also see Linne, 1976).

The movie *The Wild Bunch* caused controversy in the early 1970s because of its exceptional use of graphic violence. As we have men-tioned, a standard procedure used in psychology laboratories for assess-ing media violence effects involves the putative delivery of electric shocks following film violence (Berkowitz, 1962; Berkowitz and Geen, 1966, 1967; Berkowitz and Rawlings, 1963). This essentially uses the approach used in Milgram's classic studies of obedience (Milgram, 1965, 1974). Over many years this measure of 'aggression' had appar-ently shown the adverse effects of media violence. Zillmann and Johnson (1973) adopted this procedure and compared the effects of *The*

Wild Bunch with those of a non-violent film or seeing no film at all. Physiological arousal was lowered by the rather dull, non-violent film compared to either the violent film or seeing no film. Aggression was equally high in the violent film and the no-film conditions, but lower for the 'boring' neutral film. These findings cannot be explained in terms of the effects of media violence, since seeing no film at all had the same effect. It can, on the other hand, be explained on the basis that general physiological arousal (rather than aggression arousal) caused the differences. The arousal explanation of media violence effects was developed as the more general 'excitation-transfer theory' (Zillmann, 1978, 1979, 1982). In many ways, the theory makes good predictions about media effects as studied in the psychological laboratory. The difficulty lies in the implications of the theory for the control of violent television. Excitation-transfer theory basically suggests that physiological arousal, no matter how it is caused, leads to an increase in any activity. Thus, there is no link between the thematic type of media content which leads to arousal and the type of response consequent to that arousal. The implication is that arousing television is the problem, not violent television! One can imagine the uproar which would follow from the suggestion that television be made more boring in an attempt to reduce violence in real life!

THE KEY TELEVISION VIOLENCE STUDY?

Adults, parents in particular, may not like what the media do to children. They may be quite right to be concerned. It does not follow, though, that all possible negative influences in childhood lead to a life of crime. There are many consequences of the media which have no certain implications for later behaviour. So, for example, when researchers demonstrated what parents already knew about television's effect on bed-times or leisure habits, it would take a great deal of conjecture and supposition to relate these effects to children growing up delinquent or criminal.

Very little research attempts to draw links between childhood media use and later criminality. So it is worth noting that Blackburn (1993), a distinguished psychologist specializing in criminal behaviour, seems to accept that there is a link (see Chapter 2). Although Blackburn stresses the impossibility of isolating television from other influences of criminality, he nevertheless writes:

'... childhood viewing of violence was significantly associated with the level of aggression 22 years later, including criminal violence, suggesting that TV violence may strengthen an aggressive disposition.' (Blackburn, 1993, p. 227)

In Britain in 1994, front page lead headlines announced Professor Elizabeth Newson's claim to having been 'wrong' about video-violence (*The Daily Telegraph*, 1 April 1994, p. 1):

> 'Top psychologists blame their liberal ideals for failure to recognize danger to children
> 'NAÏVE' EXPERTS ADMIT THREAT OF VIDEO VIOLENCE'

Newson's 'report' (Newson, 1994a, b) raised considerable controversy and it was influential on controlling videos in that it led to the amendment of the Criminal Justice Bill (Barker, 1997). She argued that 'experts' like herself had severely neglected the ease with which children had access to violent videos when formulating their views on media violence (Newson, 1994a, b). Videos are readily available from local video-shops. No classification system of the sort used in Britain and elsewhere to restrict the availability of certain videos could prevent them being seen by some under-age children. Newson mentions a number of notorious cases, some involving children torturing and killing other children. These are inevitably distressing because of the youthfulness of those involved. One of her less extreme cases was:

> 'Two schoolboys were today expected to appear in court accused of torturing a six-year-old on a railway line. The youngsters, aged 10 and 11, allegedly tried to force the boy to electrocute himself on a track in Newcastle upon Tyne last week. They are also accused of stabbing him in the arm with a knife. They will appear before Gosforth Youth Court in Newcastle upon Tyne, charged with making threats to kill and three offences of indecently assaulting the youngster and his two brothers, aged 7 and 10.' (Newson, 1994a, p. 273)

A child psychologist, Newson admits to a lack of full information about the children she mentions. Nevertheless she asserts that the 'different' factor which has resulted in such cases is 'the easy availability to children of gross images of violence on video' (p. 273). She cites very little of the research evidence on media violence to support her claims.

Both Newson and Blackburn base their cases on a long-term study of media violence conducted by Eron, Lefkowitz and Huesmann (e.g. Lefkowitz et al., 1977). This study is important for a variety of reasons:

- Its status as the first and most extensive developmental study into the effects of television violence on childhood and adult behaviour cannot be denied.
- It is probably among the most influential and frequently cited research into the effects of media violence. Certainly, it is regarded by many as the most important study outside of the psychological laboratory.

• Virtually every major review and government commission into media violence since the 1960s has made reference to it.

Given the gist of the study's findings, its appeal to anti-media violence campaigners is to be expected. Newson describes the study as follows:

> 'Huesmann and Eron at Illinois published a 20-year follow-up of 400 children, and found that heavy exposure to television violence at age eight years (again remembering that the violence was by no means as extreme then as now) was associated with violent crime and spouse or child abuse at age 30—"at all socio-economic levels and all levels of intelligence... It cannot be explained away".' (Newson, 1994a, p. 274)

Professor Newson bases her knowledge of the study on Michael Medved's (1992) book *Hollywood vs America*, a popular and polemical discussion of the issue.

The Eron, Lefkowitz and Huesmann study is unusual in that it has a more than 30-year history. Numerous books and reports have been written about the details of the research findings. The study's structure is a little complex but essentially consisted of the following three stages:

• A *first stage* of data collection, using measures of media use and aggression in pre-pubescent children.
• A *10-year follow-up* of the same children as young adults using similar methods.
• A *20-year follow-up* of these same children as adults in their late twenties.

First Stage

The origins of the study were in a fairly modest survey (Eron, 1963). For eight year-olds, boys whose mothers claimed that their sons *preferred* violent television programmes were more aggressive at school, as rated by their classmates. However, perhaps counter-intuitively, the *more* a boy watched television the *less* likely he was to be seen as aggressive. No relationships were found for girls for either the preference or exposure measures. The apparent negative impact of television viewing on aggressiveness in boys, according to Cumberbatch (1989), is quite the reverse of findings from other research of the same period (Schramm, Lyle and Parker, 1961).

Ten-Year Follow-up

Eron's study might have sunk into obscurity had it not been for the longitudinal research into television's influence on the development of aggressiveness built on its foundations (e.g. Eron et al., 1972). Ten years after Eron's initial data had been collected, the children, now young adults, were re-contacted whenever possible and re-measured on aggression and television viewing variables. The researchers claimed a delayed effect of television, in which early preference for television violence correlated with aggression in the late teenage years. Once again, none of the measures showed a relationship between viewing and violence for girls.

This follow-up attracted much more vocal criticism than the original, first-wave study. The implication that youthful television viewing affects late-teenage aggression clearly has important implications. Put as simply as possible, the measures used were problematic for a number of reasons:

- Information on early television violence viewing was provided, as we have seen, by parents who may not be in that good a position to know (Kay, 1972). Who knows which programmes their children prefer out of all of those they watch? Parents might, for example, guess that aggressive programmes might be preferred by an aggressive child. We should not be surprised if aggressive children grow up to be aggressive (e.g. Olweus, 1980; Spivack, Marcus and Swift, 1986).
- Although the research seems to be about television's effects on violent behaviour, this is something of a misrepresentation, since most of the measures were of peers' assessments of assertive-type acts. They did not measure aggression alone but also perceptions of assertive behaviour by classmates (e.g. 'Who often says "give me that!"?', 'Who does things that bother others?', and 'Who does not obey the teacher?'). Out of the 10 different ratings scales which Eron et al. (1972) combined to form their measure of aggression, only 'Who starts a fight over nothing' and, possibly, 'Who pushes and shoves children?', could be classified, with complete certainty, as definitely implying violence. In other words, the violence measure may become swamped by the other items, such as, 'Who takes other children's things without asking?'. When studied in detail, the impression is that these questions describe a young tearaway with generally antisocial standards of conduct, rather than a specifically violent individual. This uncertainty between violence and other forms of antisocial behaviour muddies the interpretation of the findings of the research, probably inextricably.
- The use of peer ratings when children had left school is also problematic. An unknown number of the ratings would be of classmates at the time when they were last at school together—the best part of 10 years earlier! In other words, in this unknown number of cases it does not reflect assertiveness after 10 years at all—rather, it reflects memories from middle childhood.

Although the first phase of the study when the youngsters were eight years of age is simple, later stages add a considerable degree of statistical complexity. Non-specialists may find this difficult to follow, since the extent of the statistical detail in the reports is exceptional. The disadvantage is that many readers are forced to depend on the researchers' interpretations of the data. Sometimes the published claims of the research team appear not to match the statistical findings particularly well. For example, they write:

> 'The relation between boys' preferences for violent television at age eight and their aggressiveness revealed itself unequivocally in our study. The greater a boy's preferences for violent television at age eight, the greater was his aggressiveness both at that time and ten years later... We found that viewing was related to greater aggressiveness regardless of whether aggression was assessed by peer ratings, self-ratings, or ... the MMPI.' (Lefkowitz et al., 1977, pp. 115–6).

This would be an important finding. Unfortunately it seems not to be correct, except for peer-rated aggression, which is retrospective to an unknown degree. The researchers actually found no statistically reliable relationship between preference for violent television at age eight and aggression measured by self-ratings and the MMPI (Minnesota Multiphasic Personality Inventory) aggression scale 10 years later.

These self-ratings of aggressive behaviour are crucial to the criminological relevance of the 10 year follow-up study. It is important to note that self-ratings of aggression at 18 years of age were unrelated to past or current violence viewing. In other words, they suggest that current media violence viewing had no influence on aggressive behaviour at 18 years of age. Unlike the peer-ratings which Eron, Lefkowitz and Heumann stress, these later self-reports include acts which appear criminal in nature: 'In the last three years how many times have you done this? Used a knife or gun or some other thing (like a club) to get something from a person? Hurt someone badly enough to need bandages or a doctor? Hit a teacher?'. Once again, the researchers hopelessly confound violence against a person with other forms of 'delinquent' activity—running away from home, and staying out later than their parents said they could, for example. This is not a trivial criticism, since the media appear not to teach youngsters that running away from home is a good thing. Generally, the message of the media seems to be that dire consequences, such as life on the street, follow running away from home. Even the classic children's story about Tom Sawyer and Huckleberry Finn contains the same message.

According to the research, the danger age for the influence of media violence is eight years. Preferences for violent television at the 10-year follow-up were unrelated to aggression. This is, in a sense, a curiosity, since there is a lot of laboratory evidence to suggest that media violence affects young adults (Berkowitz, 1962; Berkowitz and Geen, 1967; Berkowitz and Rawlings, 1963). In other words, when assessing any of the media–violence relationships claimed by the Eron, Lefkowitz and Huesmann team, it should be remembered that the methodology employed in the first wave of the study at age eight years is crucial. Any problems with this may have echoes at the second or third stages.

Twenty Year Follow-up

A dramatic set of findings emerged in the final stage of this research. Aggressive youngsters of about eight years of age grow up to be rather anti-social adults (Huesmann, 1995). For example, the number of criminal convictions in adulthood is related to their childhood aggressiveness as rated by peers. Similar relationships are found for childhood aggression with the number of road traffic offences they have as adults and their punitiveness towards their own children. Of course, this may not be too surprising—it might even be expected that aggressive and ill-behaved children grow up to be aggressive and ill-behaved adults.

The more interesting and relevant question, for our purposes, concerns the relation between childhood *media violence viewing* and adult criminality. The researchers do not appear to have discussed anywhere the relationship between the *amount of television* viewed at age eight years and adult criminality. In contrast, they do report a relationship between what programmes the boys' mothers told researchers that the boys preferred when the boys were eight and the violence of the crimes that the boys committed as adults. The more their mothers claimed their sons liked television violence, the more serious their sons' criminal violence was in adulthood (Huesmann, 1995). The relationship holds even after early aggression, socio-economic status and intelligence levels are controlled (Huesmann, 1986). Huesmann (1995) suggests that this relationship emerges for boys but not for girls.

How should these findings be interpreted? There is clearly a case to be made that early preferences for television violence may lead to later criminality. It also may be true that the crucial period for this adverse influence of preference for media violence is around eight years of age. Painstaking research such as this over so many years ought to give us better answers than most short-term studies. The difficulty is that the edifice crumbles a little when we remember that everything rests on the accuracy of the boys' mothers when naming their sons' favourite programmes. It is possible that they were rather bad at making such assessments. Some of them may have been influenced by the knowledge that their sons were ill-disciplined and boisterously-behaved to assume that media violence was responsible. If this were the case, then it is hardly surprising to find that such young tearaways grew up to be criminals. One does not have to postulate an effect of media violence to explain the relationships found by Eron, Lefkowitz and Huesmann.

Whichever interpretation is selected cannot be decided on entirely rational grounds. Inevitably, what a few hundred mothers did in the years around 1960 has to be a mystery several decades later. Are there other studies which help us settle matters?

AN INTERNATIONAL PERSPECTIVE ON LONGITUDINAL STUDIES

Despite the complexity of the Eron, Lefkowitz and Huesmann developmental study of media violence, other research has followed much the same vein. Although closely tied to the above study, this later research departs in some essential details. An international series of studies was designed and coordinated by members of the original Eron, Lefkowitz and Huesmann research team (Huesman and Eron, 1986). The big question is whether the later studies reproduce the original findings. Just how robust are the findings of the original study when the methodology is altered somewhat? Do methodological improvements change the picture? Do international comparisons produce consistent findings? The answer is yes, no, or possibly depending on how exact a match is demanded. In truth, these later studies, as yet, have not reproduced the original research findings for the simple reasons that they have not involved follow-ups over a period of two decades; the newer studies took place over a period of only three years.

Although American research dominates research in this field as in many others, it is a fairly gross assumption to imply that what is true of America must be true of the rest of the world. Media systems worldwide vary markedly from American norms and the programming varies from country to country, despite the homogenizing effect of satellite television. Since crime rates vary markedly from country to country, one might assume that these 'cultural' baselines of crime may enhance or buffer media effects. Just how stable are American findings across cultures?

The basic research design included some improvements on Eron et al.'s previous procedures:

• The initial aggression levels of the children studied were controlled for. This ensured that pre-existing aggressive proclivities did not produce a spurious relationship between violence viewing and aggressiveness at the end of the study. In other words, the relationship between media violence and aggressiveness in the third year of the study was adjusted to take into account the aggressiveness of the child at the start of the study.

- Rather than viewing causing aggression (the forward pattern), the reverse may be true—aggressive youngsters may be more attracted to violent television. In order to test this, the researchers examined the patterns which emerge if one tries to predict in this reverse direction. Thus they used aggression as a predictor of viewing as part of their analysis. Did aggression in the first two years of the research predict viewing in the final year? If the reverse pattern was similar to the forward pattern, then it is impossible to say which of the two possibilities is the most adequate. In these circumstances, one is unable to decide what influenced what. In order to demonstrate media effects, there should be a better prediction of aggression from viewing than *vice versa*.

The new American study did not really replicate the findings of the famous older American one. For boys, after their initial level of aggression had been taken into account, there was no correlation of violence viewing (using own-ratings this time) with aggression (Huesmann and Eron, 1986). In contrast, but unlike the older study, for girls there was a significant relationship. In other words, what was true for the earlier study was reversed for this later study. The earlier study claimed an influence of television violence on boys but not on girls; the later study showed *no* influence of television violence for boys but one for girls! Times do change, and it may be that female violence is a much more pertinent modern problem. This notwithstanding, it is notable that the earlier findings (which were limited to boys) continue to be cited as relevant to today.

The researchers then tried a different index of television 'exposure'. This, they claim, produced evidence of the effects of media violence on boys as well. A boy's TV violence viewing was multiplied by a measure of his identification with aggressive television characters. Whether or not this is persuasive depends on what the researchers mean by identification with aggressive television characters. The concept of identification has a long history in media research but lacks a convincing research base (Howitt, 1982; Howitt and Cumberbatch, 1975). 'Identification' was measured in this case by asking, 'What we want to know next is how much you act like or do things like some of the people from TV shows... we want to know how much you act like the *Six Million Dollar Man...*' Just what the child is answering is unclear. An aggressive or active child might readily agree that they act like the television character without being affected by violent programmes at all. It may not be surprising that the researchers found that this measure led to a significant correlation with later aggression. They may be measuring basically the same thing rather than an effect of television.

The American researchers seem not to have seen eye-to-eye with all of their European co-workers over how the research should be carried out (Huesmann and Eron, 1986, p. xiii). Research findings from Holland were not included in the American report because of this. The Dutch research resulted in radically different findings from those of the American study (Wiegman, Kuttschreuter and Barda, 1992). The American and Dutch publications also describe the results of the international comparisons somewhat differently. Based on Wiegman, Kuttschreuter and Barda's summary, which seems to include more definitive statistical analyses, the findings were:

- In Holland, there emerged evidence that the youngsters' aggression levels were better predictors of their violence viewing than viewing was a predictor of aggression. In other words, aggressive youngsters tend to like violent programmes.
- In Australia there was no correlation for either sex between viewing and aggression.
- In Finland a relationship emerged between violence viewing and aggression, but not for girls.
- In Poland there were no significant correlations, although the regression analysis suggested a possible influence of violence viewing on the aggression of boys.
- In an Israeli city there was a large correlation between aggression and violence viewing for both sexes which survived controlling for initial aggression levels. In contrast, research on an Israeli Kibbutz revealed no correlations.

International comparisons beg questions about other countries—for example, the UK. Despite American studies being familiar to British researchers (Howitt and Cumberbatch, 1975), no study has directly replicated Eron's methods. Using a different method, Lynn, Hampson and Agahi (1989) studied 2000 Northern Irish school children in their early teens. No sustainable relationship was found between the amount of violent television watched and responses on a self-reported aggressive behaviours questionnaire. Rather as has been found elsewhere (Cumberbatch and Howitt, 1989), a relationship emerged between *liking* violent television programmes and aggression, but this cannot be interpreted causally.

MEDIA VIOLENCE ACROSS CULTURES

In summary, on a world-wide scale and taking the research at face value, it seems impossible to predict whether a culture will experience an effect of media violence on its children. There may be a pattern in the findings—the difficulty is establishing what it might be. What characteristics of a nation determine whether or not boys will be influenced, whether or not girls will be influenced, or whether neither boys nor girls will be influenced? It is interesting to note Wiio's (1995) claim that the USA is the only country in which the contention that media violence causes real-life violence is tenable. One would expect that high levels of both should go together if media violence is influential. Of the countries studied, only in the USA did the two things go together. Elsewhere, countries with the most violence had the fewest television sets. Japan, in contrast, is one of the safest countries in the world yet violence viewing is high.

Although the longitudinal studies have not withstood international comparison too well, the American situation might be different from elsewhere. Thus, the consistency of the American research is important. This is further undermined by the results of another American study (Milavsky et al., 1982). This was again a three-year panel study but leads to rather different conclusions from those drawn by Eron, Lefkowitz and Huesmann. This particular study has been described as being of some importance by Kenny (1984), seemingly with just cause. Milavsky et al. noted that certain children claimed to have seen non-existent programmes—fictitious television programme titles included deliberately by the researchers. Such children might be considered invalid informants. Crucially, these invalid informants were responsible for the initial findings that there is a connection between television violence viewing and aggression. When the researchers re-analysed their data excluding these invalid reporters, the correlation between viewing and violence declined markedly.

Of course, the introduction of newer media, such as video, raise questions about their effects. Very little evidence exists about video violence which does not involve generalizing from studies of television itself. Lukesh (1989) is an exception. His research was carried out in Germany on teenagers and compared their violent media use with a measure of self-reported spontaneous aggression (e.g. trying to start a brawl) and reactive aggression—essentially the sorts of circumstance in which they might be inclined to use violence. Violent cinema, violent television and violent video use all correlated with the measures of aggression. Of course, this does not prove that the media violence caused the youngsters' aggression levels. Neither does it disprove that either. In the light of all of the other research which finds a superficial correlation, it would seem that video violence is little different from other media.

We can now explore the association between the media and criminal violence.

CHAPTER 6

Violent Criminals

'The newspapers were filled with the exploits of Jack the Ripper and, in less than a year, as many as eight absolutely identical crimes were committed in various crowded streets of the great city.'
(Tarde, 1912, p. 340)

In recent times, echoing Tarde's concern, copycat crime has been in the public eye. A typical example was the British media's blaming of videos for the James Bulger murder in 1993. The infant had been led away from a shopping centre by two young boys and brutally murdered on a railway line. During their trial, the judge expressed the view that videos like *Child's Play* might have stimulated such an imitative crime (Young, 1996a). Shortly afterwards, press headlines held the video *Chucky's Children* responsible for the gang murder of Suzanne Capper, who had been found horrifically burnt, naked and on the verge of death: TORTURE MIRRORED IN 'CHUCKY' VIDEO (*Today*, 18 December 1993, p. 1). It was alleged by the press that, after seeing the video *Juice*, four teenagers beat and kicked Les Reed to death: 'The video is the story of four black youths who turn to violent crime to win respect in the ghetto' (*The Daily Mirror*, 22 March 1994, p. 5). Less seriously, when two six-year-olds claimed that they just copied kids on television when they wrecked the home of a neighbour, the press regarded the matter as proven (*Daily Mirror*, 7 April 1994, p. 1). As one of their mothers said, revealingly, 'In a way it's hard to blame them when all they see on TV whenever they switch it on is violence' (*The Daily Mirror*, 7 April 1994, p. 5).

This spate of 'imitative' actions may well be a media construction, cobbled together from dubious evidence or opportune coincidences. Nevertheless, the connection between the media and copycat crime readily resonated with public opinion.

COPYCAT CRIME

While such newspaper claims may appeal to the public, there are good reasons for caution. Despite the hyperbole of the media, it is often difficult to establish convincingly the links between a crime and media content:

- The killers of Suzanne Capper were certainly aware of the video film *Chucky's Children*—a tape repeating the phrase 'Chucky's gonna play' was played to the victim. On the other hand, there was no evidence that James Bulger's killers had ever seen *Child's Play*. Nevertheless the media blamed both of these cases on the viewing of violent videos.
- The targets for controls tend not to be chosen even-handedly. Thus, whereas circumstantial evidence that a 'video-nasty' might be implicated in a particular crime is seized upon eagerly and firm action demanded, similar links between the Christian Bible and murders of prostitutes by men hearing the voice of God are dismissed as the consequence of their madness.
- Even if the media are correct in their allegations, this is to concentrate solely on examples of the bad influence of the media. There may be such adverse influences despite the overall picture being of good rather than harm. After all, a medical drug may be beneficial to most users while having serious side-effects on a minority. Judgements about the overall worth of a drug cannot be made solely on the basis of its undesirable side-effects for certain users.

Examples of imitative or copycat crimes taken from media reports are sometimes also used by researchers as 'evidence' of waves of copycat crime (e.g. Eysenck and Nias, 1978; Liebert, Neale and Davidson, 1973).

Many imitative crimes, ranging from bomb hoaxes to suicides and sundry other aggressive acts, have been blamed on the media. Copycat crimes are essentially those in which elements of real-life criminal acts are reproduced by other offenders, usually under the influence of the media. Defining what a copycat crime is does not mean that it is possible to differentiate copycat crimes from other crimes. There are a number of difficulties which militate against doing so:

- It would seem necessary to establish that the offender is in some way aware of the original or modelled crime.
- It is not sufficient merely to show that a particular type of crime has become increasingly common, since a rise in, say, hijacking may simply be the consequence of a planned escalation of terrorism rather than imitative effects. Apparent waves of copycat crimes like these may also cease abruptly for reasons unrelated to their media coverage. For example, an increase in deterrents may cause a decline in hijacking unrelated to changes in news-media attention.
- Evidence of copycat crime is strengthened if it manifests unusual or

novel features. It is difficult to establish that an episode of car 'joyriding' is a copycat crime, since car crime, is extremely common and each episode rather indistinct from the rest. On the other hand, imagine that a movie had been released about the theft of a police car: an increase in thefts of police cars would be more convincing evidence of copycat crime, especially if thefts of other types of cars were unaffected.

• Allowance has to be made for the role of journalistic practices in the creation of apparent copycat crime-waves. Judicious selection from available news items by journalists and the police feeding them appropriate crime news can create the illusion of a crime wave (Fishman, 1981). There have been clusters of media reports about children being mauled and disfigured or even killed by uncontrollable dogs. Such stories have become increasingly newsworthy following the arousal of public interest in the topic. This would seem to be a rather more convincing explanation of apparent waves of maulings by dogs than 'copycat' savaging by canines (Cumberbatch and Howitt, 1989).

Apart from these issues, copycating following a well-publicized crime seems extremely unpredictable. Just what is it about an event which will lead to imitation by others? Is it the amount or type of publicity given, the sensational nature of the crime, the ease with which the crime can be reproduced? When Thomas Hamilton killed 16 children and their teacher in Dunblane in Scotland, the publicity surrounding the killings was massive and world-wide, leaving few unaware of the crime. Did the Dunblane massacre result in numerous copycat crimes of a similar sort? The answer appears to be no. Nevertheless, there were horrific incidents which brought attention to the possibility. The first was when, following Dunblane, Marten Bryant shot 35 people at the Port Arthur convict prison ruins in Tasmania. No evidence exists linking Marten Bryant's crimes to those of Thomas Hamilton. A second mass attack was more troubling in terms of copycat effects. Horrett Campbell carried out a machete attack on three children and four women in a class of nursery children at St. Luke's school in Wolver-hampton, England, in July 1996, a few months after the Dunblane murders. It had been planned for two months and was in no sense spontaneous, since he had with him petrol in a washing-up bottle and improvised flame-throwers made from metal tubes. Horrett Campbell said that he admired and felt sympathy for the Dunblane and Tasmania killers.

What can one make of such evidence? Assuming that Horrett Campbell had a psychological affinity for Hamilton and Bryant, why did he, alone among the millions of people who had seen news reports about Dunblane, attack school children in this way? Campbell was something of a loner, profoundly disturbed by the death of his mother, prone to walking the streets talking to himself, and subject to the belief that there was a conspiracy against him: in short, he was a disturbed individual. The question remains why this odd-ball in a world full of odd-balls carried out this sort of mass attack following Dunblane. Whatever the answer to such questions, in this context it is important to note that there was no flurry of copycat violence.

Copycat crime, of course, has had some limited theoretical support from the extensive psychological theorizing on imitation or modelling (Bandura, 1973, 1983). The early studies demonstrated that after observing a filmed or real-life adult stylistically knocking an inflatable plastic clown around to cries of 'Whack him!' and 'Sock it!', pre-school children reproduced this stylized aggression when allowed to play with the doll (Bandura and Huston, 1961; Bandura, Ross and Ross, 1961, 1963a, 1963b). It follows from this that children, and by implication adults, can imitate modelled behaviour. Probably this research finding would only have surprised the behaviourist psychologists of the 1960s who believed that children learnt through the accumulation of elements, rather than holistically (Howitt and Cumberbatch, 1975). As Bandura recognized, and others have repeatedly pointed out since, there is a crucial distinction to be made between learning and performance. Probably most of us today have a good idea of what Jack the Ripper did to women in London in the 1890s—his butchery of their genitals, as when he stole the uterus of Annie Chapman (Caputi, 1987). How many aware of the imagery actually carry it through to action? There seems to be little doubt that we may learn about how to be a mugger, a rapist or a murderer from the media; the reasons why we do not reproduce everything we see modelled are more to do with a lack of motivation to emulate these crimes than an ignorance of how to commit them. Of course, those with criminal intent might easily learn to break into a car or how to 'jam' radio intruder alarms from the media, so such details are generally avoided by the media. Nevertheless, this is not the same as saying that knowledge, in itself, is sufficient to turn people into criminals.

Claims about copycat crimes are especially disturbing as they may involve some of the most extreme, dangerous and violent situations imaginable, such as highjacking. Sometimes the word 'contagion' is used to describe copycating or modelling, especially in the research literature on political crime. According to Surrette (1990), there are two major types of copycating:

- Hoaxes or false threats of further crime following a true-life event. These can have major consequences and cannot be regarded as any other than malicious criminal acts. For example, a bomb at Kennedy Airport was followed by 500 false threats within the week. In terms of

disruption following such false threats, enormous costs can follow from intensifying security, forced cancellations and airport closures.
- Real contagion effects, in which similar real crimes follow earlier offences.

The clearest examples of media-induced copycat crime would be those in which both the occurrence and the form of a crime are affected. In this way, crime by previously law-abiding people is created which otherwise would not have happened. On the other hand, if the media influence established criminals in the form or style of their crimes then this may not result in an increase in crime, since the media have merely shaped the style of crime. Terrorists who try to reproduce a successful highjacking rather than bomb a bus are having the form of their crimes determined but not their criminal intent.

... AND STATISTICS!

Copycat crime has been extensively researched. The best known and most crucial work was carried out by the sociologist Phillips (e.g. Lesyna and Phillips, 1989; Phillips, 1982, 1983; Phillips and Hensley, 1984). Some of this research was on suicide following well-publicized celebrity suicides. Basing his claims on official suicide statistics, Phillips argued that daily suicide rates increase significantly after the suicide of a popular media personality. Of course, positive relationships such as this tend to confirm beliefs about the effects of the media on the audience which other, contradictory, results cannot easily shake (Baron and Reiss, 1985; Berman, 1988; Gould and Shaffer, 1986; Kessler et al., 1988; Kessler and Stipp, 1984; Messner, 1986; Phillips and Carstersen, 1986; Phillips and Paight, 1987). Among research which seems to negate that of Phillips's is Stack's (1992) analysis of data on imitative suicide during the American depression. With the possible but uncertain exception of the suicides of political leaders, there was no relationship between aggregate suicide rates during the period 1933–1939 and well-publicized suicides. Furthermore, Motto (1967) studied the influence of newspapers on suicide rates by comparing periods of newspaper shut-downs because of strikes with equivalent non-strike periods. Except in one case, the data solidly supported the view that newspaper coverage made absolutely no difference to suicides. The solitary exception actually showed suicide to be *commoner* when the newspapers were on strike—the exact opposite of the copycating prediction. It appears that following the suicide of Marilyn Monroe in 1962, the suicide rate for the month in question increased by 40% on normal levels. Surprisingly, in terms of modelling theory, this was largely accounted for by a rise in male rather than female suicide. There is a possibility that even if Marilyn Monroe's suicide caused imitation in the public, all that it did was to time-shift suicides; her death did not increase the overall annual suicide rate. It should have done if her suicide was causing more suicides.

Historically, suicide was a crime. For example, under religious law, it has been known for the body of a suicide to be ritually humiliated in some cultures by dragging it through the streets (Szasz, 1986). Punishing the dead body in this way was to punish the crime. Attempted suicide is, generally speaking, no longer regarded as a criminal offence in Western society but it was only decriminalized a few decades ago.

More obviously relevant to the issue of copycat crime are Phillip's views about the impact of well-publicized boxing matches on American homicide rates. One of Phillip's most celebrated studies concerns the influence of the Mohammed Ali–Joe Bugner fight of 1975. Such famous fights, Phillips claims, significantly increase homicide rates. Perhaps strangely, the increase in homicides occurred only after a few days' delay. For the white population, it took four days before the full 'copycat' effect occurred, while for the black population the peak was reached after six days. Taken at face value, as they frequently have been, these findings seem to suggest a causal influence of media violence on criminal homicide.

One difficulty with such a conclusion is that homicides vary systematically over time. They are much more common on certain days of the week, and at certain times of the year. The early part of the weekend and public holidays are peak periods for homicide. Boxing promotions are also non-random events. Promoters and media executives prefer to stage matches at times when their financial returns are maximized; so scheduling of boxing matches is an exercise in careful planning rather than in pin-sticking. Possibly these time trends in both homicide and match scheduling combine to produce a spurious relationship. Taking as far as possible the same boxing matches and homicide statistics used by Phillips, Baron and Reiss (1985) examined the extent to which factors other than copycat crime might be responsible for his findings. They introduced a simple but novel idea—they 'pretended' that the prize fights had taken place a year earlier than they actually had. For example, if a real fight had taken place on Saturday 1 June 1975, the researchers looked to see whether there was an increase in homicides a few days after the nearest Saturday to 1 June 1974 when a fight had not actually taken place. It would be illogical to claim that fights were having an effect on the homicide statistics of the previous year—before the fights had actually taken place. However, Baron and Reiss found just as strong a relationship between the crime statistics of the year earlier as they did for the year in which the fights had actually taken place. This is strong evidence that Phillips' findings were the result of a statistical artefact due to the non-random occurrence of both the boxing matches and homicides.

Actually the data which was analysed by Phillips (1983) and then reanalysed by Baron and Reiss (1985) was also analysed by Miller et al. (1991), who introduced a number of improvements. These included correcting simple coding mistakes and similar errors made in the earlier analyses. According to Miller et al., their findings broadly replicated Phillips' original ones. Not only this, they claim that there was a relationship between the race of the loser in the prize fight and the likelihood of homicide of victims of that race:

> 'Following prize fights with white losers, the young white male homicide rate significantly increased on the day of the prize fights... White homicides did not increase after fights with black losers. However, the young black male homicide rate did significantly increase on the fifth day after prize fights with black losers. Furthermore, significant fourth and fifth day effects occurred for the high publicity fights with black losers. The black homicide rate did not increase after fights with white losers.' (Miller et al., 1991, p. 127)

A great deal of caution needs to be applied to the conclusions drawn by Miller et al. Their findings reveal that the biggest increases in homicide happened on Saturdays after well-publicized prize-fights. The exceptions to this were: (a) the Thursday after a Foreman–Frazier fight, which happened to be the day after President Richard Nixon declared the end to the Vietnam war, an event likely to increase social interaction and thus potentially homicide; and (b) the Friday after an Ali–Bugner fight, which also happened to be Independence Day, the 4th of July. Again, Independence Day, being a public holiday, was also likely to be associated with increases in homicide. Thus Miller et al.'s findings agree with Baron and Reiss's critique better than the notion of copycat crime. In support of this, when one examines the prize fights studied by Miller et al., there were only highly-publicized fights showing the four-day time delay on a Saturday or Sunday—peak days for homicide anyway. That is to say, the effects of publicity themselves may well be an artefact, since there are no comparable low- to medium-publicity fights.

Some researchers, on discovering trends similar to Phillips', have expressed considerably more caution about the interpretation of the findings:

> 'All of the studies of the effects of media events on violence raise more questions than they answer. Certainly, the nature of the spacing of homicides over time has not been explained, nor has the process by which the media violence is converted into actual violence. It is clear that the

content of the media and sporting events, are only the precipitators of violence. The more significant influences on violent behavior are embedded in the immediate social support systems and emotional states of the actors.' (White, 1989, p. 432)

These comments were made following White's (1989) copycating study of championship professional football games in the USA. For a period in the late 1970s, he examined the relationship between the occurrence of play-off games and standard metropolitan area crime data (crime rates in particular areas). If frustration was the cause of the homicides following football games, then homicides should only increase in areas where the home-team loses. In contrast, if the imitation of aggression is the reason for the increase in homicides then this should be largely independent of home-win or home-lose.

The initial analysis of the data suggested that the games increased homicides six days afterwards. The day of the week also made a difference, since matches occurring on Monday to Friday produced decreases in homicide; only matches on a Saturday were followed by an increase in homicide a few days later. Generally speaking, the effects of the game were only comparable in size to, for example, the effects of the month of the year in which the game was played. However, stronger effects of the games were found when broken down into home team win or lose. Losing the match led to a significant increase in homicides six days later:

'The aggregate level data employed in this study is not adequate to determine how homicides get conveyed from football games to the public. Why homicides peak on the sixth day following a losing game is not known. It is possible that a sense of loss reaches its zenith on the day before the [next] game...' (White, 1989, p. 432)

To complicate matters further, White, Katz and Scarborough (1992) provided data which showed that victories in American football games led to increased levels of emergency hospital visits by women due to gunshot wounds, stabbings, assaults and the like. Of course, this is aggregate data which cannot be directly linked to the women's partners' exposure to the football games. Furthermore, it is also difficult to regard these findings as evidence of copycat crime, since the football games, no matter how violent they may have been, did not model shootings and stabbings and many of the other sorts of violence perpetrated against these women. The study does cause us to question the extent to which imitative processes are responsible for increases in crime in other studies.

Surrette (1990) suggests a theoretical model of copycat crime in which the following are key steps:

- Certain 'select' crimes which are usually newsworthy and successful become available as candidates to be copied.
- The initial copycating comes from 'identification' with the original crime by members of a pool of particularly 'at-risk' criminals. The extent of this 'pool' is largely determined by social context factors such as norms on deviance and violence, and the realistic opportunities for copycating. There are obviously more possibilities of car thefts than aircraft highjacking. The type, extent and persuasiveness of media coverage may also influence copycating. Furthermore, communities with a sizeable criminal population are more at risk of copycating than low criminal areas.
- Imitation then leads to copycat crimes depending on opportunity.
- These initial copycat crimes may result in secondary copycating if they receive media attention.

It should be fairly obvious that most of the research on copycat violence significantly fails to meet the requirements of Surrette's model or even the basic requirements which might distinguish a copycat crime from other crimes. So, for example, most of the research based on aggregate statistics fails to establish that the form or style of the original violence is being reproduced. This is very clear from the studies of prize fights on homicide statistics. Here all homicides are considered, although the idea of copycating suggests that only batterings to death with the fists ought to be considered. Furthermore, there is no evidence that the perpetrators of the homicides actually saw or were particularly aware of the prize fights. Since some of the key fights were not broadcast on national television, it is hard to explain the sophisticated processes by which these may have resulted in copycat crimes. Given the strong evidence of the artefactual nature of some of the most famous copycating 'effects', it is uncertain that violent crime levels are the result of this process.

There have been few attempts to examine seriously the copycating incidents identified as such by the media. One exception is Wilson and Hunter (1983), who searched for movie-related incidents in national publications. They found 58 reported 'copycat' episodes in the 12-year period beginning in 1970. In these there were 83 different victims, 13 different films and 13 different television programmes listed. About half of the incidents involved aggression of some sort. The most commonly mentioned movie was *The Deer Hunter*, which contains a Russian roulette scene. Virtually all reports in which the imitation was directed by individuals against themselves (i.e. suicides) involved hand-guns and this particular film. In contrast, putative copycat situations in which there was a perpetrator and a victim involved a wide variety of films and television programmes, but none in particular. Of course, this merely shows which movies and television shows are accused of copycat influences—it is not evidence of the validity of such claims.

CORRELATIONAL STUDIES

Direct imitation or copycating is just one process by which media violence may increase levels of violence in real life. Many of those concerned about media violence point to rising crime statistics as evidence that media violence is causing the problem. Crime statistics are flawed indicators of crime since they underestimate several-fold the levels of victimization assessed from surveys (Maguire, 1994). There are other difficulties. Changes in the law may redefine an act as a different category of crime or create new crimes; e.g. developments in British law which reclassified forced anal intercourse with a man as rape may result in a misleading increase in rape figures unless this is noted or adjustments made to take it into account. Given these limitations, it is tempting to reject research based on crime statistics as invalid. This may well be to overestimate the level of the problem. So long as the biases are constant and consistent over time, criminal statistics may be reasonable indicators of fluctuations in crime levels despite being an underestimate of 'true' or underlying crime levels.

Messner (1986) argued that 'once the focus of attention shifts from "aggression" to "violence," and to "criminal violence" in particular, the evidence on the effects of television viewing becomes much less conclusive' (p. 220). If he is correct, then this reinforces the view that studies involving criminal acts of violence warrant greater attention than is customarily given them. Showing the extent to which crime statistics correlate with the amounts of television violence watched in different communities is one such criminologically relevant approach. Curiously, although this strategy has been employed quite frequently in relation to pornography (Chapter 8), it is rarely employed in the study of non-sexual violent crime. In the UK, despite there having been a decline in the levels of violence in the media (Cumberbatch, Hardy and Lee, 1987), these appear not to have been matched by similar reduction in the levels of violent crime. In the USA, year-by-year variations in US television violence levels showed no relationship to national rates of criminal violence (Clark and Blankenberg, 1971). Similarly, Hennigan et al. (1982) studied the effects of the introduction of television into different American communities during the 1950s and found no evidence of increases in violent crime. In a meta-analysis of the effects of television on anti-social behaviour, Paik and Comstock (1994) found little to suggest that criminal violence against a person, as opposed to property crime, was related to television exposure.

There are difficulties, of course, with this sort of argument. If media violence has its effects through a slow and fairly lengthy socialization process, then we would not expect rapidly changing levels of real-life violence to accompany changes in the level of media violence. If developmental processes are involved, then variations in media output may not immediately alter the levels of criminal violence. This perhaps makes a study by Messner (1986) particularly pertinent. Apparently beginning with the assumption that media violence does lead to criminal violence, Messner correlated indices of the amount of exposure to violent television programmes in different parts of the USA with levels of crime. The average audience for the most violent television series was used as the measure of exposure to television violence. Messner took criminal statistics for various violent crimes (criminal homicide, forcible rape, aggravated assault) and examined whether they were higher in regions with the most media violence viewing. They were not. Indeed, there was a *negative* association between the two; violent crime was *less* common in areas watching greater amounts of violence; that is, watching television violence is associated with lower levels of criminal violence! A causal interpretation of these findings would suggest that television violence lowers criminal violence. Messner preferred to interpret these relationships in terms of a sub-cultural theory (Howitt and Cumberbatch, 1975; Howitt and Dembo, 1974; Roe, 1995, adopts a similar sort of approach). Basically, the subcultural argument is that criminal and delinquent subcultures are not television-oriented but instead tend to be oriented to the culture of the streets and youth. This means, put crudely, that youngsters who are the most likely to be involved in criminal activity are the least likely to spend their time watching television. They are more likely to be in public places putting themselves at increased risk of offending.

Although Hennigan et al. (1982) found no relationship between the introduction of television in the USA and changes in crime statistics for violent crime in a sophisticated time-series analysis, this has not prevented others from attempting radically different interpretations. Centerwall (1993) makes a remarkable and dramatic claim:

> '... the evidence indicates if, hypothetically, television technology had never been developed, there would today be 10,000 fewer homicides each year in the United States, 70,000 fewer rapes, and 700,000 fewer injurious assaults. Violent crime would be half what it is.' (pp. 63–4)

Now these are the very sort of figures that appear to be vital. Instead of giving the usual highly abstract statistical summaries, here the data are translated into a specific number of victims of television each year. The figures are indeed frightening.

How did Centerwall reach his conclusion that television has doubled the number of violent crimes? He used graphs showing the relationship between annual rates of homicides of American (and Canadian) white people during the period 1945–1975. From 1949, television spread rapidly through households in America, reaching near-saturation levels by the mid-1960s. Growth in ownership then slowed down as full saturation was approached. If television has any immediate effect, then there should be an increase in the homicide rates following the introduction of television. Just as Hennigan et al. (1982) found, nothing much happened to the homicide statistics immediately following the introduction of television. Homicides at the end of the 1950s were much the same as they had been at the start of the decade. Indeed, not until about 1965 did homicides reach the level they had been in the mid-1940s. From that point on they practically doubled in a period of five years. So, if one assumes that the effects of television on homicide are lagged or delayed by about 15 years, and if one assumes that all of the increase is due to television, then Centerwall's argument about fits the trends shown in his graphs. As Centerwall points out, one would not expect the effects of television on homicide to be immediate if television's influence is on pre-adolescent children. It would take several years for such children to develop into violent young adults in the age group most likely to commit homicide. On the other hand, this neglects to explain why the children do not become killers at an early age. Guns are the commonest weapon in homicides and are found in a great many American homes, so would be available to some children.

Centerwall compared the American data with homicide rates for white people in South Africa over the same period. There was no television in South Africa until 1975. Thus, one could compare changes in homicide over time in the USA (with television) with those in South Africa (without television). According to Centerwall, the interpretation is clear:

'From 1945 to 1974, the white homicide rate in the United States increased 93% ... In South Africa, where television was banned, the white homicide rate declined by 7%.' (p. 61)

So that appears to clinch things. However, an examination of Centerwall's data suggests that his interpretation is somewhat selective. The crime statistics in South Africa in 1974 were exceptionally low compared to the previous long-term trend. The South African trend is actually more like a 30% increase in homicide *without* television between 1945 and 1969. The corresponding increase for America *with* television was approximately 57%. This, in itself, suggests that the statistics are quite capable of yielding other interpretations far less extreme than Centerwall's.

In a fuller account of his research, Centerwall (1989) claims that it is possible to exclude some of the main competing explanations of the data, such as differential age distribution, urbanization, economic conditions, alcohol consumption, capital punishment, civil unrest and firearms. There is also evidence that his lagged effects model might work quite well. This model is summed-up by the hypothesis that television would affect violent crime initially in the younger age groups and then the older ones. This seems to be true, since for several years after 1958, the urban arrest rates for violent crime in the USA grew greatest in the youngest age group.

Possibly Centerwall inadvertently capitalized on social trends which have nothing directly to do with television as such. After all, it is not usual to compare American crime trends with those of South Africa. What, for example, of other countries where television was introduced later? Trends in the British statistics on violent crimes known to the police in the same period suggest that Centerwall's interpretation should be regarded as extremely tentative. Britain had the first television service in the world, but it was not until the early 1950s that television began its relentless penetration of households throughout the country. Thus, Britain is an analogous country to the USA for the purposes of Centerwall's claims. Indeed, one would expect the rapid escalation which Centerwall identified in American homicide statistics around the mid-1960s to be matched, more or less, in Britain. Homicide in Britain is a composite of murder, manslaughter and infanticide. Combining these categories together, for 1955–1959 there were 291 homicides per year on average in England and Wales; for 1960–1964 there were 289 homicides per year on average; 1966, 364; 1967, 412; 1968, 425; 1969, 392; 1970, 393; 1971, 459; 1972, 476; 1973, 465 (Command Papers, 1971, 1978). So British homicides increased over roughly the same time period as the American data. However, there was no break in the trend to show a rapid escalation in violence rates 15 or so years after the introduction of television. Thus, *with television*, British trends look more like the South African trend, which Centerwall attributes to a lack of television!

Even if we assume that Centrewall is correct in identifying television as the cause of homicide, there is no reason to assume that the violence of television is responsible. He provides not one jot of evidence linking any sort of media content with the crimes. The number of religious broadcasts could just as well be the cause of these trends. There may be unknown effects which lead to the changes. Centerwall puts his case against this as follows:

'Because television sets are a luxury commodity, it is amusing to speculate whether the key variable might not be some luxury commodity other than television (backyard barbecue grills? four-slice toasters?). Because ownership of these other luxury items would be correlated with the ownership of television sets, it is a priori likely that they would also correlate with subsequent changes in rates of violence. Such speculation must necessarily ignore the large body of empirical knowledge relating exposure to television and audio-visual violence with subsequent aggression...' (Centerwall, 1989, p. 45)

Nevertheless, despite Centerwall's claims, it is known that crime statistics follow economic cycles to a degree (Barlow, Barlow and Chiricos, 1995). His case rests on making assumptions about the sorts of contents of television which might lead to increases in violence in society. Television's effects on consumerism might be responsible—those who could not obtain wealth any other way may resort to violence. Overall homicide statistics do not tell us what sorts of crimes are increasing or decreasing.

STUDIES OF DELINQUENTS

Some researchers have attempted to fill-out the picture somewhat by studying the use made by delinquents of the media. No signs emerge of youngsters helplessly addicted to media violence which they play out in fantasy. Halloran, Brown and Chaney (1970) studied the use of television by youngsters on probation, whom they compared with a control group of middle-class and working-class youngsters. In comparison after comparison, manifest differences emerged between the delinquents and the middle-class controls. On the other hand, the delinquents were little different from their working-class controls and what differences there were often seem gratuitous. Thus, social class appears to explain more variation in television use than delinquency does. According to the authors, 'specific characteristics of delinquents' viewing behaviour can be accounted for in ways that have little bearing on the validation or disproof of simple, causal models' (Halloran, Brown and Chaney, 1970, p. 180). About a quarter of a century later, the Policy Studies Institute in London published the conclusions of a similar study, which compared young offenders and (poorly) matched controls in terms of the use of violent media material (Hagell and Newburn, 1994). Although the authors were disinclined to interpret their findings causally, they suggest that young offenders demonstrate an extremely low level of interest in video-nasties and similar types of material, compared with the control group. Their favourite television broadcasts were popular mass-audience soap opera programmes with no particular emphasis on violence.

Perhaps the only major exception to the trend is a study of over 2000 adolescents in Maryland, in which both television viewing habits and various delinquent behaviours were assessed (McIntyre and Teevan, 1972). Preferences for violent television programmes correlated with serious and violent delinquent acts rather than petty delinquency. But boys, black youngsters and those from the lower social-economic classes contributed most to overall delinquency levels. When these obvious control variables were taken into account, the reported correlations between television and delinquency became weaker and statistically unreliable. Thus, when allowance is made for various socio-economic factors, the evidence from this study is that delinquent and non-delinquent youths do not differ in terms of their preferences for violent media.

Another study took a sample of young adult men incarcerated for violent offences and matched them with non-offenders from their community (Kruttschnitt, Heath and Ward, 1986). Television use was measured by the somewhat dubious procedure of having them report their viewing habits when they were aged 8, 10 and 12, as well as a number of other background experiences. Who can recall accurately their television viewing of four years ago, let alone longer? Overall findings suggested that alienation from school and parental use of physical violence in relationships were fairly good predictors of violent crime. Violence viewing during childhood was a poor predictor which failed to reach the normally accepted standards of statistical significance, although the authors erroneously describe it as 'a weak media effect'.

Arguably, one of the most ambitious correlational studies of media violence investigated over 1500 London boys in the 13–16 year age-range (Belson, 1978). The basic strategy was to measure the boys' exposure to television violence in their younger years and relate this to their self-reported violent behaviour. Methodologically, the research employed a sophisticated system of matching heavy and light television viewers on large numbers of control variables which might otherwise have produced spurious relationships between television viewing and subsequent aggression. Belson concluded that boys with high levels of exposure to television violence commit nearly 50% more acts of serious violence than those who see little. He included in his list of policy recommendations the suggestion that violence should be reduced on television, especially in 'plays or films in which violence occurs in the context of close personal relations, programmes presenting fictional violence of a realistic kind...' (p. 520). Superficially, these are extremely impressive findings because they give details of the number of violent acts which potentially might be avoided by reducing viewing of television violence.

This is to take Belson's analysis at its face value. Others have dug a little deeper. Belson's measures of exposure to television violence seem seriously flawed. The list of programmes given to the boys to measure their television violence viewing included ones which had not been broadcast since the boys were three years of age (Murdock and McCron, 1979)! Given this, the validity of the measure is in serious doubt. Belson did not adopt the sort of procedure used by Milavsky et al. (1982) and so failed to exclude these invalid respondents from his analysis.

Other aspects of Belson's study encourage more circumspect conclusions than his own. For example, when exposure to television violence is plotted against aggressive behaviour, it is clear that the relationship is curvilinear—an inverted U-shape. This means that boys who watched medium amounts of television violence are the most aggressive, low *and* high viewers showing the least aggression. Very high viewers of television violence were 50% *less* aggressive than those watching medium amounts of violence. So it would be an equally appropriate policy recommendation to argue for an increase the violence in television programming and to encourage youngsters to watch it more. Watching either more or less could change the levels of violence in society! Moreover, in Belson's data, exposure to *non-violent* television was also linked to aggressive behaviour, as indeed was comic book and even newspaper readership. Thus, there is as strong a case to be made that the use of any media, irrespective of the violence or otherwise of the content, leads to aggression! Or, of course, we might prefer to disregard the research as unhelpful as a consequence.

THE VERDICT?

When considering research on the effects of media violence on violent crime, it might be useful to reflect on Lande's (1993) comment that, in the USA, no court has attributed liability for harm resulting from a video. This suggests that detailed study of individual cases raises sizeable doubts about any involvement of the media. Copycat crime may occur, but the evidence in its favour is more than occasionally flawed. Copycating is a largely unpredictable phenomenon and many real-life crimes which have been held to be copycat incidents have only tentative links with the media. Generally, studies of media violence based on crime statistics show little evidence of media influence—sometimes the very reverse of the expectations of those concerned that media violence causes violence in society. Studies demonstrate that delinquent youngsters have no particular involvement with or interest in media violence. Claims have been made that half of the violent crime in American society may be due to the television, do not seem to generalize to other countries and may be a gross exaggeration or even unfounded.

CHAPTER 7

Sexual Crimes and the Mass Media

'I remember seeing a nine-year-old chase a girl and catch her, shouting "I want a baby". He didn't know what he was doing, but it was part of a natural development—seeing what it felt like physically to hold a girl.' (Driscoll, 1997, p. 6)

To many people, and the media for that matter, rape is largely about sexual gratification. It is then easy to associate anything which causes sexual arousal with sexual assaults; pornography, manifestly designed to be sexually arousing, then becomes implicated in rape. There are a number of difficulties with these assumptions. Why don't legally defined acts of rape occur much more frequently than they do? Why are sexual dysfunctions, such as impotence, common in sexual assaults? Why do these crimes involve force way beyond that necessary to obtain sex?

The capacity to commit rape is universal (Russell, 1988, 1992); virtually all men have the strength to enforce a sexual assault against someone, albeit a child. Despite this, conviction statistics for rape suggest that the majority choose not to do so (Groth and Hobson, 1983). Nevertheless, some men show a pattern of 'repetitive offending' for rape, although there is some evidence that this may not be typical of those imprisoned for rape. Most rapists seem to be more likely to repeat-offend with offences such as burglary rather than more sexual offences (Lloyd and Walmsley, 1989). Possibly, repeat rapists offend as a result of acting out problems which have lain unresolved throughout their life-span; due to current life events these problems become resurrected. An obvious source of such unresolved problems is their own sexual and physical abuse in childhood (Freund, Watson and Dickey, 1990; Greenberg, Bradford and Curry, 1993; Groth, 1979; Howitt, 1995a). In keeping with feminist views, Groth and Hobson (1983) define rape as 'the sexual expression of aggression' (p. 160): thus, rape is not aggressive sex but aggression against women expressed sexually. Lust is not the key to rape; rape's causes are more likely to lie in the dynamics of hostility and control:

> 'Contrary to the common impression that rape is a sexually satisfying experience for the offender, there is little subjective sense of sexual pleasure in rape. As one offender put it, "Rape is lousy sex", What the offender finds satisfying in rape is the discharge of anger and/or the feelings of power, but sex *per se* affords little pleasure.' (Groth and Hobson, 1983, p. 171)

Aggression can be expressed in rape in a variety of ways, according to Groth and Hobson:

- *Anger rape.* This involves physically damaging the victim beyond the level required to overpower her and obtain sex. Abusive, obscene and degrading language accompanies this form of rape, which tends to be episodic and unplanned.
- *Power rape.* The offender uses little more force than is required to gain control of his victim. However, rape fantasy precedes the offending, as does a degree of planning. The offences are repetitive and may increase with time. The offender's language is more about control than anger, so is commanding or inquisitive.
- *Sadistic rape.* In this, either power is eroticized and the victim involved with ritualistic sexual activities, such as bondage or genital shaving, or anger is eroticized and the victim tortured or subjected to bizarre sexual acts. Again, the offending is pre-planned but the language alternates between reassurance and threat.

This indicates that rape cannot be understood in terms of sexual desire alone. Others (e.g. Ellis, 1989), while having some sympathy with such views, suggest that the sexual gratification motive in rape may be underplayed. Still, the details of many rapes seem to imply a great deal of anger and desire to humiliate the victim (Burgess and Holmstrom, 1979; Clark and Lewis, 1977; Sanders, 1980). It is difficult to regard a rape in which a woman is penetrated anally and then forced to fellate the rapist as a purely sexual episode rather than an attempt at psychological destruction.

The issue is complicated by claims that sexual motivations underlie some non-sexual crimes, such as burglaries and thefts. Of course, legally these would not be regarded as sexual crimes at all (Schlesinger and Revitch, 1983). So rape may be a sexual crime not motivated by sex, but some non-sexual crimes are motivated by sex. Obviously there are considerable difficulties in verifying this latter proposition. Limited evidence in favour of the idea can be gleaned from cases in which offending initially shows a non-sexual pattern which eventually becomes much more clearly sexual. Revitch (1983) provides a good illustration of this. He describes a compulsive burglar for whom an overt sexual motivation eventually emerged:

> 'Within approximately one month following his discharge from the state prison, he entered a dwelling on November 12 and grabbed 72-year-old woman by her throat, and then, smothering her with a pillow, he either raped her or made an attempt to do so. He left when the victim gave him all the money in her possession, amounting to $86.' (p. 181)

After a truth-drug (sodium amytal and methedrine injection) administered for therapeutic purposes, the burglar revealed a great deal about the depth and extent of his sexual drives:

> '... his spontaneous revelations dealt with sadistic fantasies and experience, voyeuristic impulses, his attitudes toward women, and sexual preoccupations. He reminisced the killing and mistreating of animals since his childhood. Thus, he inserted fuses into horses' rectums and lit them. He cut cows' teats off, and he wantonly killed chickens, dogs, and cats... In sexual relations with women he experienced either retarded ejaculation or could not ejaculate at all. "After intercourse," he said, "I get vicious. I then do not want to see the woman again, and I hate the world." The first attempt at intercourse at age twenty-four, he defecated while ejaculating. He then had an impression that the woman either tried to kill him or "to mess up my privates". He expressed dislike and distrust of women. He said he preferred masturbation to intercourse, since the result was the same. The only woman he ever respected was his grandmother. He spontaneously admitted to strong urges to enter dwellings with intent or fantasies of rape.' (pp. 181–2).

Of course, this is an extreme example. None the less, it shows why assumptions about the sexual motivation of crimes need to be treated carefully.

SEX AND THE MEDIA

The media contained scandalous accounts of sex crimes even in Victorian times (e.g. Gorn, 1995). Despite these historical antecedents, there has been a change in the way in which we find out about sex crimes over the last 50 years (Soothill and Walby, 1991). Once, sex crime news was not a staple of all newspapers, it was largely confined to just a few notorious prurient publications. The *News of the World* in the UK was the archetypal newspaper whose 'select' audience was privileged to read what was available about sex crimes. Since the mid-1970s, sex crime has become a common feature of all newspapers. This is partly the consequence of the way in which feminism shaped sexual violence into a political issue. Irrespective of this feminist influence:

'The major theme of the coverage of sex crime is the construction of the sex beast, the sex fiend or the sex monster. We have indicated that the manifestation of the sex beast in florid form does not happen that often in the media, but the endeavour is consistently geared up to sponsoring the arrival of the sex fiend on the national scene ... Only a few major sex offenders dominate at every juncture, whether it be the search, the arrest, the trial, the aftermath of the trial, the prison sentence, or the parole decision.' (Soothill and Walby, 1991, p. 145).

Such a narrow concentration on sex crimes with these particular features obstructs a fuller understanding of sex crime by the public. Stranger attacks seriously distort the picture of sex crime. Sex crimes perpetrated by men known to their victims are treated differently by the media, partly because they are more likely to be contested if they go to court. Furthermore, the offences are often re-construed by the men, defence and media as consensual sex reneged on by the woman (see Chapter 9).

Early researchers into the effects of movies on young people were quite forthcoming about sexual matters, possibly more so than modern researchers. The Payne Fund studies *circa* 1930 included interviews collected from young people, of which the following is fairly typical:

'At present I don't go to the movies very often as I prefer dancing, and anyway girls think that a movie date is too cheap. It was, however, during my college career that I went to the movies with some other fellows to learn how to do a very disgusting act. This act was a French kiss where you put your tongue in the girl's mouth and slobber around, saliva dripping from both your mouth and the girl's, as you try to see how far you can get your tongue down her throat and she her tongue down your throat. We were told that this was the next thing to sexual intercourse and that actors and actresses did it when they kissed in order to create passion. After seeing it done I used the same means in attempting to get a girl "hot" enough that I could engage in sexual intercourse with her; but it didn't work.' (Unpublished Payne Fund Material from the 1930s, eventually published in Blumer, 1995, pp. 289–90)

While through modern eyes such comments seem somewhat quaint, these interviews should not be regarded merely as amusing diversions. At that time in the USA, a girl who engaged in this sort of sexual licence may well have been charged with sexual delinquency.

Since then, research has largely ignored the issue. Certainly, the portrayal of sexual behaviour on broadcast television has been little researched, despite it being a common source of complaint. Most of the research that is available consists of rather simplistic analyses of things like the amount of hugging and kissing on American television (Franzblau, Sprafkin and Rubinstein, 1977; Greenberg, 1980; Sprafkin et al., 1983). Following a study of American magazines, Scott (1986) argued that the coverage of sex had remained much the same for a period of several years. The consistencies and similarities make it difficult to hold this coverage responsible for the general liberalization of sexual attitudes of recent decades. There is some recent research on the content of broadcast television. Sapolksy and Tarbalet (1991) studied sex in US prime-time television in 1979 and again 10 years later. Sexual behaviour and language remained relatively constant. On the other hand, suggestive sexual episodes and non-criminal sexual acts declined in frequency during this period. Explicitly depicted intercourse and sexual touching both increased. Sex was commonest between unmarried people and tended to be initiated by males. Given the radical increase in the awareness of sexual health following the publicity given to AIDS, it was notable that safe sex, venereal disease and contraception were rarely addressed topics.

There is also very little research to suggest that regular media portrayals of sex and sexuality (as opposed to explicit pornography) have an effect on the audience other than to cause some people offence. An important exception is that, according to Brinson (1992), rape myths are fairly common in American prime-time dramas. Rape myths are beliefs which are conducive to rape (Burt, 1980), such as those which imply that rape victims are at least partly responsible for their victimization. The average number of rape myths per story line in drama was 1.5. Gender of the character made no difference to the frequency with which it was suggested that a rape victim causes the attack on herself (this study did not deal with male rape). This is important since it is a common complaint against pornography that it promotes these rape myths. There is some evidence that a television programme about acquaintance or date rape had an effect on the awareness of adults (Wilson et al., 1992).

Research on sex, the media, and children is even rarer. Peterson, Moore and Furstenberg (1991) detected no relationship between the extent of television viewing and early initiation of sexual intercourse, although Brown and Newcomer (1991) showed that adolescents who watched sexy television programmes were more likely to have had sexual intercourse, irrespective of their social class and physical maturity. It was not possible for the researchers to say whether this indicated a causal influence of the media on sexual behaviour or merely an association. Mostly this research indicates little or nothing about explicit material shown in late-night time-slots. Although segments, or entire videos, of the sort available from sex-shops are used by researchers into the effects of pornography, the vast majority of sexual material shown by terrestrial broadcast media is rather different. It is a big step from the effects of out-and-out pornography and serious treatments of sexual matters which may sometimes include explicit scenes. The non-pornographic sexual representations seen in the media have largely been ignored by researchers. This is curious, since complaints are regularly made to television companies and independent watch-dogs about sexually explicit scenes and themes on television; for example, gay kisses and incest.

Similarly, anyone wishing to know the effects of indecent or obscene language on youthful viewers will find little media research to help them. While researchers have not been tardy in exposing pre-school children to violent film, video and television material, ethical consider-ations have prevented them from showing children even the mildest forms of sexual material, not even the pictures of semi-naked women which litter the tabloid press in some countries and which they prob-ably could see at home. Even such 'erotica' are controversial; there have been unsuccessful attempts to control such topless depictions in news-papers as well as attempts to remove so-called men's magazines from newsagents' racks (Short, 1991).

Of course, hard-core pornography is available on subscription satel-lite services in parts of Europe and elsewhere, although effectively controlled in some countries such as the UK. The extensive research evidence about pornography of this sort deals with its influence almost exclusively on adult men.

ORIGINS OF PUBLIC CONCERN ABOUT MEDIA SEX

There is little doubt that sexual incidents, assaults and threats are fairly common and that their extent may vary culturally. Sex crimes are commonest in Australia at 7.1% of the population sampled; the figure for the USA was 6.3%; England and Wales 3.5%; the lowest level of all was for Japan at 0.7% (Mayhew, 1994). Concerns about pornography may not simply follow from beliefs about the extent of sexual crime, they may also be related to an individual's political orientation. For example, Fisher, Cook and Shirkey (1994) studied the factors which lead to support for the censorship of sexually explicit, sexually violent, and violent materials. These categories have been put forward by re-searchers as having differential effects and dangers for their users. In a random telephone survey in Florida, sexually explicit materials were more acceptable than sexually violent materials—whereas 47% wanted to ban sexually explicit magazines, this figure increased to 77% for sexually violent magazines. A similar pattern was found for movies and videos. Indeed, a complex statistical analysis suggested that the desire to censor sexually explicit materials was to a degree independent of the desire to censor sexual violence. Different predictors were related to the desire to censor these two different categories of pornography; the best set of predictors of being in favour of the censorship of sexually explicit materials was concern about pornography's effects, high sex-role stereotyping, and being female. It was not so easy to identify the distinctive characteristics of those wishing to censor sexually violent materials; the best set of predictors was concern about the effects of pornography, being female and right-wing authoritarianism. Interestingly, those with the least sex-role stereotyping (the authors call them 'feminists') scored lower than religious fundamentalists in terms of support for censoring sexual explicitness, sexual violence, supporting anti-pornography campaigns and concerns about the effects of pornography.

Schell and Bonin (1988) studied the factors which were associated with the tolerance of pornography. They found the best predictors of this to be:

- Belief in freedom of personal choice.
- Self-reported use of pornography.
- A lack of exaggerated concern about sexual goings on in the world around them.

Other factors associated with tolerance of pornography included a lack of religious behaviour and being male, young and better educated.

THE POLITICS OF SEXUAL IMAGERY

Psychological research is sometimes rather more of a product of its time than a 'science' seeking timeless basic truths. This is certainly true of research on pornography and its effects, where research seems to trail behind changes in ideologically-based concerns. Research into the effects of pornography was virtually non-existent until the latter part of the 1960s, when mega-buck US government funding became available for research in this area. The overriding concerns of politicians at the time reflected the then major social anxieties about 'sexual liberation and free love'. Furthermore, Western society was yet to become accepting of divorce, and 'living in sin' or even 'trial marriage' were the common phrases for cohabitation. Much of the research enterprise at this time focused on matters such as the influence of pornography and other erotic materials on the sexual conduct of individuals. This early research commissioned by the Commission on Obscenity and Pornography (1970) in the USA, mainly concentrated on whether pornography was responsible for a decline in the moral standards of adults. Did pornography make them feel sexually aroused? Did it make them want to have more sex? Did it make them want sex outside of marriage? Did it make them want kinkier sex? Relatively little of the research commissioned—and there were volumes of it—wondered whether sexual crime was a consequence, let alone whether pornography made ordinary men rape.

As with most subsequent research on pornography, controversy reigned. Close examination of the research evidence, covering several large volumes, gleaned sufficient evidence of risks for critics to dispute the main conclusions of the committee—which amounted to pornography being made freely available to adults (Cline, 1974; Eysenck and Nias, 1978). Radically new findings undermined beliefs about men, women and pornography. For example, despite women's apparent lack of interest in buying pornography at the time, when they watched explicit pornography of the mating variety they seemed nearly as likely to be aroused by it as men (Byrne and Lamberth, 1970). Of course, this would not be such a radical idea nowadays, given the availability of explicit pornography for women. Nevertheless, it was surprising at a time when women's sexuality had yet to become public knowledge, despite the infamy of the Kinsey studies of two decades earlier (Kinsey et al., 1948, 1953). The first American pornography report, then, demonstrated that pornography aroused both sexes. The overwhelming consequence was that they were more likely to masturbate (Amoroso et al., 1970) or, perhaps, to have sex with their customary partner (Davis and Braucht, 1970). Pornography was not much of a stimulus to sexual experimentation. Very few of those who watched pornography in the interests of science tried new forms of sexual activity, even with their regular partners (Kutchinsky, 1970). While this makes perfect sense within a framework of the uses-and-gratifications of media (see Chapter 1), it is far from startling or significant evidence of an anti-social effect of pornography. Only if sexuality itself is regarded as undesirable could this be seen as anti-social. Of course, in Victorian times, moral entrepreneurs from medicine and elsewhere would have been set firmly against anything which encouraged even masturbation (Haller and Haller, 1974).

The group of eminent researchers and others who comprised the Commission gave pornography a clean bill of health except in relation to the matter of children, who could not be researched. This conclusion disappointed many, including one president and some researchers. The findings and political shenanigans of this committee were the focus of a number of critiques (e.g. Cline, 1974; Eysenck and Nias, 1978). Critics of the Commission on Obscenity and Pornography did not take a value-free stance on pornography. Eysenck and Nias (1978) misled nobody, since they clearly stated the ideological foundations of their position. More to the point, they accurately reflect the basic political beliefs of those who see pornography as a symptom of a more general malaise. Pornography is a symptom:

'... of a much more widespread disease, namely a general loss of values, Christian, moral, or social. Being born of this general loss of values, it in turn feeds into it a kind of positive feedback cycle.' (Eysenck and Nias, 1978, p. 273)

Of course, what one researcher may see as a loss of values, another might regard as a blow for sexual liberation.

The so-called sexual revolution of the 1960s was not in retreat during the early 1970s, but newer ideological concerns began to dominate. Of particular importance were those associated with the upsurge of feminism and the women's movement. Sexual politics gained a great deal of attention. The emphasis on male aggression (and sexual violence in particular) as weapons to maintain male dominance over women was crucial. Brownmiller's (1975) thesis, describing the world-wide and history-long use by men of rape as artillery in the subordination of women, contained the quintessential argument. Thus, the ideological ground underlying the new debate about pornography had shifted away from issues of personal morality to the more consensually abhorrent arena of sexual violence. Pornography, especially when labelled as sexually violent, was capable of uniting feminists and fundamentalists to speak with one voice, despite their radically different views of the traditional sex roles, marriage and the family (Downs, 1989).

The new anti-pornography rhetoric held that to be concerned about pornography was not simply to meddle in individual freedom, since there is no moral freedom to harm others. The concept of social harm is central to modern debates around issues of social control (Howitt, 1995a). Various 'harm conditions' are postulated for which controls are advocated—drugs, media violence and pornography are alike in this respect. Children were no longer the only potential 'victims' to be protected from pornography, since its effects on adult men and women were also salient. In this way, feminist concerns provided a unified and consensual way of framing pornography as a danger to a wide range of innocent parties. No longer could previous worries about the effects of pornography on unbridled sexuality hold sway.

The infusion of feminist gender politics into the pornography debate led to a reawakening of interest in the effects of pornography. The issues were now conceived differently and so the nature of the problem had changed. Now the issues were sexual violence, such as rape and, to a lesser extent, child sexual abuse. The question of who was influenced by such pornography was muddied. Was it the rapists who carry out specific crimes? Was it all men, who not only exert power in their sexual relations but also benefit from rape and pornography as means of clinging to that power? Researchers in the early 1980s began to incorporate notions derived from feminism into research paradigms that were becoming traditions as they dated back to the 1950s and media violence research (Berkowitz, Corwin and Heironimus, 1963; Berkowitz and Rawlings, 1963). Even research which had initially made no claims to being feminist was seized upon to bolster the feminist case against men and pornography. With various government initiatives in the USA, Canada and elsewhere, the renewed interest of the state in pornography research was confirmed.

The US Attorney General's Commission on Pornography (1986), otherwise known as the Meese Commission, did not fund new research but considered much of the then available research. It was no faint-hearted assembly: 'bellicose' seems a better term. It was sued by several reputable major companies (Paletz, 1988) over its threats that they disavow involvement with pornography or else be branded as pornographers in the Commission's report! This was hardly the cool, detached arena for debating the intricacies, subtleties or otherwise of research studies. Once again, not only was the cavalier use of research data by the commission of concern to the research community (Wilcox, 1987), but there were internecine conflicts among researchers and others between researchers and their critics (Brannigan, 1987; Christensen, 1986, 1987; Zillmann and Bryant, 1986a, 1987a, b).

The Meese Commission concluded firmly that 'the available evidence strongly supports the hypothesis that substantial exposure to sexually violent materials ... bears a causal relationship to antisocial acts of sexual violence' (US Attorney General's Commission on Pornography, 1986, p. 326). This is a clear statement, albeit controversial (Einsiedel, 1988; Nobile and Nadler, 1986). Just a year earlier, the Canadian Fraser Committee had concluded that 'the research is so inadequate and chaotic that no consistent body of information has been established' (Committee on Pornography and Prostitution, 1985, p. 99). In Australia, the government reviewed much the same research evidence and, according to one observer, was 'split right down the middle' on the matter of pornography's effects (Brannigan, 1991). To correct this slightly in the interests of precision, there was in fact a minimal majority broadly favouring the US Meese Commission position.

Feminists had new means of promoting their messages about pornography. In the public arena, feminists, fundamentalists, researchers and other pressure groups had now joined forces to push for legislation. Particularly noteworthy were attempts to introduce legislation to hold pornographers responsible for the harm done by their activities. The most important initiative of this sort was the 'Minneapolis Hearings' of 1983 (Everywoman, 1988). In the short term this was successful, although in the longer term the legislation was ruled unconstitutional. The same fundamental idea was inherent in the *Pornography Victims Compensation Bills* which were put before Congress for consideration in the early 1990s (Bullis, 1995).

The UK had no such public review of pornography research, since the Williams Committee report (Williams, 1979), which concluded that 'the only objective verdict must be one of "not proven"' (p. 68). On the other hand, Howitt and Cumberbatch (1990) were commissioned to review the accumulated research evidence on the effects of pornography on sexual violence for the Home Office. They concluded that: 'It would be a rather selective use of the evidence to make a strong case that pornography is so influential as a cause of sexual and other forms of violence against women and children that its elimination would result in a diminution in such attacks' (p. 95). Both this and the Williams report were received with a good deal of hostility by some sectors of the community (Howitt, 1994). Lobbying anti-pornography groups in the UK, as elsewhere, have generally been convinced that research on pornography unambiguously supports their views. Among the best known of these groups were the Longford Committee Investigating Pornography (1972), Barlow and Hill (1985) and Itzin (1992).

Only a trickle of pertinent research on pornography is British or European in origin. Mostly it is American. The vast bulk of the research consists of laboratory experiments along the lines of those used in television violence studies (Chapter 5). There are several parallels between pornography research and media violence research. Two main factors account for this: (a) there is a considerable overlap of the researchers doing the two types of research, so it is hardly surprising that preferred methods are carried over from one area of research to another; and (b) only a limited variety of styles of research are feasible. Laboratory studies form the nucleus of the 'hard' evidence of pornography's effects. As we will see, laboratory experiments into the effects of pornographic material have produced rather mixed results which have been attributed to differences in the types of pornography involved—the erotic, the sexually violent or the sexually degrading (Check, 1992).

The parallels between media violence research and pornography research can be over-emphasized. So, for example, although there is a considerable body of research on the role of pornography consumption on the offences of adult sex offenders, there is little research on the use of violent media by violent adult criminals.

WHAT IS PORNOGRAPHY?

The definition of pornography is a complex matter. Pornography is not illegal as such, so legal definitions do not apply. Obscene materials which deprave or corrupt ordinary mortals is the test in some countries. Researchers have tended to look for different categories of sexually explicit material rather than dwell on defining what is precisely meant by pornography. Different sorts of pornography have been claimed to influence sexual aggression differentially (Check, 1992). The classification depends upon the presence or absence of thematic content which (a) involves violence against women in a sexual context, or (b) degrades or humiliates women in a sexual context. There is an additional category, erotica, which is sexually explicit and can be arousing but involves neither violence nor degradation. Usually, 'erotica' is defined as having a degree of mutuality and consensuality in the sexual activities of the participants. The sex in erotica may well be raunchily and explicitly presented, since it is the absence of violence and humiliation which define it as erotica. It should be noted that very much the same violent or humiliating thematic content may exist, but without a sexual explicitness in its presentation (Howitt and Cumberbatch, 1990). Laboratory researchers, in particular, have claimed that sexually violent and degrading depictions are especially likely to have damaging effects, such as encouraging sexual violence against women and children (e.g. Baxter, 1990).

There is very little research which supports these feminism-based claims. There is plenty of evidence to suggest that non-violent non-degrading pornography—i.e. erotica—is harmless in the sense of not increasing aggression against women (Howitt and Cumberbatch, 1990). The difficulty lies in whether or not pornographic materials which contain violence or degradation against women actually have the effects that have been ascribed to them. According to Donnerstein, Linz and Penrod (1987), the violence in some materials is the key to their effects; sexual explicitness of the material is not essential in producing adverse effects. Furthermore, the evidence which is claimed to show that sexually degrading pornography increases aggression against women is not statistically significant (Check, 1992; Check and Guloien, 1989). There are other problems which set this in context. Fisher, Cook and Shirkey (1994) point out that this research had to use selected individual sex scenes, since degrading and dehumanizing materials are usually found along with egalitarian and non-exploitative scenes in pornographic videos.

PORNOGRAPHY—JUST WHAT HAS CHANGED?

It is hard to understand why the question of whether pornography has become more violent and degrading should be difficult to answer. Violence has always been a part of some pornography. Research based on archives of pornography suggest that around 10% of pornography includes some violent imagery (Slade, 1984). There are a number of studies which suggest that violence in pornography has increased over the years or is at high levels (Baxter, 1990; Cowan et al., 1988; Itzin and Sweet, 1989; Malamuth and Spinner, 1980; Smith, 1976). Other studies suggest rather lower levels of violence, or even that it has declined over time (Kutchinsky, 1985; Scott and Cuvelier, 1987; Soble, 1986). Relatively little of the disagreement can be accounted for by researchers studying dissimilar types of pornography or pornography obtained from different sources. Much more important are the problems of defining what is meant by violence. If a female performer or model is dressed as a soldier, does this constitute violent imagery? Perhaps we have fewer doubts when Itzin (1992) writes: 'Struck by the images of violence in this "child pornography": close-up of knives and scissors, poised with points over clitoris or entrance to vagina ... overt sadism' (p. 41). The trouble is that we have not seen the images which are being reported and so are rather limited to the reporter's description. However, the term 'child pornography' is very much an interpretation since it actually refers to cases where adult women appear with shaven pubic hair—it has nothing to do with children as such, except that the researcher has a theory that depilation makes the adult women child-like in the eyes of men. What, then, is meant by the knife and scissor points being poised over the clitoris or entrance to the vagina? The choice of a word like 'poised' suggests that they are about to be used to inflict physical harm, but we do not know that, and if that is the intent, then why are they not inserted into the vagina in the pornography? Had a word such as 'near' been used instead of 'poised' the implication that sadistic violence is to follow would be far weaker. Itzin may well be correct in her interpretation. The point is not to challenge that but merely to demonstrate that content analysis can involve the active construction of impressions. Gross and imaginative assumptions about the contents of pornography are easy for those of us largely unfamiliar with such material. Doubtless, legal restraints have an effect on the types and contents of pornographic material freely available in any community. For that reason it is not easy to generalize from country to country.

Definitive conclusions about the contents of pornography are enormously difficult, since much is in the eye of the beholder. In this context, one important study is that of Thompson (1994). He reports the findings on legally available pornography in Britain from 1960 to 1990. This matches a period of great concern about the effects of pornography. In terms of crusades against pornography, the legally available material is particularly relevant to the debate about further controls, since illegal material is already subject to penalties. The lack of the violent and demeaning imagery which feminists have suggested characterize pornography was striking. Nevertheless, there was plenty of evidence that the gynaecological explicitness of the nudity in the magazines grew markedly over the three decades studied. Only 3% of pictures showed the women's vulvas in 1960s magazines, whereas such open-legged shots reached 22% by the 1990s.

The US Meese Commission defined sexually violent pornography as 'material featuring actual or unmistakably simulated or unmistakably threatened violence presented in a sexually explicit fashion with a predominant focus on the sexually explicit violence. Sadomasochistic themes, with the standard accoutrements of the genre, including whips, chains, devices of torture, and so on...' (US Attorney General's Commission on Pornography, 1986, p. 323). This sort of imagery was virtually absent from British soft-core pornography. What little there was involved five simulated spanking photographs, four pictures of bondage scenes from a general release movie, and a simulated boxing match. Similarly, Meese defined non-violent materials depicting degradation, domination, subordination or humiliation as: 'The depiction of people solely for the sexual satisfaction of others. The depiction of people engaged in sexual practices that would to most people be considered humiliating' (US Attorney General's Commission on Pornography, 1986, p. 331). Thompson found it difficult to relate such a definition to the contents of soft-core pornography at any stage in the three decades studied. The definitions of these things can be as wide or narrow as the mind of the analyst. Some people would regard posing nude and open-legged as humiliating. If such a definition is adopted, then all sorts of legally available material can be regarded as 'demeaning imagery'.

Thompson experimented with what he terms 'an ideological reading' of the magazine contents. This means that, although there was little which fitted Meese's violent and demeaning categories, one could stretch their definition considerably, as some anti-pornography lobbyists have. What happens if one regards imagery involving couples, masturbation, open-legs showing genitals, the vulva held open, or shaven pubic hair as demeaning? What if anything that could be remotely construed as violent was designated violent? The trends in Thompson's study remained less than dramatic, even after this. Demeaning imagery would be down in recent years; violent imagery has declined over the three decades studied!

Of course, the imagery of soft-core British pornography is unlikely to match that of hard-core pornography from continental Europe, for example. Thompson assembled samples of this sort of European material using catalogues and other historical sources for the period 1972–1983. He found instances of: "Fem-Dom" (women dominating men); "fifteen" (implying virginal status); "fist-fucking" (by one woman of another); "gang bang" (four or more males to one female); group sex (four participants of any gender combination); he/she (pre-transexual); homosexual; incest (implied); "irreligion" (imagery involving religious paraphernalia); leather (person/s engaging in sexual activities wearing leather clothing); "lesbians", "lolitas" (female child pornography)...' (Thompson, 1994, p. 173–4) and numerous other categories. According to an analysis of the time-trends in the data, violent imagery declined in this hard-core material over time, demeaning but non-violent imagery increased but then decreased to hold at its initial levels in recent years. Non-violent and non-demeaning imagery has substantially increased over time.

It is similarly remarkably difficult to match the contents of hard-core pornography with the Meese-type definitions of violent and degrading pornography. Some researchers (e.g. Check, 1991) are adamant that it is a straightforward matter and that the general public can differentiate erotica, sexually violent and sexually degrading materials from each other. However, this has only been demonstrated for materials which are precisely matched to their genres by the researcher in the first place. That is, if the researcher chooses a rape scene and shows it to the public, it is less than surprising that the public match this to the category of sexually violent pornography. Problems arise when one tries to apply the Meese-type definitions to unselected pornography. This is best illustrated with an example. In 1996 I was invited by the defence in a pornography case to evaluate the likelihood that certain hard-core videos would be 'degrading and corrupting', the British test of obscenity. Conscious of the Meese definitions and the considerable emphasis given to the distinctions between erotica and violent and degrading pornography in the effects research on the effects of pornography, I became concerned by several entries in the police itinerary which detailed the contents of these videos. To take one example, at one point a broom handle is inserted into a woman's anus. Reading this suggested a violent and painful act which certainly would seem to be sexually violent and, possibly, sexually demeaning. Viewing the video suggested otherwise. The broom handle is clearly and graphically seen entering the woman's anus, but it is inserted carefully and apparently gently by another woman. There are no indications of coercion, let alone violence, since the woman has positioned herself appropriately for anal penetration by the broom handle. There are no signs of pain or resistance, her facial expression is of pleasure. Furthermore, the handle is not inserted in a violent or probing manner but gently and minimally; when it is moved it is with the gentlest of movements.

While it is likely that most of us have no interest in and would reject having a broom handle inserted into our anuses, just how should one classify the events depicted? It is difficult to construe them as violent, since force or coercion is not seen to be used, the woman seems willing, and the operation is actually carried out delicately. Is it degrading? Again, in terms of what is seen on the screen there are no signs that the woman is otherwise humiliated. Is it erotic? While the depicted scene is not reciprocal, there is no evidence that the women are doing things other than for their mutual pleasure. Indeed, throughout 12 hours or so of video featuring a wide variety of sexual acts, there are no more than a few seconds of footage which might imply coercion or unwanted force.

COMMUNITY STANDARDS

Another way of understanding what pornography is involves finding out what the public regard as unacceptable. Essentially, pornography can be seen as an offence against good taste; good taste is, though, not an objective matter. Not surprisingly, psychologists have sought to objectify such subjective judgements by compiling aggregate data from members of the community. Among the first to do this were Eysenck and Nias (1978). Their idea was simply to get people to rate elements of pornography in terms of how acceptable or unacceptable they were. In this way, a rank ordering of imagery could be drawn up in terms of the degree to which it offends people. Are bare buttocks more acceptable than men's genitals or women's breasts? Quite obviously this is to decontextualize the imagery from any story-line or other redeeming features. To many media researchers, especially those working from a cultural studies perspective, for whom intent, meaning and context are vital, such approaches are ludicrously reductionist. As such they can gravely distort the essential meaning of media content.

Schell and Bonin (1988) describe the trial of an Ontario businessman, eventually acquitted of distributing pornography. The judge in the case claimed to have been more impressed by the testimony of psychologists based on the 'community standards' approach than that of other experts. Twenty-two different elements of 'pornography' had been rated by members of the community in terms of how 'tolerable' they were—100 indicating the most tolerable. Thus 'kissing between consenting adults' tended to have high tolerability rating of about 87, irrespective of whether it was in a magazine or a movie. The acceptability figure declined to about 30 if the kissing was not consensual. Consenting intercourse was rated at about 39, but non-consenting intercourse at about 12. Scenes of bestiality and incest were even lower on acceptability.

ENDING CONTROVERSY?

If the issue is good taste, there is probably no end to the debate about pornography. Pornography latches on to too many ideologies to be resolved—feminism, libertarianism and fundamentalism are unlikely to abandon pornography as an issue. Indeed, it is unlikely that the nature of the debate will remain static. But what of the effects of pornography on its user? Again, this is unlikely to be easily resolved —deprivation and corruption are ideological concepts rather than psychological or social scientific ones. We can now turn to one issue which seems more amenable to research, the question of the role of pornography in the lives of sex offenders.

CHAPTER 8

Pornography and Sexually Violent Crime

'... for some of these people, their criminal behaviour itself may
have become addictive. By this I mean that they are as addicted to
their particular form of criminal activity, as is a heroin addict to
smack or an alcoholic to alcohol. This implies that they may have
the same difficulty in resisting committing criminal acts as would
other addicts in resisting their own cravings, and it means that they
would show the same apparent indifferent to consequence as do
other addicts.' (Hodge, 1991, p. 92)

Robert Black was a lorry driver who abducted girls from far-flung
places and discarded their corpses on isolated waysides in Britain.
Nobody knows for sure how many murders he committed (Wyre and
Tate, 1995) although the police achieved no further successes in an
investigation lasting for several years after his trial. Like many offenders, there was a pattern to his offending; the consistency of the ages of
his victims and his *modus operandi* is striking. Black's basic offending
blueprint was established by the age of 16 when he committed a sexual
offence which illustrates the elements of his later offending:

'I picked her up by the knees and she was hanging down... Her head
wasn't touching the floor. Her skirt fell down and I could see the hole in
her vagina was gaping, like it must have been well relaxed, and it was
wide open and I put my finger straight in, all the way in. I took it out
again, just the once, and I laid her down on the floor and masturbated.
When I'd done that I put her knickers back on.' (Wyre and Tate, 1995,
p. 94)

Just what reduces a man to this? Was there ever a more noble Robert
Black? Probably not.

Black's early life was far from idyllic; he was born to a lone parent and
given up for adoption about a year later. He could recollect vividly his
first sexual encounter. As a child, he had taken a walk into the Scottish
hills with a young girl where, mutually, they removed each other's
clothing. Despite the fact that Black could remember nothing else of the

first five years of his life, he could recall this girl's name. Wyre and Tate (1995) argue that this experience had penetrated Black's psyche. However, this sort of precocious sexuality may also be a sign of early sexual abuse (Howitt, 1995a). Both of his adoptive parents died by the time he was 11 and, from then on, Black entered a cruel world of children's homes. In the first of these he assaulted a young female resident, which forced his removal to another children's home. According to Black, at this second children's home he was subject to sexual abuse by a male member of staff. Although none of his contemporaries there recall any signs that he was affected by this abuse, Wyre and Tate (1995) explain that it had happened in an era in which silence was an appropriate strategy for abused children. Such a silence may have been destructive, so damaging that it led to him acting out his silent turmoil. In this way, new young victims were created by this cycle of abuse. At the age of 16, Black was convicted for the sexual offence against a young girl. When he was 21 years of age, Black returned to the area in which this offence had been committed and was charged with an indecent assault on a six-year-old girl shortly afterwards. It is virtually self-evident from all of this that Robert Black's sexually deviant, criminal career had become entrenched well before he reached adulthood. The pattern of his childhood offending established a motif for his adult life—his erotic fixation was young girls. The quest to digitally penetrate their vaginas was crucial to his sexual fulfilment.

There is no evidence that Black was a serious user of pornography in his early years. Indeed, it is not known precisely when he first saw such imagery. The significant steps towards pornography occurred in his adult life. According to Black, his earliest experience of pornography was:

> 'I was getting on for 30. There was a place I used to go to where I first discovered the child pornography: a shop down near King's Cross in London. It didn't have a name—it was just like a shop front. You went in and there was, like, old books lined up, but if you wanted to get something else, you went in the back. They used to give you half price on what you brought back.' (Wyre and Tate, 1995, p. 160).

To what extent can we generalize from cases like Robert Black when estimating pornography's role in sexual offending? No matter how compelling the political case against pornography, it remains controversial whether there is a demonstrable causal relationship between pornography and sex crimes. Would there be fewer rapes without pornography's influence? The question of the effects of pornography is a profoundly politicized matter, as we saw in Chapter 7. Some construe the evidence on pornography's effects as analogous to the evidence of smoking on health (Itzin, 1992); pornography is seen as a pathogen which causes socially diseased individuals and communities. Furthermore, all sides in the debate see their opponents as hopelessly biased when faced with the 'facts'.

SEX OFFENDERS AND PORNOGRAPHY

Some therapists who treat sex offenders are convinced of the causal role of pornography in offending (e.g. Wyre, 1987, 1990, 1992). Unfortunately, despite claims like this, few published case studies exist which convincingly support assertions about the causal influence of pornography on sex crime (Howitt, 1995b). Newspapers, at the time of his conviction, suggested that Robert Black was driven to his crimes by pornography as in the headline FROM PORNOGRAPHY TO CHILD MURDER: ANATOMY OF A MONSTER (*The Daily Mail*, 20 May 1994, p. 1). That newspapers blame pornography for creating sex monsters like Black does not prove that it is true. The biographical details of Black's life show that his deviant sexual behaviour was established in childhood, long before his first exposure to child pornography.

Similar doubts about the causal influence of pornography on sex offending are encouraged by the extensive case study reported by Kutchinsky (1976). To be sure, this offender was aware of pornography but nevertheless his sexually deviant history preceded his first exposure to erotic materials. Such case studies are illustrative but are not in themselves definitive evidence. Case study evidence may be contaminated by all sorts of factors—the denial of blame and responsibility is common in offenders (Howitt, 1995a). What better excuse than to blame pornography? Some offenders proactively implicate pornography in their offending. The notorious American killer Ted Bundy made death-cell claims that pornography was responsible for his murderous, raping, criminal ways (Brannigan, 1991):

'Those of us who are... influenced by violence in the media, in particular pornographic violence, are not some kind of inherent monsters. We are your husbands, and we grew up in regular families.' (Lamar, 1985, p. 34)

Does systematic research support the idea that pornography has a causal influence on sexual deviant criminality? Inevitably such research relies on retrospective reports of childhood experiences obtained from offenders some years into adulthood. This has to be regarded as inherently risky evidence, simply because of the difficulty of remembering back to childhood days as adults. Furthermore, research inevitably takes place in a social context, which may encourage truth-telling or obfuscation. The institutional settings in which research is conducted may not be conducive to truthful accuracy; offenders in prison or undergoing therapy may have a vested interest in blaming factors out of their control for their offending. Bearing all of these things in mind, the thrust of the evidence concerning the childhood role of pornography in sex crime is unusually consistent.

Research into the childhoods of sex offenders has been available since the earliest studies of pornography's influences. A fairly modern investigation of this type by Nutter and Kearns (1993) seems to epitomize the field. Sex offenders (including rapists, exhibitionists, voyeurs and cross-dressers) were compared with community controls. Sex offenders, in general, started masturbating at a younger age than controls and were likely to use pornography in masturbation once they had access to pornography. Child molesters, however, were no different from the controls in these respects. Usually, masturbation preceded exposure to pornography in the offender group—that is, they were not stimulated to masturbation by exposure to pornography. Indeed, apart from first seeing pornography *later* in life, child molesters did not differ from controls. Based on the authors' clinical experience, it would appear that most offenders report having had deviant fantasies or behaviours prior to any exposure to pornography. If anything, then, it would seem that sex offenders are less precocious than non-offenders in relation to pornography. Rapists first see pornography a year and a half on average later in childhood than controls (Walker, 1970). Condron and Nutter's (1988) findings suggest much the same. There is evidence of a lower incidence of exposure to pornography in the early lives of sex offenders than others (Cook and Fosen, 1970; Goldstein et al., 1970; Goldstein and Kant, 1973). For rapists and child molesters alike, exposure to violent pornography tends to be low (Carter et al., 1987). These trends have been consistent enough over a range of studies, the findings of recent research being little different from those of earlier studies. A difficulty in assessing the role of pornography in sexually deviant careers lies in the frequent exposure of ordinary men to such sexually explicit material. In other words, if exposure to pornography in childhood is the prime cause of sexual offending, it is difficult to see how it leaves so many men seemingly unaffected. Thus, exposure is very high in young people in general and not just among juvenile offenders (Propper, 1970) and sex offenders (Gebhard et al., 1965). What is more, sex offenders are more likely to have begun masturbating before they ever see pornography. This makes distinctly untenable the view that offenders become deviant because they masturbate to deviant thoughts stimulated by pornography. That is, there is no evidence that they undergo a process in which sexual arousal becomes conditioned to deviant thoughts (Condron and Nutter, 1988).

So it would appear that sex offenders are relatively late developers in relation to pornography. Only one study can be regarded as a significant departure from the general run of research findings. Marshall (1988) found somewhat more sexual molesters of adult women or children claimed to have seen hard-core pornography during puberty than controls. This was not true of incest offenders, none of whom reported exposure to this material. Nevertheless, taken overall, the data provide little or no evidence especially conducive to the view that pornography in childhood leads to later sexual offending.

Pornography may be influential in ways other than affecting psychosexual development in youngsters; are sex offenders more aroused by pornography (or particular types of pornography) than non-offending men, for instance? Frequency of adult use of sexually explicit material does not differentiate offenders from non-offenders (Nutter and Kearns, 1993). Similarly, Langevin et al. (1988) found that exposure to various sorts of pornography (magazines, videos, movies) was much the same for sex offenders and community controls. A number of studies (Cook and Fosen, 1970; Gebhard et al, 1965; Johnson, Kupperstein and Petters, 1970) seemed to suggest that sex offenders were more aroused by particular types of pornography. Later research also found similar trends in various types of sex offenders. For example, rapists show more arousal to rape pornography than non-rapists (Abel et al., 1977; Barbaree, Marshall and Lanthier, 1979; Quinsey, Chaplin and Upton, 1984). Clinically, this has been used to develop a rape index (Abel et al., 1977) and, in a similar way, a dangerous child molester index (Avery-Clark and Laws, 1984).

Despite this, care needs to be taken to avoid the assumption that offenders with a specific type of victim are only aroused by pornography which reflects their preferred type of victim (Howitt, 1995a). If this assumption is correct, it seems only to apply to rapists. Freund and Blanchard (1989) compared child molesters with offenders against mature women. Videos of nude mature women, early adolescent girls, pubescent girls and 5–8 year-old girls were shown. Whereas nearly all non-paedophile men were accurately classified as being sexually attracted to women, only about half of the paedophiles were correctly identified as such, since they tended to show genital enlargement to pictures of nude adult women as well. Another study found that, on average, a sample of normal men had substantial erections in response to pictures of pubescent and younger girls which were on average more than 50% of the size of their erections to pictures of adult women (Quinsey et al., 1975). Hall et al. (1988) compared rapists of adult women, sex offenders against under-12-year-olds, and offenders against adolescents. No differences were found in sexual arousal to pictures of nude children. Similarly, those who used violence in their crimes were not especially excited by sexually violent materials. Wormith (1986) found considerable misclassification of different offender types on the basis of their response to various sorts of sexual imagery. Approximately one-third of non-sexual offenders were wrongly classified as rapists and over 40% of paedophilies were categorized as normal men!

In line with these findings, Marshall (1988) found no clear links between the type of hard-core pornography offenders had used in adulthood and their type of offending. Rapists, however, did have significantly greater access to rape pornography, thus supporting some of the above physiological studies. Quite high proportions of child molesters and rapists claimed that pornography had a role in their offending. Similar proportions of offenders blamed pornography in Condron and Nutter's (1988) study, although these researchers felt that these might have been self-serving excuses. Much lower figures were obtained by Becker and Stein (1991) in a study of sexually deviant adolescent boys. The boys mostly claimed that pornography had no role in their sexual offending and the exceptions to this were very tentatively phrased. It is, of course, difficult to interpret such claims on the part of offenders who might well have their own reasons for blaming pornography or, indeed, not blaming it. Similarly, claims that arrested sex offenders usually have collections of pornography at home (Everywoman, 1988) are difficult to evaluate, given the general availability of pornography throughout the community.

In keeping with Groth and Hobson's (1983) view that rape is the result of developmental difficulties, most offenders they studied began their sexual offending history by the age of 16. Often their offences were labelled by those in authority as being little other than youthful sexual curiosity. Groth and Hobson also suggest that since aggressiveness in men declines with age, rape should become less common following middle-age if it is primarily a violent crime. The evidence suggests that rape is indeed a youthful crime (Office for National Statistics, 1997) and that the age profile of rapists is much the same as that of violent offenders. If sex were the major motive, then rape should not show such an age profile, since sexual interest in men is maintained past middle-age. For Groth and Hobson, because rape results from the arousal of aggression, not sexual arousal:

'... the majority of offenders report no significant exposure to or preoccupation with pornography or erotica, which is predominantly sexually oriented...' (p. 162)

SELF-CREATED PORNOGRAPHY

Sex offenders certainly have deviant sexual fantasies. Denial of such deviant fantasy is common in untreated sexual offenders (Howitt,

1995a). Consequently it is somewhat problematic to assess the extent to which deviant sexual fantasy is universal in offenders, whether or not fuelled by pornography. There is implicit recognition that fantasy is regarded as crucial, since most modern therapeutic programmes for sex offenders involve exercises about the role of sexual fantasy in sex crime (Howitt, 1995b). Bates (1996) studied a sample of men in a British therapeutic prison who had been convicted for sexual offences against women or children. All but one of the men had experienced deviant sexual fantasies before committing their first offence. The one exception had first offended at the age of 14 years and recalled no fantasies up to that time; nevertheless, the subsequent escalation of his offending was accompanied by sexual fantasy. Most of the offenders were able to identify the approximate time that their deviant sexual fantasies began. Nearly 80% of the men began their deviant sexual fantasies during puberty (11–15 years). A small number started to fantasize earlier than this; only about 17% identified the start of their fantasy as *above* the age of 15 years. Deviant sexual fantasy had emerged long before first offending, according to the Bates' data. Only about a quarter offended within a year of first having the deviant fantasy.

In this sample of offenders, pornography seemed to have a role in fuelling or sustaining fantasy; 58% had used pornography in this way. Just about 20% had used soft-core pornography, they said, to enable them to view women as sexual objects. Another 20% used hard-core pornography to 'reinforce' their preference for aggressive sexual behaviour:

> 'Other men, variously, reported other sources of material which they had used in order to become aroused and sexually fantasize. These include: newspaper accounts of rape, rape scenes from commercially available films, general scenes of sex and violence in horror films, horror books, "death metal" music (an extremely loud and aggressive form of rock music, with lyrics explicitly about death, sex and sadism) and the works of the Marquis de Sade.' (Bates, 1996, p. 10)

A majority of the men mentioned the sense of power, control and mastery as the enjoyable or arousing aspect of their deviant fantasies.

Erotic imagery can be manufactured from other types of imagery, so reducing the dependence of offenders on pornography. Howitt (1995b) suggests that for some offenders the offence itself may provide sexual imagery for later masturbation. Another source is non-sexual depictions taken from the mass media, which can be re-processed into a sort of pornography. Paedophiles may be affected by legal sanctions against child pornography, which act as a deterrent to possessing such material. In some countries, the possession of child pornography attracts severe penalties. Howitt (1995a) found that some paedophiles expressed relatively little interest in pornography and that, in general, child pornography was regarded as a very risky commodity. A much safer alternative is to collect innocuous pictures of children from newspapers, magazines or advertisements, which can then be used to feed sexual fantasies about sex with children (Holmes, 1991). Other offenders use normal heterosexual pornography as an initial source of imagery, which they then manipulate into fantasy about children. It is wrong to assume that nudity in imagery is essential to its transformation into deviant fantasy. The non-sexually explicit and non-pornographic imagery which some offenders use to generate fantasies about children include such things as Walt Disney videos which feature children, or pictures of children modelling underclothing in mail-order clothing catalogues (Howitt, 1995a). Some offenders use imagery from broadcast television programmes for children to generate fantasy. Programmes about schools or schoolchildren would be one source of such stimulation. None of this seems particularly odd if one considers the wide range of non-sexually explicit imagery which normal adults find arousing. There is other evidence that the sexual explicitness is not always the key feature determining sexual arousal. Hinton et al. (1980) describe how rapists found 'stalking' scenes prior to a rape more sexually arousing than the subsequent violent rape in video.

PORNOGRAPHY CIRCULATION AND SEXUAL VIOLENCE

The above studies concentrate on offenders who may or may not be reliable sources of information about the role of pornography on their offending. There are other ways of studying sex offending which do not rely on information obtained from individual offenders. Sexually violent crime statistics for different geographical areas can be correlated with the amount of pornography in circulation in those areas. Alternatively, changes over time can be studied. There have been a number of investigations of this type. Typical of them is Gentry (1991) who took the official rape statistics for different metropolitan areas of the USA in order to see whether the corresponding circulation figures for mass market soft-core pornographic magazines supported the pornography-causes-rape thesis. She found that they did not when appropriate statistical controls were employed—no more pornography was sold in areas where sexual violence was commonest. The proportions of divorced people and young adults in the areas in question predicted rape rates rather better.

Several other studies point to much the same conclusion. Baron and Straus (1984, 1987) were the first to employ such an approach. Their complex statistical analysis actually did show a relationship between rape rates and the circulation of sex magazines in the initial statistical analysis. This was not a causal relationship in the researchers' view. They pointed out, for example, that the circulation of *Playgirl* magazine, aimed at women readers, actually correlated better with rape rates than did male-oriented magazine circulation! It is difficult to explain how reading magazines featuring naked men encouraged women to become rape victims! Equally, it is difficult to imagine men buying *Playgirl* magazine and being driven to rape after seeing pictures of naked men. Baron and Straus (1989) followed this with an even more sophisticated analysis, which led them to the same 'no effect' conclusion about pornography. Jaffee and Straus (1987) found a relationship between pornography circulation and rape rates. Howitt and Cumberbatch (1990) showed that this correlation could actually be accounted for by the high correlation of both of these variables—pornography circulation and rape rates—with the proportions of divorced males in the area. Taking this into account reduced the correlation to insignificance, much as Gentry (1991) found. Another study following this style (Scott and Schwalm, 1988) initially found a relationship which became statistically insignificant when the three areas with the highest rape and pornography circulations were taken out of the analysis; so just a few areas were responsible for the apparent association. Furthermore, non-sexually violent magazine circulation correlated better with rape rates than that of sexually violent magazines! This further undermines a causal explanation which would have predicted the reverse.

The authors of these studies are all disinclined to interpret their data as evidence that pornography is implicated in sexual violence. Intriguingly, some authors have prematurely (Russell, 1988, 1992) or one-sidedly (Baxter, 1990) interpreted the data as support for their well-publicized views about the damaging effects of pornography on women.

A variant on this approach adds to the confidence in the no-causal-effects interpretation. Winick and Evans (1996) studied the effect of the non-enforcement of laws dealing with pornography in various states of the USA. The laws on pornography were suspended in North Carolina, Pennsylvania and Washington State at different times in the period 1973–1986. Increased circulation of sexually explicit materials seems to have occurred when the risk of prosecution had been reduced by these suspensions. Arrest rates for different types of crimes, including prostitution, sex offences and property offences, were studied for these states for the periods. There were *no* changes in the rates of these various types of crime in the states in question during the period of the suspension of the laws; however, in the other states the sex crime rates continued to increase. Whatever the interpretation one prefers, it is impossible to construe these changes as support of the argument that pornography leads to sexual crime.

Before moving on, it should be stressed that this type of survey does involve empirically based estimates of the actual circulation of pornography. The next approach simply *assumes* that the amount of pornography in circulation is directly linked to legislation against pornography.

TIME-SERIES ANALYSES

Time-series analysis also provides no convincing evidence that pornography leads to sexual violence. The best known study of the relationships between changes in the availability of pornography and sex crime rates is Kutchinsky's (1973) Danish investigation into the effects of liberalizing pornography. The evidence from this research suggests that sex offences declined as pornography became freely available. However, at best, this is probably only true for trivial, nuisance, sex crimes (Howitt and Cumberbatch, 1990). It simply did not apply to rape. Furthermore, the increased circulation of pornography in the USA during the same period was associated with more sex crimes (Cline, 1974). However, growth in sex crimes and of crime in general were similar (Kupperstein and Wilson, 1970). It is doubtful whether pornography could be the cause of both of these; why should pornography affect general crime in the same way as sexual crime? Consequently, this is weak evidence of an influence of pornography on sex crime.

For the modern period in Britain, according to the best estimates of the circulation of pornographic magazines and videos possible (although these are fairly poor), the increase in officially recorded crimes of sexual violence does not parallel trends in the circulation figures of soft-core pornographic magazines and the numbers of obscene publications (Howitt and Cumberbatch, 1990). Kutchinsky (1991) covers similar ground by collating aggregate data on officially recorded sexually violent crimes. Data for the USA, Denmark, Sweden and West Germany were considered for the 20-year period ending in 1984. As with other research, there was no evidence that violent sexual crime was increasing faster than crime in general, despite apparent increases in the availability of pornography. In West Germany there had even been a substantial decline in the numbers of reported rapes by strangers and groups of men, despite the rise in pornography in circulation.

The trend to find no relationship between sex crime and changes in the availability of pornography is only bucked by Court's (1977, 1984) analyses. He puts forward a number of propositions about the relationship between controls on pornography's availability and sex crimes, which he tests against data from different parts of the world. So, for example, he mentions Singapore, South Africa and South Australia as places where pornography was not liberalized, and found that rape rates in these places increased far more slowly than other places which allowed increases in the availability of pornography. The reporting of rape is subject to the influence of changes in practices and policies, such as court procedures (Howitt, 1982). So, perhaps it is not surprising that the reporting of rape changes less in repressive societies which have tough penalties for the crime. The problem with Court's data is not so much that there are reasonable alternative interpretations—although this is true of several of the studies—but that his views are so out of line with others adopting a similar style of research.

Generally speaking, the evidence from recorded crime rates casts cold water on the assertion that a 'steady' rise in the availability of ever more violent and degrading pornography is reflected in changes in the rates of sexually violent crime. Indeed, it is questionable what the trends in pornography circulation actually are. If so many systematic studies of sexual crime rates suggest no evidence of a role of pornography, there seems little room for the untrained eye to spot relationships overlooked by statisticians.

PRIORITIZING RESEARCH

As a body of research, studies of pornography in the lives of sex offenders seem remarkably consistent in their implications. There seems to be very little to suggest that substantial reductions in sex crimes could be achieved if the world were rid of the last vestiges of pornographic imagery. The reasons for this partly lie in the early origins of proclivities to sex offending, which seem to pre-date even the earliest experiences with pornography in childhood. This does not mean that offenders do not use pornography, merely that they use pornography which often is little related to their offending style. Furthermore, although deviant sexual fantasy characterizes many sex offenders, this fantasy has many sources, including seemingly innocuous imagery from regular broadcast media which is not sexually explicit or erotic in intent.

Despite the relative clarity of the research evidence on sex offenders, there exists a vast body of other research on students and other adults in the community, some of which is suggestive of an adverse influence of pornography on some men. This cannot and should not be denied, since it reinforces the importance of considering the criminological pertinence of research. Part of the fascination on the research is that it is subject to different interpretations, partly based on ideological considerations. If there is to be criminologically relevant media research, this issue is among the most urgent to be addressed.

CHAPTER 9

Women and Crime

'Four days after a network had shown the television movie *Born Innocent*, three teenage girls attacked a nine-year-old girl on a California beach. While a teenage boy kept watch, the girls apparently attempted to approximate a scene from the movie to rape their victim, Olivia Niemi, artificially. One girl was quoted in a deposition as stating that during the rape her boy-friend had called out, "Hey, are you doing it just like they did in the picture?"' (Wilson and Hunter, 1983, p. 435)

The heroine is no longer tied to railway tracks, a hapless victim. She has kicked over the traces and rarely screams in helpless fear while men sort out whatever needs sorting out. While old-fashioned gender stereotypes may be on the wane, new questions arise about the media, women and crime. One thing is certain, men and women do not share a level playing field when it comes to media representations of their involvement in crime. The inequalities portray one perspective on the ways in which men and women are framed as both victims and offenders. Simply put, women are likely to be blamed because they are victims and blamed because they are women if they are perpetrators of crime. Essentially, explanations are pushed to their ideological extremes when women are involved. Media criminology has to draw on feminist sources to understand the nature of the inequalities.

Characteristically, women's fears are encouraged by the media which stress women's special vulnerability to the most horrific crimes. Not surprisingly, therefore, women's fear of crime is about three times the level of men's (Stanko, 1995), although this is more to do with women's social position than the statistical likelihood that they will fall victim to crime:

'The fact is that many still place what endangers women the most—familial and familiar violence—on an agenda often separate from that of crime reduction. Others may suggest that better lighting, repairing broken windows, or cleaning graffiti is sufficient for creating an environment that is woman friendly and thus less fear producing. (Stanko, 1995, p. 58)

This sort of avoidance of structural issues in favour of palliative measures is to be found in media coverage of crimes against women. Men who commit atrocious violence against women are marginalized as bizarre monsters.

Even when women are neither victims nor perpetrators, they risk being held responsible for the acts of others. In recent years, our concepts of childhood innocence have been severely tested by grotesque murders by children in ways which have traditionally been regarded as the prerogative of deranged men. The British murder of James Bulger, the two-year old who was abducted from a shopping centre by the 10-year old boys, Jon Venables and Robert Thompson, is a case in point. They left James Bulger's body a few miles away on a railway track to be decapitated by a passing train. Our framing of childhood makes it difficult to reconcile such barbarism with the ideology of childhood innocence. Blame has to shift elsewhere. Although the media blamed violent videos, they also blamed the mothers of his young killers—in the case of Jon Venables' mother for giving him too much 'motherly' attention (Young, 1996b).

Women, then, are blamed as victims, offenders and mothers of offenders. It might be said that the media's response to them implies that they are a greater threat to society than men. All of this is unified under the issue of how crime is gendered in society in general and in the media in particular. In terms of media criminology, we are moving into a domain dominated by feminist theorists. The quantitative, empiricist concerns of the last few chapters have to be eschewed in favour of substantially more qualitative approaches.

In a rare quantitive study, Weimann and Gabor (1987) found that the amount of coverage of a victim of crime was best predicted by the interaction of the offender's sex and the type of crime. Women perpetrators of violent crime were associated with increased media coverage of the victim. References to the victim's contribution to the crime were commonest for a female perpetrating a violent crime. Holding the victim responsible was uncommon when the perpetrator was male. In other words, maleness of the perpetrator may be in itself sufficient explanation of male offending to the journalist.

SEXUAL OFFENCES AND THE MEDIA

Rape is an obvious but important example of a crime for which women are held responsible for their own victimization by the media and society in general. The classic example of this is the way in which women are described as provoking their own rape, perhaps by wearing short skirts. Systematic research has confirmed that this sort of victim-blaming strategy underlies the media's treatment of women victims of rape. The representation of crimes against women was studied by examining three newspapers in Toronto (Voumvakis and Ericson, 1982). Items concerning sexual attacks on women characteristically implied that the women were at fault for placing themselves at risk—for example, they had gone to dangerous areas or premises. Nevertheless, the danger was not from ordinary men but from immensely troubled and pathological individuals; the insinuation being that rape is perpetrated by mentally sick or bizarre individuals. This is the wrong message according to many feminist writers and crime statistics which suggest, for example, that in America strangers are responsible for only one-third of rapes and sexual assaults on women (US Department of Commerce, Economics and Statistics Information, 1996). Recommended solutions in the media to the problem of attacks on women involved escalating coercive actions by the criminal justice system against individuals. In other words, whatever validity there may be in the newspaper explanations of rape, ideas about gender inequality are consistently excluded from news stories. Curfews on men in general are not seen as the solution (cf. Lederer, 1980).

It has been shown that even the syntax of news reports is biased against women and can have a profound impact on perceptions of crimes against women (Henely, Miller and Beazley, 1995). When the active voice is used, as in 'In the USA a man rapes a woman every 6 minutes,' a different impression is created in the reader than with other forms. For example, the passive voice 'In the USA a woman is raped by a man every 6 minutes.' can be truncated to the following simply by omitting the agent (a man): 'In the US a woman is raped every 6 minutes'. These changes in syntax, superficially slight, substantially affect the subjective meaning of the crime report for readers, viewers and listeners. For stories using the passive voice there was a tendency for men (but not women) to attribute less harm to the victim and less responsibility to the perpetrator of the violence against a woman. Both sexes were more accepting of the violence against a woman if a passive voice rather than an active voice was used. It is of some significance that the passive voice is more common in stories about violence against women and non-sexual violence (murder) stories than any other type of story. In other words, not only could these syntax variations make a difference to the impact of a story, they actually are more commonly used when women are the victims.

Social and legal changes in the Western world and elsewhere have eased some of the difficulties experienced by victims when reporting rape. This does not mean that women's interests have been well served. One particularly important change has been the marked reduction in the amount of unwanted publicity given to identified or identifiable rape victims by the media, despite some infamous cases in which intrusive publicity has been given. The number of reported rapes has increased in the last 20 years or so, partially as a consequence of such changes. Nevertheless, this increase in reports of rape is not associated with an increase in the numbers of convictions for rape everywhere. Despite an increase in the number of rape trials, convictions have declined proportionately in the UK. In England and Wales, for the period 1985–1993, convictions reduced from 24% to 10% of verdicts, which just about balanced the increase in crimes reported to the police. Consequently, the number of *convictions* for rape has kept more or less steady, despite the increase in court cases. Thus, there is no increase in the number of women who have the satisfaction of seeing their attacker convicted and punished. Other parts of the world have shown different trends. In Canada over half of alleged rapists are convicted and in Australia 80% of men brought to court are convicted (Mills, 1996).

One continuing feminist concern about the criminal justice system involves the distress and injustice caused to women giving evidence about their own rapes. Notorious examples illustrate the problem well, for instance, the case of a rapist who cross-examined his victim, Julia Mason, at great length in court over a period of six days. Not only this, but he wore the same clothes for this cross-examination as during the rape. Such situations are not alleviated by the media's characteristic perspective on such crimes. Conventions and practices employed when reporting sexual attacks characterize such crimes in basically anti-women ways. One study of the reporting of rape in British newspapers took place in 1993 during the period of time when the issue of 'date rape' was gaining some prominence (Lees, 1995). The press characterized rape in ways which distorts the social reality of the crime and its victims:

- Rape is often portrayed as an exclusively sexual event. The violence and coercion, which are a feature of the typical rape, are either ignored completely or minimized. A victim's account, as presented in court, is frequently disregarded. Instead, the media structure their accounts of rape around how the defendant 'misunderstood' the victim's behaviour. What the victim may have seen as an innocent act of friendliness, say, is reported in the press as a confusing signal of sexual interest.
- Complainants are stereotyped as one or more of three basic types: (a) hysterical women; (b) promiscuous sluttish women; or (c) manipulative women. There are different 'explanations' of why each of these three different types of women make false allegations against a man or why a sexually naive woman might inadvertently encourage her own rape. The press is likely to adopt the defence's strategy of questioning and undermining the victim's credibility or scapegoating as

some sort of unreliable slut. This is not easily explained away, as it reverses the findings of other studies of the media and crime which demonstrate a clear affinity between the media and the prosecutor or prosecution case (see Chapter 3).

- Different parts of a newspaper are used to report convictions and acquittals. The placement of a news story in a newspaper signals the importance of the item. Acquittals tend to be given great prominence by, for example, making them front page headline news. In contrast, rape convictions are tucked away towards the middle of the newspaper, thus de-emphasizing them. The underlying message is that acquittal is a more significant event. One exception to these trends occurs when a man fitting the stereotype of a psychopathic, stranger rapist is convicted. In these circumstances the story may dominate the front page, emphasizing the dominant view of rape as 'stranger-danger'.

Of course, news reports are merely part of the total media coverage of rape—films and drama may also have their distinctive messages. The media, taken as a whole, do not represent a single hegemonic view of the sexual victimization of women. Entertainment shows, for example, may operate to a different agenda from news. This is clearly apparent if in-depth research into rape in movies is considered. A good example of this is Cuklanz's (1996) cultural studies approach to the study of 'fictional' rape trials. She describes famous real-life rape trials which resulted in fictional (or fictionalized) films. A key example is the 1988 Hollywood film, *The Accused*. This attracted attention and criticism from several different perspectives. It concerns a rape trial presented with flash-backs to the events leading up to and culminating in a gang rape. Cuklanz (1996) writes:

'Public trials are about power. They serve as the terrain on which ... opposing discourses do battle, and as such they are about the effort to determine definitions and truths central to our understanding of ourselves and our culture. Public trials are also about power in that their very existence is the result of conflict. In issue-oriented trials, social movements have won a place on the national agenda for their issues and concerns, and specific cases are taken up in the context of their struggle and arguments against mainstream ideas.' (p. 117)

So the legal victory is not crucial, as the trial enables a number of disparate ideologies to be brought into focus. Issue-oriented trials reveal and highlight significant areas in which society is troubled; possible future changes in dominant ideology are signalled as a consequence. Issue-oriented trials provide an arena in which the powerless can raise issues which otherwise escape general attention—they are 'sites of ideological accommodation', according to Cuklanz. So the media begin to concentrate on such newly emerging issues in measured ways which involve slight or grudging acceptance of minority points of view. This process of slow accommodation is vital to alterations in the dominant ideology. In turn, journalists' preferred mode of representing real-life rape trials may also change to have a less hostile perspective on the women victims.

Tobias, the central female character in *The Accused*, essentially characterizes radical feminist views about rape. These include rejecting the familiar claim that the victim of rape precipitates her own rape. Tobias refuses to comprehend that her past life has any bearing on her being raped. To her, her frequent use of drugs, including alcohol, living with an alleged drug-dealer boyfriend, her prior police record, or when she admits saying 'I'd like to take that guy home and fuck his brains out right in front of Larry. . . So what? It was just a joke' have no relevance to the crime. Furthermore, her desire to have her experience validated, both in public and in court, was based on radical feminist thinking of the time.

If Cuklanz is correct in her assertions about the role of trials in changing dominant ideology, research on the effects of pornography (Chapters 7 and 8) may have similarly served to highlight social contradictions and the nudging aside of previous dominant ideologies. Consider how research into pornography, for example, was effectively transformed into a feminist issue. The academic evidence on pornography's effects are being hotly debated and variously interpreted, especially in feminist terms.

A CASE STUDY IN THE GENDERING OF CRIME

'Importantly, the social significance of crime is never inherent in the event itself. There is a whole fabric of forces that act upon crime, designating the nature of its deviance, the understanding of those victims and perpetrators involved, the appropriate social response, and the associated punishment. News reporting is an important initial moment of this definitional process. Events do not speak their newsworthiness; rather, this culturally defined category stands as an informal set of criteria informing what is to enter a position of public and popular scrutiny.' (Acland, 1995, p. 46)

The preppy murder took place in Central Park, New York in 1986. Extensive media coverage over nearly two years kept it in the public eye. It illustrates some of the processes by which a crime may become gendered. Eighteen-year-old Jennifer Lewin was killed by Robert Chambers, who confessed shortly afterwards. He killed her, he claimed, because he had to defend himself from her predatory sexual advances.

This provided much of the framework for her media representation, in which her corpse symbolized the dangers to women created by feminism, which had 'defeminized' her by making her aggressive, demanding and desirous. She had failed to adhere to 'gender's natural order' and so brought about her own downfall. Jennifer would not have been dead but for the 'fact' that she had pushed Robert Chambers beyond the limit. In his own words:

> 'Jenny excused herself and then came up behind me. She messaged my shoulder and said I looked cute, but I would look cuter tied up. Jenny began cackling and tied me with her panties...She pushed me down and took off my pants. She grabbed my dick and jerked me off. I said it hurt. She picked up a stick and hit my dick with it. I yelled out, and a jogger passed and asked if everything was alright. She sat on my face and dug her nails into my chest. I screamed, and she squeezed my balls... I couldn't take any more. I got a hand free and around her neck. She flipped over and landed on her side, twisted next to a tree. I stood up, pulled on my pants, and said, "Let's go" ... I shook the body, but it didn't move.'
> (Acland, 1995, p. 79)

Robert Chambers was six feet four inches tall and Jennifer Lewin just over half of his weight! In many respects this is a variant of one male excuse for rape—we were lovers—but this time extended further in an attempt to justify the homicide. Of course, his confession was also central to the defence case. The American tabloid newspapers translated this into SHE RAPED ME and WILD SEX KILLED JENNY. Jennifer Lewin's murder was important because of the ideological concerns about gender which Robert Chambers' confession amounted to.

ANOTHER SIDE TO ANOTHER STORY

One of the curiosities of the media's treatment of women and crime is that certain feminism-inspired ideas become routine in the media, whereas others are virtually ignored or ridiculed. So while the press has largely continued to portray rape from the male viewpoint, not all feminist crime issues have so doggedly failed to gain prominence. Conceptions of female violence are a good example of the profound influence of feminist perspectives. The history of female violence is long—there is an abundance of cultural stereotypes which portray violent females. In Britain, examples include seaside postcards and cartoons featuring women awaiting their men with rolling-pins in their hands, or phrases like 'battle-axes' implying combative women. Nevertheless, female violence against men has been largely ignored in modern times. The public may take media silence as an indication that there is no problem. For instance, a survey by Stalans (1996) in Georgia, USA, asked the public to estimate the percentage of domestic violence calls which involved injuries and who was injured. Two-thirds, on average, were thought to involve injury to the wife, 17% to involve injuries to the husband, and 17% injuries to both. In other words, men are the main perpetrators of domestic violence which results in injuries. This may or may not be so in reality; our concern at the moment is the way in which the media contribute to this view.

Murray Straus was one of the architects of research into domestic violence. His work was among some of the earliest and most important demonstrating the extent of violence in the home. Straus (1992) argues that the media have failed to communicate effectively the extent and seriousness of female violence against their male partners. In contrast, very similar findings about men's violence to their sexual partners became a staple of media coverage of gender relationships from the 1970s onwards. According to American family violence surveys, violent abuse of partners is almost equally common in women as men. Although the issue has only recently entered into the public debate through the media, the extensiveness of women's violence against their men was established by some of the early domestic violence surveys. Men's violence against women created enormous press and public interest but domestic violence by female perpetrators had remarkably little impact.

Of course, this was not solely a media phenomenon. 'Husband-battering', according to Straus, was derided, opposed and derogated by crucial opinion-leaders on domestic violence. Public lectures on the topic were sabotaged by disruptions of various sorts; bomb threats hit conferences at which it was discussed. There are other, more studied, responses to Straus's claims. Some argued that his measures of violence were so general that they failed to distinguish between a slap by a woman of a man and several beatings of a woman by a man (Scott, 1994). Others felt that women were being unrealistically idealized, which led to a disbelief that women could be dangerously violent. Nevertheless, even when the notion of domestic violence by women was accepted, it was explained that such women were likely to have been acting out their own abuse (e.g. Kelly, 1991).

Lucal (1995) sought to explain the slow emergence of 'battered husbands' as a social issue. In her view, things are not defined as social problems merely because they are common. The 'tagging' or promotion of social phenomena as social problems is much more to do with the activities of claims-makers than numerical frequencies. One can, Lucal suggests, identify the beginning of concern about 'battered wives' with Erin Pizzey's 1974 publication, *Scream Quietly or the Neighbours will Hear*, and the ensuing academic research. The gathering dominance of feminism and the women's movement led to a new conceptualization of women's domestic experience of violence as 'wife-battering'. Steinmetz's article, *The Battered Husband Syndrome* (Steinmetz, 1977), provided the equivalent starting point for 'husband-battering'. The feminist gender politic holds that male violence against women is a means by which men achieve and maintain power over women. This violence includes sexual attacks, physical violence and the fear of these things. In this context, routine female violence against men is rendered inexplicable, since it should not exist other than as irrelevant, trivial episodes. Women mercilessly abused by their violent partners might eventually 'snap' and kill their tormentors, but they are the exception which proves the rule. Feminism developed an infrastructure which included a network of support and pressure groups. As a consequence, feminist claims-makers were readily accessible to journalists to provide feminist explanations of male violence against women.

In contrast, there were no analogous organized groups promoting 'husband-battering' during the same period of time. Professionals, such as psychologists, counsellors and social workers, who had made claims about 'wife-battering', had no incentive to stake a claim in the 'husband-battering' debate; men simply were not approaching professionals in substantial numbers seeking help to deal with violent partners. Furthermore, some women's groups were antagonistic to the very idea of 'husband-battering' because of its potential to detract attention and funding from women—the 'real' victims of domestic violence. The task of getting women's violence on the agenda was made no easier by the image of men as tough, forceful and powerful. This made it difficult to construe them as anything other than deserving victims of their own excesses.

There is a further issue related to this. It is claimed that women who are violent, for example those who murder their abusive partners, are treated much more severely by the courts than men who murder their partners. McNeill (1996) argues that men routinely get away with murdering their wives and girlfriends. She suggests that the exceptions in which life sentences are given prove the rule. These exceptions include the man who robbed a financial institution managed by his wife. He tied her up and killed her and then tried to blame a gang of criminals for this deed. Most times when a man kills his wife he gets away without a life sentence for very ordinary reasons such as the woman nagged or she taunted him sexually. Less than one-third of men in Britain who killed women known to them were convicted of murder in 1994 (Roberts, 1995). Forty percent of women who killed men known to them were convicted of murder. The trend is not great and is better illustrated by specific cases. Sara Thornton was convicted of murder in 1990 and released by the courts in 1995, to be eventually acquitted. She had killed her violent and drunken husband who, among other things, had knocked her unconscious. The killing, however, had an element of premeditation, since there was evidence of planning rather than immediate retaliation for one of his violent attacks. Much of the evidence against her painted her as a bad person—abortions, suicide attempts and smoking drugs. Furthermore, just as in the preppy murder, she had high sexual needs—she even did not wear underwear! Sara Thornton became a feminists' *cause celebre* and her case led to the very sort of public trial and publicity which Cuklanz (1996) identified as vital to changing society. Legal definitions in Britain may have changed in ways which encompass delayed responses to intolerable violence as a consequence.

FEMICIDE AND FEMINIST CLAIMS-MAKERS

Ideas about women as victims do not simply hark back to bygone ages, since they still manifest themselves in a variety of different contexts. Walter (1996) makes this very clear when she points to the great emphasis given to murders of Britons in foreign countries. For example, *The Daily Mail* carried the headline WHY DO YOUNG GIRLS RISK THEIR LIVES ON THE BACK-PACK TRAIL? However, when set against the reality of the situation, this is to neglect that men are several times more at risk of being illegally killed abroad. Less than one-fifth of the 40 or so Britons killed overseas in a year are female. Such a killing of a man is far less newsworthy; neither is it presented as a crisis of male behaviour as it is for females. The underlying agenda is the reaffirmation of the belief in the vulnerability of women and the importance for them that they keep within 'natural' boundaries.

More of the intricate interplay between representations of crime in the media and feminism is revealed by considering *serial murder*, as documented by Jenkins (1994). Serial killing is probably age-old and not merely a media creation. The Monster of the Andes, Pedro Lopez of Bolivia, for example, killed nearly 400 girls in the 1970s, although serial killing first became identified as a major social problem in the USA in the 1980s, when it gained a great deal of media attention. Some of the modern imagery about serial killing is reinforced by fictional representations of serial killers in movies, such as those based on *Dracula*. Epstein (1995) studied 155 serial killers in 172 feature-length films issued from 1930 to 1992. (Some, such as Freddy Kruger, might be described as serial serial killers, since they appeared in several films.) Although the film representations of the serial killer may accurately portray them as typically middle-aged and white, they misrepresent other significant features of serial killing. So, despite the fact that famous American serial killers such as Jeffrey Dahmer were involved in homosexual killings, homosexuality is severely under-represented in these films. Consequently, movie serial killing is tied to heterosexuality and, thus, the feminist notion of femicide (Radford and Russell, 1992) is better supported in the cinema than in real-life. Sexually active couples, however, are typical victims of serial killers in movies, partly because they can provide gratuitous nudity. Movie serial killing often involves a sense of moral fortitude which legitimates the violence.

Movie representations of *female* serial killers imply that they are morally driven avengers of a gang-rape or a wrong done by a significant male character, or motivated by bad supernatural forces. In real life, the female serial killer is more typified by such cases as Beverley Allitt, a British nurse who was given life sentences for the murder of four, and the attempted murder of three, sick children in her care. Naylor (1995) suggests that Allitt was portrayed by the tabloid media as a 'not woman':

'The tabloid coverage of Beverley Allitt combined the broad-brush "monster" image with one which emphasized her 'masculinity'. She was big, she was butch, she beat up her boyfriend, who became (according to *The Daily Mirror* 18 May 1993) "a sex-starved target of her ugly violence". And for good measure, she is a lesbian.' (p. 89)

This is quite different from the case of the American serial killer, Aileen Wournos, who admitted killing seven men. That she was a lesbian prostitute helped to make her something of a feminist cause (Deem, 1996). Perhaps things would have been different had she been a child killer.

For more than 100 years, multiple-murder cases have been linked together; Jack the Ripper being the most infamous example. Nevertheless, serial murder as a general phenomenon only approached 'panic' levels in America during the 1980s. In previous decades, serial killers would have been seen as the responsibility of psychiatrists or other therapists. Thus, conceptions derived from the medical model of construing social problems (Howitt, 1991, 1992) governed understanding and disposal of repeat killers. They were not seen as a problem warranting the special attention of the criminal justice system. Over time, serial killing and serial killers became redefined or reconstrued as instances of a general problem with wide social ramifications. Culturally, Jenkins argues, serial murder is held in heavy contradistinction to the innocence of the victim (such as a child). Such a dichotomy can be used politically to justify the most extreme policies, including draconian punishments.

It remains to be explained just how serial killers became elevated to a major issue of social concern in America. Jenkins (1994) takes the view that the crucial step is to identify those 'claims-makers' who present issues in a particular way. Understanding such claims-makers is central to social constructionist approaches to social problems. Social constructionism assumes that social knowledge is created socially, usually by groups or institutions with a particular vested interest in a particular way of construing reality. Jenkins lists what he sees as the important groups of claim-makers which emerged in the 1980s with a particular stake in the idea of serial killers: (a) feminists and their concerns about serial femicide in the context of the broader problem of violence against women; (b) religious groups with concerns about ritual murders; (c) children's rights activists worried about missing or exploited children; and (d) black groups who saw serial murder as systematic racial exploitation. Each of these used the media to promote their cause.

Concern about serial killers may have had roots in American culture, but it spread elsewhere. For example, Jenkins argues that the case of the Yorkshire Ripper in Britain gave credence to the feminist notion of femicide. The 13 known victims of Peter Sutcliffe, the Yorkshire Ripper, were young women, including prostitutes. However, the serial killer Dennis Nilsen, who strangled 16 young men, has the greatest number of convictions. Nevertheless, serial killing was construed in terms of sexual politics: some men kill some women but, in effect, womankind is terrified into submission to all men. The concept of femicide not only shaped media coverage but also criminology and law enforcement practice (Jenkins, 1992). The neologisms *gynocide* and *femicide* essentially re-define serial murder as a crime which is at the core of feminist concerns. In femicide, both the killer and his victim are merely representative of wider social categories determined by gender. This is seen by Jenkins as a grave misrepresentation:

'In reality, women, and especially white women, are by far the least likely segment of the population to fall victim to homicide. For Americans in the 1990s, the lifetime chance of becoming a murder victim is about 1 in 150, but this ranges from a high of 1 in 21 for black men to 1 in 104 for black women, one in 131 for white men, and 1 in 369 for white women.' (Jenkins, 1994, p. 156)

Jenkins suggests that there has been 'immense ideological value' attached to serial murder for feminists in recent years. He argues that it is as important as a rhetorical device as rape was in the 1970s. Rape and serial murder have provided feminists with powerful and potent images which serve crucial rhetorical purposes. In this way, serial murder has contributed to the dissemination of feminist beliefs about the extent and causes of sexual violence. Some feminist writers are dismissive of the notion of female serial killers, arguing that this is a male phenomenon (Cameron, 1996). The difficulty can be in how the term is defined. According to Cameron, we should restrict it to sex killings, which obviously excludes women such as Beverley Allitt, who murdered in the context of caring for children for whom there was no obvious sexual motive. Serial sadistic sexual homicide may amount to fewer than 10 females world-wide. Rose West and Myra Hindley were committed 30 years apart and seem to be the only obvious British examples of serial *sexual* murderesses. On the other hand, neither were lone offenders and both were in relationships with a male co-offender. No matter, feminist ideas of femicide are compromised by such female serial killers and the homosexual serial killers who are high on the lists of prolific offenders.

Socially constructed statistics may accompany socially constructed facts. The flaws of mainstream crime statistics based on numbers of crimes known to the police pale into insignificance in comparison to the statistics on serial homicide. For example, newspaper reports claimed that serial murder amounts for about one-fifth of homicides in the USA. It was being suggested in the American media in the early 1980s that there were over 3500 senseless, random murders annually in the USA. In contrast, the FBI official estimate put the figure at approximately 200 such crimes. How could estimates vary so much? The high figure was obtained by massaging of the available statistical information. So:

- There was *nothing* known about the circumstances of 17% of homicides.
- In 29% of homicides there was *no* available information about the relationship between the offender and victim.
- In 16% of cases the killer was a stranger to the victim.

Adding each of these percentages together yields a estimate of the extent of serial-killing which is bogus and misleading. It is bogus because it is not based on known multiple killings and because it assumes the worst possible scenario without any justification. Since the 'unknown' categories described had increased since the 1960s, they may be partially responsible for the additional dubious claim that serial homicide has 'exploded' in recent years.

The ramifications of the serial killer phenomenon are many and sometimes unexpected. For example, Sanders and Lyon (1995) describe how the media represented the unsolved murders of women from minority groups who were found left in the streets. The media suggested that they were involved in prostitution and consequently constituted a group of victims 'undeserving' of sympathy. This representation treated each death as an individual event, thus overlooking strong patterns in the incidents. Sanders and Lyon argue that the creation of social reality is a political act; the media are an important political tool for claims-makers to manipulate our understanding of the world and so influence social and political agenda. Their example shows how a group such as women from minority groups can be ignored by claim-makers.

DISCOURSES OF GENDER IN CRIME

Mainstream media coverage of women and crime does not routinely involve all of the discourses discussed in this chapter. For the most part, significant attention is only drawn to these fundamental matters in exceptional circumstances. The mainstream media may be unable to respond to aspects of crime which feminists, for example, see as crucial. Take the case of Jennifer Saunders, who was convicted of indecent assault and initially sent to prison for six-years. She had had penetrative sex with two girls of 15 and 16 years of age using a strapped-on dildo. Saunders, herself, was a girl of about this age at the time. She was alleged to have hidden the fact that she was female from them and somehow convinced them that there were good medical reasons why she had women's breasts and that the dildo was a real penis. Jennifer Saunders claimed that the girls were aware of her sex and that she only posed as a male with their families. The trial judge expressed the view that her offences were worse than rape. In British law, lesbianism has been 'erased' from the official legal discourse for centuries (Smith, 1995), in contrast with male homosexuality which is still punishable in certain circumstances. For Smith, Jennifer Saunders's treatment by the court can only be understood by reference to this. Saunders had, after all, initiated several sexual episodes with other girls, so violating the assumption of passivity in representations of women's sexuality:

'There were only three pre-authorized positions in legal discourse which could have accommodated Saunders's sex subjectivity—the heterosexual male, the dangerous gay man, and the heterosexual female prostitute. The heterosexual female prostitute is of course one of the very few women figures who are recognized as sexual subjects in official discourse; she owes her specificity precisely to the fact that she threatens to disrupt the exchange of women between men along patriarchal familial lines.' (Smith, 1995, p. 173)

This process, by which traditional views of women are imposed and alternative constructions of femininity ignored, is recognizable in many popular media issues. So when gendered excuses for female crimes of violence become popular in the media—pre-menstrual syndrome or battered-woman syndrome, for example—they essentially marginalize female violence to exceptional but feminine circumstances. In this respect they can each be anti-female constructions (Kendall, 1991), despite their superficial pro-women aspects.

Other issues of female dangerousness are neutralized by the media. John Wayne Bobbitt is said to be more famous than the American President among Americans. Presumably this is partly because of the intense media publicity given to the trial of his wife, Lorena Bobbitt, for slicing off and disposing of his penis (which was eventually found and re-attached). Frequently in media reports, the feminist implications of the case are lost in favour of its bizarre novelty value. Lorena Bobbitt claimed that she had been frequently raped by him within marriage and that she had retaliated violently following such an assault. The media tended to represent the problem as being caused by his philandering (Coles, 1996), thus casting her as a woman spurned who acted out of jealousy. Of course, to some feminists, such events should have provided the opportunity to broaden the stage for a debate about feminist discourses on female violence (Deem, 1996).

Other, more systematic, research suggests that the way women are portrayed when they kill their male partners is somewhat different from men who kill their female partners. According to Wykes (1995), the crucial difference is that men killers are portrayed as breaking the law, whereas the women are portrayed as breaking the taboos of behaviour appropriate to their gender:

> 'Thus the press accounts manage to perpetuate the legitimacy of male violence in gendered terms while castigating it in legal terms, and castigating female violence in legal terms whilst "resurrecting old stereotypes about appropriate female behaviour"... What is missing is any critique of violence as associated with masculinity.' (p. 69–70)

Clearly, a feminist criminology is needed which brings the media to a more central position in order to understand better and in more detail just how media gendering of crime is achieved.

CHAPTER 10

Acquisitive Crime

'... any simple conclusion that economic hardship leads to crime is undermined by the fact that there does not appear to have been anything other than a steady growth of offending during the inter-war period, in spite of the acute depression of many of the largest and traditional centres of industrialization.' (Emsley, 1994, p. 153)

Property crime is under-represented in the media (Chapter 3). The evidence from published statistics suggests that the crimes which have most exercised media researchers are the least likely to happen to people. Violent crime in the USA affects over 700 people per 100 000 of the population each year (US Department of Commerce, Economics and Statistics, 1996). In contrast, the rates for property crimes are about 4700 people per 100 000 of the population. The greatest rates for these crimes are found in metropolitan areas and the least in rural areas. Victim surveys suggest that burglary is likely to affect as many as 8% of households with the lowest incomes; it is only half as frequent for the richest households. Similarly, in England and Wales there were more than five million notifiable offences in 1995 (Office for National Statistics, 1997). Of these, nearly half were theft and handling stolen goods and a quarter were burglary. Out of the five million crimes, only 213 000 involved violence against the person. There are signs that the public are anxious about property crime, although violence receives dispropor-tionate attention. About one-fifth of men reported that they were very worried about the possibility of theft of their car, theft from their car or burglary. Only one-eighth expressed such fears of mugging. Generally speaking, more women were very worried about the possibility of prop-erty offences—about a quarter of women were afraid of these. A quarter of women were very worried about the possibility of being mugged and one-third about the possibility of being raped (Office for National Statis-tics, 1997). There are about 30 000 sexual offences annually in England and Wales, of which 5000 are rape.

It is curious, therefore, to find that property crime is not only ignored by the media but that media researchers have neglected research into the effects of property crime in the media. In contrast to the thousands of studies on pornography and violence, it is difficult to find more than a handful or two of studies which involve property crime.

INSTRUMENTAL VS EXPRESSIVE CRIMES

Payne and Payne (1970) made a number of theoretical suggestions of how the levels of crime in society related to the newspaper coverage of crime:

• The news media provide a cathartic release of tensions which otherwise might result in crime.
• The news media provide information about the sorts of people who commit crimes and the methods they use to commit crime.
• Newspaper publicity given to crime encourages attention-seekers to actively court such publicity.
• Newspaper publicity given to criminals is a deterrent to crime.

The latter two hypotheses are clearly direct opposites and involve different motives.

In the 1950s, several newspaper strikes lasting for periods of up to several months took place in Detroit. Payne and Payne examined crime trends when newspapers were available compared with when they were unavailable. If newspaper reports were affecting crime levels, then it would be expected that statistics on crimes known to the police would differ during newspaper strikes compared with normal periods of production. Did crime rates fluctuate in the absence of newspaper coverage of crime? The researchers, in analysing the crime data, divided crime into two types: (a) expressive crimes such as rape, murder and assault; and (b) non-expressive crimes, such as burglary or motor car thefts. It is not altogether certain how Payne and Payne defined the difference between the two concepts. They did, however, explain that there is a distinction between crime which is instrumental in that it is *an end in itself* and crime which is *a means to achieving other ends*. There may be problems with this, since it is far from clear that the motivations for the so-called non-expressive crimes are always extrinsic to the individual's psychological needs (see Chapter 7). Payne and Payne hypothesized that expressive crimes would be unaffected by newspaper strikes, since their motivation was intrinsic to the individual, whereas non-expressive crimes would be influenced. Their predictions were supported by the evidence. Car thefts, robbery and burglary (the non-expressive crimes) were about 10–20% lower during strike periods. The so-called expressive crimes demonstrated no consistent trend in any direction. Thus, Payne and Payne found some support for their hypothesis about the effect of the media on instrumental crime.

It has become increasingly clear that Payne and Payne's conclusions are not quite so exceptional as they might once have appeared (Howitt, 1982). Television reached virtually saturation penetration of its potential market during the 1960s; nearly all households have had at least one television set since then. There were a number of studies which researched the impact of television's arrival as a truly mass medium in the 1950s (Himmelweit, Oppenheim and Vince, 1958; Schram, Lyle and Parker, 1961). These, with the exception of minor excursions into media violence effects, ignored the impact of the introduction of television on levels of crime. It was not until many years later that Hennigan et al. (1982) somewhat retrospectively examined the trends in American crime rates for the period of time before and after the introduction of television during the 1950s. It should be stressed that there was no instant at which television was suddenly switched-on throughout the country. Technical and practical factors ensured that some areas had television several years before other areas. This provided Hennigan et al. with the opportunity to carry out a sophisticated analysis of the effects of the introduction of television. In this, they could compare time-trends in television and no-television areas, and then time-trends in no-television areas when they were finally linked-up. Hennigan et al.'s argument about their strategy was that 'To be convincing, an effect found at the earlier time in one sample must be replicated at the other time in the other sample' (p. 464). In other words, if television causes crime, then increases in crime should occur sooner in areas which adopted television first, and later in areas which adopted television later.

Crime statistics were obtained for a variety of different types of crimes—criminal homicide, forcible rape of a female, robbery (using force, violence or fear), aggravated assault, burglary (breaking and entering), larceny/theft (but not of a motor vehicle), and motor vehicle theft. Generally, the evidence only implicated television in less serious property crime, such as larceny. In keeping with other research, it was far from clear that television had any effect at all on more serious crimes, including violent ones. Because Hennigan's et al.'s conclusions have not always been precisely reported, it is useful to note their exact words:

'The fear that television has increased crime in the United States is indeed well founded. For the first time, a study directly assessed how the introduction of television affected crime and strongly suggested that television increased larceny. Although no firm conclusions were possible about television's effect on other crimes, it seems warranted to suggest that television's impact may have been stronger on less serious crimes like larceny than on more serious crimes like murder, aggravated assault, or burglary.' (p. 475)

These findings are essentially compatible with those of Payne and Payne—if we take a reasonably broad view. It should be noted that Clark and Blankenburg (1971) studied the relationship between the amount of violence shown in television programmes yearly between 1953 and 1969 and levels of violent crime in the community. Much as Payne and Payne (1970) and Hennigan et al. (1982) concluded, there was no relationship between levels of violent crime and the media.

In their meta-analysis of the effects of television, Paik and Comstock (1994) found that the available research showed moderate effects of television on crime. The exception to this was criminal violence (which they defined as homicide, suicide, stabbing, etc.) for which the trends were the weakest in their analysis. On the other hand, crimes like burglary and grand theft tended to show relationships with the media. This again fits in well with Hennigan's careful conclusion. A possible exception to this sort of trend is the study by Davis (1952). He related the amount of crime coverage in newspapers to the amount of crime reported in the Uniform Crime Reports of the FBI during 1948–1950 inclusive. For the four Colorado newspapers studied, it was clear that there was no relationship between newspaper reports about crime and the actual amounts of crime committed, as indexed by the criminal statistics. This is very much a rogue finding compared with the general trend of what is, admittedly, a rather limited number of studies.

OTHER EXCEPTIONS TO THE RULE?

So, there seems to be a relationship between the levels of property crime and the media; this is not the case for violent crime (see Chapters 5 and 6). At first sight, a number of studies appear to be relevant to this argument. Unfortunately, closer examination shows that they do not distinguish between property or acquisitive crime and other forms of crime. There may be a number of reasons for this—these particular studies tend not to rely on official crime statistics.

As discussed in Chapter 6, Halloran, Brown and Chaney (1970) compared the television viewing habits of delinquents reporting to probation officers with those of a matched sample of non-delinquent youngsters, equated in terms of age, social class, sex, intelligence and performance in school. The sheer quantity of exposure to television did not reliably differentiate between the delinquent and non-delinquent youngsters. Nevertheless, there was some hint in the data of a prefer-ence of delinquents towards 'exciting' programmes. In the USA, Pfuhl (1960, 1970) investigated data from a large sample of boys and girls who anonymously completed a questionnaire about their delinquent behav-iours, such as wanton destruction of property. According to Pfuhl, the amount of exposure to television and radio did not differentiate between self-reported delinquents and non-delinquents. On the other hand, there did appear to be an association between the use of some media and delinquency—particularly the motion-picture theatre. Howitt and Dembo (1974) and Howitt and Cumberbatch (1975) argue that this is much what one would expect in terms of delinquent sub-cultures. Certain media serve as a focus for the social activities of delinquent youth. Delinquency is itself a social activity (most delinquent acts being committed by groups of young people, rather that youths acting in isolation), so one might expect the delinquents to choose the movies as a base for their recreation. They probably frequent bars and street corners for much the same reason. Unfortunately, these studies do not allow us to distinguish among different types of delinquent behaviour and so it is impossible to know from them if property crime, in particular, is associated with media use.

DECISIVE STUDIES?

One major and crucial study did directly investigate the relationship between the media and juvenile theft (Belson, 1975). Belson took a large sample of 1500 London boys in the age range 13–16 years in order to find the factors which led to theft in this age group. Many different types of theft were included—buying stolen goods, avoiding payment of fares, stealing money, stealing cars, cheating someone out of money, stealing milk, stealing from family or relations and stealing from shops. The research, although based on essentially simple methods, was extremely thorough and exacting. The researcher went to considerable lengths to ensure that the boys' self-reports of thefts were as honest as possible. Since the study basically involved assessing the correlation between media use and theft, as wide a range of competing explanations for the findings as possible were taken into account by controlling for numerous third-variable effects. Working class youngsters may, for example, watch more television and steal more without television being the cause of that stealing. Thus, the researcher needed to control or equate for differences in social class associated with both viewing and stealing. Belson's *Stable Correlate Method* weights the distribution of the group of light viewers such that it matches the distribution of heavy viewing in terms of numerous extraneous variables which might cause a spurious, non-causal, relationship between viewing and crime.

After these adjustments, there was no hint in the data that television schooled children into theft. In the early stages of the analysis it was found that the more a youngster was involved in stealing, the *less* interested he was in watching television and the *lower* his actual television viewing time. However, this difference disappeared once the full set of control variables were employed. Television was not the cause of juveniles stealing. In contrast, activities such as going to the cinema, getting the latest fashions, dancing, riding a motor bike or scooter, going around with mates, getting into fights with other youngsters, and having a bit of a wild time were associated with thieving, whereas gardening, welfare work, reading and going to church or chapel were uncommon in thieves. Again this pattern fits in well with Howitt and Dembo's (1974) subcultural account of apparent media influences, discussed earlier (Chapter 6).

Further evidence casting doubt on television's influence on theft comes from a series of experiments by Milgram and Shotland (1973). These studies involved manipulating the contents of regular broadcast television transmissions. In other words, unlike most experimental studies of the mass media, they were extremely naturalistic and realistic. In one of their experiments, a special version of a programme, *Medical Center*, was produced. In this episode, a character made an abusive telephone call to a medical charity. Milgram and Stotland wished to know whether this caused 'anti-social behaviour' in the form of similar telephone calls to an authentic medical charity. This authentic charity had some public service advertising during the programme. The researchers compared abusive telephone calls directed to the charity following a 'neutral' episode of the programme (i.e. one not including fictional abusive phone calls) with those received following the experimental version. Not only were abusive calls very uncommon indeed, but they were just as infrequent following the experimental episode compared to the neutral episode. The researchers carried out a range of studies along these lines, which also included theft from charity boxes as the dependent variable. There was little or nothing to implicate the media in crime.

WHICH PROCESS OF MEDIA INFLUENCE?

Just what is the interpretation of the apparently contradictory trends emerging in different types of research? Carefully controlled studies of offenders seem to suggest that property crime is not related to media use. One implication of this is that media use does not influence people to steal. The types of study which do implicate television and newspapers in crimes against property are those which involve crime statistics based on offences known to the police. These studies are essentially time-series analyses of the availability of media and the levels of crime. They indicate a relationship between fluctuations in media availability and levels of property crimes.

What confidence can be placed in these somewhat anomalous findings which imply that the media are associated with theft but, apparently, not through direct effects on individuals? One possibility is that the public are simply less inclined to report crimes to the police in the absence of crime news in the media. In other words, the media make people concerned about crime and so more likely to report a property offence. It may also not be surprising that the more serious crimes, such as murder, rape and assault, are less affected by such considerations, simply because they are much more serious. Similarly, without the pressures of media coverage, the police may be less inclined to classify a minor incident as a crime or to proactively engage in crime sweeps. In short, the more media coverage there is of crime, the more likely it is that crimes will be reported to and recorded by the police.

But what if this is not the case? What if we are dealing with the indirect media effects on crime that were mentioned in Chapter 2? Most models of media effects assume that the media influence individuals directly through processes such as imitation or attitude change. Thus, criminal acts by individuals are responsible for variations in crime statistics. However, things do not necessarily have to be like this—the process could be substantially different. For example, the assumption that media cause change by acting directly on individuals is not shared by research into the diffusion innovations in society. Concepts such as *opinion leader* (a person with a significant role in leading change) and the *two-step flow of communications* (the media may operate through such opinion leaders, rather than directly) are elderly ones in media research, but perhaps very pertinent to indirect influences of the media on crime levels (Katz and Lazarsfeld, 1964). So, an indirect model of communication effects would suggest that a youngster who is vulnerable to peer pressure would not even have to watch television to be persuadable into crime by someone who had been influenced. Furthermore, since the media overwhelmingly promote consumption and consumerism, it may be that people learn to want from the media, theft being a consequence of that rather than of crime shows. Just what sort of media content do we expect to be criminogenic in these circumstances? The answer must be anything that encourages wanting.

If the media do influence the audience to be criminal, but not directly, then it is perfectly feasible that media use by individuals fails to predict their crimininality, whereas criminal statistics respond to the introduction of the media or periods of media strikes. The pattern of the evidence supports the indirect effects thesis better than it does a direct effects model. The evidence is far too weak to suggest that media crime shows or crime news reporting are directly responsible for property crime.

CHAPTER 11

Race and Hate Crime

'It is not their blackness that has made them commit crime, but we cannot ignore the fact that many of the youngsters we are going to be arresting are going to be black.' (Sir Paul Condon, Commissioner of the Metropolitan Police, *The Guardian*, 29 July 1995, p. 3)

'The Metropolitan Police will not identify the source of their figures about mugging in the capital, because they apply to a very few areas of London. And surprise, surprise, these areas are populated largely by black residents. Amazingly, therefore, both the perpetrators and the victims of street crime are black.' (Philip, 1995, p. 10)

The hate crime question is simple: do the media, by promoting anti-minority feelings, sentiments and beliefs, contribute to crimes against minorities? There has been steady and consistent criticism of the media from black individuals and groups concerning biased and racist coverage of black people and black issues (Yeboah, 1988). Not only have the media perpetrated gross injustices in their treatment of black peoples, minorities continue to be represented in fundamentally hostile ways despite evidence that crude misrepresentations of black people have declined. While the very first study of the role of the media in racial issues (Thurstone and Chave, 1929) investigated cinema effects, since then the effects model has been adopted infrequently by media researchers. Content analysis studies which quantify the representations of race on television and in newspapers are more prevalent. Consequently, comparatively little is known about the effects of racial imagery in the mass media on the audience and how media representations of black people become incorporated with other culturally-based beliefs.

Characteristically, race issues in relation to the media change over time, although there are some continuities. Is the research carried out in earlier decades still relevant? Are lessons from the past still pertinent? Should we disregard the routine racism of children's books from bygone times, now that they have been purged or rewritten (Zimet, 1976)? For those interested, useful summaries exist of earlier content analyses of minorities and the mass media (Durkin, 1985; Greenberg, 1986; Wober and Gunter, 1988). Some might find Signorielli's (1985) comprehensive annotated bibliography of role portrayal and stereo-typing on television still useful. Older research will be referred to in this chapter when it has things of theoretic importance to say or when it contrasts markedly with modern practices.

Racially motivated attacks are known to be on the increase in vir-tually every public setting that one would wish to consider. So, for example, it has been demonstrated that racial minorities are much more likely to suffer racially motivated attacks (Home Office, 1981), that racial violence and harassment are increasing in the housing sector (Commission for Racial Equality, 1987a), that racial attacks have become commoner in educational settings (Commission for Racial Equality, 1987b) and that racial assaults known to the police are in-creasing (Runnymede Trust, 1993). Generally speaking, of course, these are crimes which are rarely covered by the media except for exceptional cases.

Race is not the only area in which the media may contribute to hate-crimes. The anti-gay sentiments characteristic of much media output (Sanderson, 1995) cannot be ignored when cataloguing violence against other minorities such as homosexuals (Herck and Berrill, 1992; Kitzinger, 1994). As yet the evidence implicating the media in hate crime other than race is circumstantial.

RACE AND CRIME

In some ideologically-based beliefs, black people and crime are asso-ciated (Yeboah, 1988). Whatever the complete explanation of this, the belief is, in part, a socially constructed 'fact' to which the media contrib-ute. The idea of black crime serves wide ideological functions. As Hall et al. (1978) argued, African-American and African-Caribbean young-sters, in the USA and UK, became identified with the media-created crime of 'mugging'. Mugging has characteristically urban and inner-city connotations. African-Caribbean youngsters were (and are) readily identifiable as victims of unemployment and cycles of poverty which characterize the inner city where they tend to be found. Although not the only victims, these black youngsters epitomize inner-city problems. Furthermore, beliefs about black families stress many of the factors which are associated with crime. Black families are regarded as patho-logical—incapable of meeting the needs of their own offspring (Howitt and Owusu-Bempah, 1994; Robinson, 1995). Other beliefs add to this anti-black family mythology—they are held to have lost their cultural roots and are structurally unstable. African-Caribbean children are thus believed to manifest difficulties such as 'broken families', father absence and worse (Hall et al., 1978). These routine images of black families provide us with 'common-sense' notions about the risks of crime in such children. In other words, mugging and race are associated in this ideologically-founded perspective.

Concern about black criminality is sometimes expressed in other ways. An extreme example is the right-wing politician's claim that there are groups of violent black criminals who rob white people and rape white women (Stark, 1993). 'Ghetto sickness' is one phrase used to describe this so-called malady, putatively afflicting this black under-class. This is redolent of the 'disease' *drapetomania* (literally, running away disease), which was used in the nineteenth century to stigmatize and blame black slaves for their resistance to slavery (Fernando, 1988; Howitt and Owusu-Bempah, 1994)! There is little doubt that official crime statistics record more crime by black people relative to their numbers in the general population. However, crime statistics are, at best, a summary of discrete acts by individuals reporting crime and the police recording crime; they cannot represent the realities of crime precisely. So, for example, if black people are over-represented in statistics on crimes known to the police, greater police activity in black areas may be responsible. Other factors which may lead to this over-representation include racial biases in reporting by victims, prosecuting black people more readily and charging black people's crimes as a more serious offence. All of these things would create a distorted impression of the extent of criminality among black people. Furthermore, they also feed back into the system as grounds for policy initiatives targeted against black people and their families. Agencies such as the police or courts may do more to create the image of a black criminal underclass than could ever be warranted by the objective situation.

In an important analysis, Stark (1993) chose to explore what he describes as the 'myth of black violence'. He identified sources of crime information he believed to be less biased than official statistics. Examples of this less (or differently) biased information include self-report studies of criminal activity and systematic surveys of victimization. In the American National Crime Survey of 1987, victims of violence were about two-and-a-half times more likely to be attacked by white rather than black assailants; furthermore, two-thirds of attackers were white. So, the typical violent attacker is *not* a young black male. Despite the fact that black men are twice as likely as their white equivalents to commit a violent crime, they are *four* times more likely to be arrested than white men.

Another fallacy suggests that homicide by black males is an increasing problem in the USA; black homicide figures have fallen by 40% from their peak in 1970. The belief that black males are more likely to be victims of violence is also of dubious validity. The rates of victimization by aggravated assault are no different for black and white males—this is somewhat remarkable given the concentration of black people in urban areas prone to violent crime. A national survey of youths obtained confidential self-reports about offending. Black youngsters had only marginally higher rates of general delinquency and serious offences, and even these slight trends were somewhat inconsistent for different age groups. Finally, surveys reveal no evidence that hard drug use is commoner among black people. Stark (1993) argues that the publicity surrounding violent crimes serves racist beliefs:

> 'When heinous acts of violence are committed by whites or by blacks who do not fit the stereotype, these exceptions are publicized in ways that reinforce racist imagery... Similarly, the Los Angeles "riot" in 1992 was universally identified with black gang violence, but the majority of those arrested were Hispanic or white, there was little evidence of gang activity, and gun-related violence was committed mainly by Korean store owners.' (p. 488)

RACE AND RACISM

Racism as it occurs in modern society can be difficult to define. Dictionary definitions indicate that racism is the belief in the innate superiority of one race over another, but many modern manifestations of racism simply are not included within this (Howitt and Owusu-Bempah, 1994). Some who think and behave in a racially discriminatory way do not subscribe to a belief in innate racial superiority. They may accept, for example, that all people are equal; thus they cannot be racist according to definitions which involve a *belief* in racial superiority. It has been argued in recent years that traditional forms of racism have partly been replaced by what is described as new, modern or symbolic (Kinder, 1986; Sears, 1988) racism. Although fundamentally all of these involve racially antagonistic feelings, their mode of expression is in certain ways 'subtler' than old-fashioned or traditional racism. Concepts such as fairness and justice are the lexicon of these new forms of racism. Some writers prefer to subdivide racism into a variety of component forms. Halstead (1988), for example, specified six different types of racism which are more easily applied to the analysis of contemporary media than any definition involving beliefs about genetic racial inferiority:

- *Type 1: Pre-reflective gut racism.* This is race hatred based on emotive reactions which have not been articulated into ideas and beliefs.
- *Type 2: Post-reflective gut racism.* This is based on a completely

unfounded and arbitrary set of beliefs which might be used to justify discrimination.

- *Type 3: Cultural racism.* This debases the social customs, manners and behaviours of other races. Religious and moral practices and beliefs, language, aesthetics and recreational activities are regarded as strange, barbaric or in some other way inferior.
- *Type 4: Institutional racism.* This involves the institutional arrangements which lead to discriminatory employment practices and other inequalities in the distribution of resources.
- *Type 5: Paternalistic racism.* This is the sort of racism in which, perhaps, well-intentioned white people decide what is best for black people without even consulting their representatives.
- *Type 6: Colour-blind racism.* This is based on a belief that to recognize differences between different racial groups is divisive and an obstacle to progress. In this way, the specific needs of different racial groups are neglected.

Other ideas ought to be considered. For example, Joseph, Reddy and Searle-Chatterjee (1990) stress the concept of *Eurocentrism*—the tendency to perceive the world solely through the white Western standpoint.

Once it is understood that racism has many forms, it is possible to look beyond crude racial bigotry when considering media racism.

RACISM AND ENTERTAINMENT

Complaints about the press by black people are almost as old as the truly mass media. In 1827, the launch of the very first newspaper for black Americans was accompanied by the complaint, 'From the press and the pulpit we have suffered much by being incorrectly represented' and 'Too long have the publick been deceived' (Cumberbatch, 1989, p. 17). The rhetoric of racism historically has changed when it has been challenged (Howitt and Owusu-Bempah, 1994). A review of studies of racism and the mass media over the last three or four decades would show how racist imagery has been reformulated during this time. There have been advances is legislation against racial discrimination and other developments which have changed how we think about race issues. This does not mean that the cruder forms of racism are gone—the process is not quite like that; older ideologically-based perspectives tend to be overshadowed by newer ones, rather than being completely replaced.

An indication of the extent to which things are different can be gained by examining a study of television advertisements from two decades ago. Pierce et al. (1977) developed a theoretical account of racism which they applied to television commercials:

'The chief vehicle for proracist behaviors are microaggressions. These are subtle, stunning, often automatic, and non-verbal exchanges which are "put downs" of blacks by offenders. The offensive mechanisms used against blacks often are innocuous. The cumulative weight of their never-ending burden is the major ingredient in black–white interactions.' (p. 65)

A number of predictions were made about how the media perpetrate such microaggressions: black people (a) would appear less often than animals, (b) never teach white people, (c) have fewer positive contacts with each other than have white people, (d) are rarely initiators or controllers of events, and (e) have poorer grasp of technology. For commercials shown during prime-time television in the early 1970s, their analysis confirmed many of their hypotheses:

- Disproportionately more white people were shown exerting authority or demonstrating their superior knowledge.
- Disproportionately more white people were portrayed as dispensing goods and favours, black people appearing not to have anything to give.
- Disproportionately more white women were used to represent ideal beauty and sexual attractiveness.
- Disproportionately more black people were portrayed as dependent on or subservient to white people. For example, disproportionately more worked for wages.

These sow seeds of anti-black sentiments. However, they have become much more difficult to see reflected in current media output. What was apparently acceptable when the study was carried out is no longer acceptable. Racism is generally expressed in less obvious ways in the media nowadays.

One way in which the media have contributed to racism is through a subtle support of what has been described as aversive racism (Gaertner and Dovidio, 1986). Aversive racism reflects the discomfort white people experience about mixing with black people; they prefer to psychologically distance themselves from black people and black communities. Indications of aversive racism emerged in two major studies, each covering approximately a decade of television entertainment programmes. Research into American television found that the representation of African-American males fluctuated from 6% of all male characters in 1971 to 9% in 1980. At the same time, the representation of white males increased from 81 to 88%. Black females were just 5–6% of all female characters over that decade Seggar, Hafen and Hannonen (1981). A similar figure of 8% black characters was reported by Gerbner and Signorielli (1979), based on the decade beginning 1968, and this general trend was confirmed by Weigel and Howes (1982). The racial population of television differed from real life—something like 12% of Americans were black. Given this baseline, the under-representation of African-Americans in the American media was striking. Black people were not portrayed as central to the community; instead, they appeared mostly in minor or supporting roles. As a proportion of major roles, black males accounted for only 4% and black females only 2% of their respective sexes (Gerbner and Signorielli, 1979). Furthermore, there was also a 'clustering effect' which is obscured by these global percentages (Baptista-Fernandez and Greenberg, 1980). Forty percent of black people appearing on television did so in groups of four or more black characters. This appears to have been an undesirable 'ghetto-ization' of minorities—that is, confining black people to associate solely with their own race. The mixing of black with white people was avoided. In over 80% of children's programmes of the time, white and minority children did *not* appear together (Barcus, 1983). This contrasts somewhat with the greater levels of racial mixing on modern television.

Sometimes racism occurs in the media in ways too subtle to be detected in content analysis. Rainville, Roberts and Sweet (1978) showed that this occurs in American football broadcasts. Transcripts of the commentaries were matched into pairs on the basis of the position played by the key player, the number of words spoken about the key player and the key player's performance statistics. The player was white for one of the pair, and black for the other. Clues to the race of the player were removed by calling all of the key players John Smith. Students read the transcripts and guessed whether John Smith was black or white. White participants in the research, especially, were able to recognize the player's race more accurately than would be expected on the basis of chance. The authors argue that this linguistic bias in favour of white players is unlikely to be perceived as such since it is embedded in a welter of other audio and visual information. Nevertheless, viewers would routinely absorb a more favourable impression of white players.

A common stereotype of black people involves the idea that they are exceptionally good at sport and music, but little else. Not surprisingly, this sort of stereotyping of black people has been found in British television (Branthwaite and Peirce, 1990). Black people tended to be shown in the context of popular music or as celebrities or sportsmen in advertisements. They were infrequently portrayed in a home environment, perhaps reflecting the myths about the inadequacy of black families, once again.

The debate about racial stereotyping on television has been a long-standing one. The question is more of the nature of the stereotyping than whether stereotypes are used. Generally, the evidence is that the crudest forms of racial stereotyping may have declined over the years. Following the growth of the black civil rights movement during the 1960s, it has been suggested that:

> '... significant changes in both recognition and respect were accorded on television ... whereas they had been cast as entertainers, servants or buffoons during their rare appearance in the 1950s and early 1960s, a decade later they were more likely to be cast as "regulators" of society, typically playing such roles as teachers or policemen.' (Liebert and Sprafkin, 1988, p. 190)

The image of the black family in popular programmes such as the *Cosby Show* is more positive now than previous studies suggested (Merritt and Stroman, 1993), with both the husband and wife present in the family and loving, egalitarian relationships portrayed. Such examples are important, since they counter stereotypes of black family pathology (Howitt and Owusu-Bempah, 1994).

No British study has the scope and magnitude of American content analysis. Indeed some of the earliest British studies of racism in the media simply rely on illustrations to make their points rather than aggregate statistics from content analysis (e.g. Anwar and Shange, 1982).

RACE AND NEWS

The most convincing studies documenting the nature of racial stereotyping in the British media concern newspapers rather than television. The most systematic is van Dijk's (1991) analysis of the press coverage of a number of significant racial episodes. These include the case of the Bradford head teacher who caused consternation among parents at a multi-racial school by writing articles flagrantly antagonistic to multi-culturalism in education (Honeyford 1983a, 1983b, 1984, 1986) and insulting of immigrant communities. The British press, nevertheless, frequently portrayed him as a paragon of common-sense and a victim of the anti-racist faction:

> 'There is something decidedly rotten about education when a mob of adults pretending to be caring parents picket a school.' (*The Daily Telegraph*)

In other words, ideologically the newspapers aligned themselves with the racism of the new right (Barker, 1981). Van Dijk used discourse analysis rather than conventional content analysis. In this context, discourse analysis is concerned with the textual devices used to achieve a particular (racist) end (cf. Wetherell and Potter, 1992). A rather less formal study is *Your Daily Dose*—a review of the racism and jingoism of the daily tabloid newspaper *The Sun* (Searle, 1989), which puts even the worst excesses of the broadcast media into the shade. Mainly it concerns the crudest, and most overt sorts of cultural stereotyping—cartoons about white people being boiled in pots by cannibal Africans, for example. Such racism continues to be represented by jingoistic and nationalistic displays, such as those associated with international sporting events.

The texts of news stories may contain anti-black messages which are far more subtle and insidious than any of this. According to Campbell's (1995) study of race in local television news in America, racism persists in this coverage in two ways:

- The lack of attention given to minorities and minority ways of life. This marginalizes black people to the edges of society; they are separated from mainstream society and so are not deserving of attention.
- Occasionally the media reflect traditional racist views of black people. Take, for example, the following account of media coverage of celebrations of the life of Martin Luther King:

> 'Hutchins (a African American reporter) says the participation of young people—and almost all of those we have seen are black—in the day's events "was a great example . . . of kids not on the streets but actually performing and participating in activities all throughout the city". And Brown adds that participation is "the kind of thing that you don't expect young people to do, given so much of what we cover every day and so many of the problems that we have with our young people".' (Campbell, 1995, p. 104).

In this way, the story dwells on stereotypes which are not necessary for reporting the story itself. By suggesting that the celebrations were essentially one-off, not typical of black community life, negative stereotypes of black youth are reinforced.

Campbell accepts that there is a 'dangerous myth' that racism is now non-existent in mainstream society. For example, the media may fail to recognize the role of racism in the debilitating social conditions experienced by many black (and other minority) people in Western societies:

> '. . . when news organizations—however well intentioned—implicitly accent the values and determination of socially and economically successfully minority Americans, they feed the mythological notion that success is equally accessible to all. So when the majority of news accounts of people of color show them to be anything but socially and economically successful—killers of pizza parlor employees, mothers who leave their children home alone to die in fires, and so on—the implication is that those people had the same options and preparation necessary to seize The

American Dream yet chose a life of savagery and/or destitution instead.'
(Campbell, 1995, pp. 132–3)

There is, Cambell argues, a difficulty associated with reporting crimes perpetrated by black or ethnic minority people compared to those of white people. An asymmetry exists which stems from routine features of the news. Because the vast majority of on-air reporters and presenters are white, these people immediately counterbalance any tendency to see white killers as typical of white people. On the other hand, a brutal murder by a black person is not contradicted in this way, nor by the large numbers of white people who appear in a more positive light in the news.

Another researcher specifically linked three key aspects of modern racism with news coverage (Entman, 1990):

- *'Anti-black affect' or emotive hostility towards black people.* The emphasis on crime committed by black people in local television news encourages this ill-feeling towards black people. A number of factors create this feeling:

  '... the accused black criminals were usually illustrated by glowering mug shots or by footage of them being led around in handcuffs, their arms held by uniformed white policemen. None of the accused violent criminals during the week studied were shown in mug shots or in physical custody.' (Entman, 1990, p. 337)

- *Resistance to political demands by black people.* This is based on the belief that black people want and get more of their fair share of benefits than their hard work justifies. The media promote this belief about black people by presenting black politicians solely addressing black audiences and only on black sectional interests. So black politicians arguing the cause of the black community was typical of their coverage in the news:

  'Even though white leaders in Chicago typically come from recognizable ethnic power bases, they were more often presented as if they represented the entire community. The news equated black political action almost exclusively with special interest politics and white political action most frequently with public interest politics (Entman, 1990, p. 339). Sound bites usually depicted the black person talking loudly, often in what might be termed a "harangue" or "tirade," employing an emotional, rhetorical appeal rather than a calm, deliberative one. Such images may bolster the image of black political figures as more emotional and angry than white ones...' (Entman, 1990, p. 340).

- *The belief that racism is dead and that there are no impediments to black people's progress caused by racism.* The use of black journalists and authority figures reinforces this view that racism is no longer a problem:

  'Paradoxically, the images sustaining the modern racist notion that racism has ended may work at the same time to suppress old-fashioned racism.' (Entman, 1990, p. 333)

There is a lot of work to be done before we fully understand these broader implications of media coverage of race, racial beliefs, and racial imagery.

MEDIA, RACE AND THE AUDIENCE

In his discussion of hate speech, Calvert (1997) contrasts the *transmission* effects of communication with its *ritual* role (Carey, 1989). The transmission effect amounts to changes in the beliefs or behaviour of the audience. The ritual role is essentially how the media may reproduce or rehearse crucial aspects of the culture, thus reaffirming cultural values. This distinction is important, since it forewarns us that media messages may be so in tune with dominant beliefs in a culture that change is unlikely. Evidence of the direct effects of the media's treatment of race on the viewer is not extensive and is rather circumstantial, although it has taken new directions recently. Some of the earliest research examined the relationship between television consumption and self-esteem among white and black viewers of American television (Tan and Tan, 1979). For white viewers, watching news and public affairs programmes was associated with higher self-esteem. For black viewers, the more entertainment programmes watched, the lower was their self-esteem. This would be expected in terms of Gerbner's cultivation analysis (Chapter 4), given the racial stereotyping in entertainment programmes of the time. The relationship between news viewing and self-esteem in white people may have reflected white dominance in the content of news programming. Much more recently, Armstrong, Neuendorf and Brentar (1992) studied white American university students and found that the extensive viewing of entertainment television was associated with the view that black Americans have a relatively high standard of living. In contrast, heavy viewing of television news-type programmes was associated with the opinion that black Americans were not well-off socio-economically. The trends were stronger among white students with very little direct experience of or contact with black people.

A major British study on the media and racism focused on children's knowledge of ethnic minorities (Hartmann and Husband, 1974). It asked the extent to which children were influenced by the media or by personal experience in terms of the sources of their ideas about 'coloured' people:

> '... the media do not seem to have any direct influence on attitudes as such. It would appear that the media serve to define for people what the dimensions of the situation are. How they feel about the situation, thus defined, would appear to depend on other factors, particularly where they live.' (p. 108)

In some instances the media appeared to alert youngsters to the social disadvantages experienced by black people (Howitt, 1982).

Modern research on racial stereotyping suggests reasons why Hartmann and Husband (1974) detected little direct negative influence of the media on racial attitudes. It has been found that, irrespective of people's racial attitudes, knowledge of negative stereotypes of black people such as 'they are lazy' is ubiquitous and extensive (Devine, 1989; Gilbert and Hixon, 1991). It is not surprising, then, that the media are rather ineffective in extending this repertoire of hostility. It should not be assumed that media-derived stereotypes are benign, even though they do not appear to relate to racial attitudes. People, irrespective of their attitudes, can be influenced by stereotypes, especially in circumstances in which they are not 'on guard' (Gaertner and Dovidio, 1986; Rogers and Prentice-Dunn, 1981).

Of course, it is argued by some that the media can be used to undermine racism by holding it up to ridicule. The classic example of this is the use of humour to make fun of grotesque racist bigots of the likes of Alf Garnett (*Till Death Us Do Part*) or his American equivalent Archie Bunker (*All in the Family*). Vidmar and Rokeach (1974) assessed the impact of the American series on adolescents. Both high-prejudiced and low-prejudiced adolescents saw the programme as funny and enjoyable, while Archie Bunker was the most admired of the characters portrayed. The majority thought it was wrong to use racially derogatory expressions like 'coons' and 'chinks', but still saw Archie Bunker as a winner and sympathized with him to a marked degree. White people were more favourable to the Archie Bunker and his views if they were racially prejudiced (Brigham and Giesbrecht, 1976). Commitment to black power did not predict black people's antagonism to the series. In Holland, racially prejudiced people thought Archie Bunker's racism was reasonable (Wilhoit and de Bock, 1976). This is an example of selective perception (Cooper and Jahoda, 1947), i.e. the idea that people interpret communications differentially according to their pre-existing beliefs and perspectives. However, it is unlikely that selective perception alone accounts for all of the findings from this research. For example, those high on racial prejudice were the most likely to claim that the programme had made them uncertain about their beliefs. Amusement at the humour of the series was determined in a very complex way by culture, sex and authoritarianism as well as at the target for the joke in the series (Surlin and Tate, 1976).

EFFECTS ON THE AUDIENCE

An experiment carried out by Peffley, Shields and Williams (1996) demonstrates just how stereotypes affect viewers. They argued that the visual image of a black person as a crime suspect activates a number of racist stereotypes among white viewers. This process of activation should be strongest in more racially prejudiced viewers. Racial stereotypes were assessed as part of a battery of measures. On another, apparently unconnected occasion, participants in the research saw a video of one of two crime-news stories; these were identical except that in one case it was a white male suspect being led away in handcuffs, whereas in the other case the man was African-American. Following the video, the participants were asked a number of questions about the suspect, such as his guilt and likely future criminal behaviour. The black suspect was more likely to be judged guilty, recommended for a longer sentence and expected to carry on with his criminal ways in the future. The more racist the viewer, the more guilty he/she saw the black suspect as being. One of the implications of this study is that visual imagery may affect the viewer despite the journalistic convention that the race of an accused person is irrelevant to the reporting of the crime and so should not be mentioned in a story.

Racism can affect crime-news stories in somewhat complex and unexpected ways. Winkel (1990) systematically varied the contents of news stories; the perpetrator of a crime was described as either an Amsterdam resident, a German migrant or a Turkish migrant. The news report concerned a rape which was described as follows:

'WOMAN RAPED BY AMSTERDAM RESIDENT

By our reporter, Duivendrecht, Wednesday

A 19-year-old woman who stepped out of the night bus last night around four o'clock at the Van der Madeweg stop in Duivendrecht was addressed by a fellow passenger after she had gone a few yards. He threatened her with a large screwdriver, struck her, and raped the woman, who later had to undergo medical treatment. Based on the description she gave, the 31-year-old Amsterdam resident, Gerard K., was taken into custody by the police as the suspect a few hours later.' (Winkel, 1990, p. 92)

The two alternative versions of this were the same but for the nationality of the offender being changed to a German or a Turk.

Responses were affected by the nationality of the perpetrator:

'... information about crimes committed by foreigners is perceived as "informative" in the sense that such information says something about the disposition of foreigners to criminal behaviour.' (p. 95)

So, for example, when people were asked to assess the subjective probability that Dutchmen will commit rape their responses varied according to the nationality of the rapist in the news story. A lower probability was given if the suspect was Dutch than if he was foreign. This implies that only information about foreigners was considered 'informative'—that is, affecting the probability of men committing a rape. Newspaper stories dealing with the Dutch rapists did not generalize to the men of Holland in general; 'In other words, unjustified generalizations are not made to other Dutchmen when the suspect is Dutch' (p. 95).

There is evidence of a growth of ideological racism in Europe in the early 1990s when racial attacks became more common. One of the most disturbing studies of the media and racism is that of Esser and Brosius (1996) who examined the spread of violence in Germany following racist attacks on migrant workers. The researchers were testing a version of contagion or copycat theory which, essentially, claims that events publicized in the media are likely to be reproduced in real life (Chapter 6). Esser and Brosius measured news coverage of the issue of xenophobic assaults in the German media. Six different types of news were involved:

• *Xenophobic attacks or assaults* on foreigners.
• *Counteractions*, including demonstrations by the public opposed to such racism.
• *Political activities*, such as reports of parliamentary debates about the offences or legislative initiatives against such xenophobic violence.
• *Prosecutions*, including news stories to do with trials, sentencing or police activities and initiatives to counter xenophobic violence.
• *Right-wing radicalism*, which basically included stories relating to the writings, political parties and marches associated with right-wing radicalism.
• *Background information*, which included news stories about the social and other problems of foreigners in Germany.

A week-by-week count was made of these six types of news stories broadcast on German television. Some parts of Germany recorded statistics on xenophobic attacks on a weekly basis, enabling comparisons between race coverage in the media and racial crime to be made for relatively short time intervals.

What was the relationship between the amount of reporting and the numbers of xenophobic attacks as assessed from public statistics? The trends over time were very similar for the television news stories and xenophobic crimes; news stories increased at about the same time as attacks increased. The question is whether this indicates a causal relationship, since there are a number of different possibilities:

• The news stories might be causing the attacks.
• The attacks might be causing the news stories.
• Both of these may be partially true.

A statistical technique known as *lagged-correlations* was used to prioritize these possibilities. The data had been adjusted in the following ways:

- Media coverage is correlated with *crime rates for the following week*. Since logically crime cannot influence media coverage in the previous week, a correlation in these circumstances is evidence that media coverage causes crime rates.
- Crime rates are correlated with the *media coverage for the following week*. Since media coverage cannot influence crime during the previous week, a correlation in these circumstances suggests that the media merely reflect what is happening in real-life.

There were no strong correlations for either of the above. That is, the media did not inspire or lead to imitative crime during the period studied. However, the analysis was not left at this.

The researchers carried out the subsidiary analysis in two phases. The first phase, August 1990–September 1992, was a relatively successful period for the racists. Their activities had resulted in the foreign workers in hostels being moved to other places. After November 1992, racist violence ceased to benefit the racists. Counter-demonstrations by the German public against the xenophobic attacks were gaining strength, for example. Violence that is rewarded is more likely to be copied than violence that is unsuccessful. The researchers claim, as a result of analysing these two separate time periods, that when the violence was rewarded (as in the first phase) there is a causal association between media content and later violent behaviour. In this first phase, news coverage from the week *before* the racial crimes predicted the rates of xenophobic assaults the best. This was not so in the second phase. (It would appear that the influence of the media was for events like prosecutions, right-wing radicalism and background information. Specific news about the arsons did not seem to have a causal influence. This would suggest that imitation of aggression was not the mechanism by which the news media had their effect.)

TAKING THE HATE OUT OF CRIME

There is some agreement that minorities suffer propaganda, subtle or otherwise, against them by the mass media. People who are different because of their race, sexuality and ethnicity are particularly prone to this. Generally speaking, however, there is probably too little evidence yet to hold the media directly responsible for crimes against such minorities. The most convincing evidence is to be found in the research on the media and race although this, unfortunately, contains only the merest smattering of studies which investigates the role of the media in racial victimization. Although the media may be used to promote a favourable image of minorities, it is not clear that this is more effective than the negative stereotyping which has been found in so many content analyses. Hate-crimes need to be an important research priority for media criminologists given that the media are engaged in an ideologically-based dialogue with their audience which is to some extent racist, sexist and homophobic.

CHAPTER 12

Drug Crime

'... the pursuit of truth about drug trafficking is one way of thinking, whilst the question of the purposes served by any particular
grasp of truth may be just as important.' (Dorn et al., 1992, p. 205)

If the media were responsible in any way for people using illicit drugs,
the potential criminogenic effect of the media could be immense. Crime
and drugs are intimately connected, at least for some illicit drugs. In
recent years, the percentage of people who believe that cannabis causes
crime and violence has declined (Gould, Shaw and Arendt, 1996). Despite this, nearly three-quarters of adults in the UK are convinced of the
substance's criminogenic properties. Although it is a little surprising
that there is such a consensus about the implications for crime of this
relatively benign and inexpensive drug (Home Office, 1982; Kleinman,
1989), the association of drugs and crime in the public mind is deep and,
seemingly, intractable. Public opinion can be puzzling, as the trends in
beliefs about legalizing the drug illustrate. In the period 1983–1995, the
proportion of the public in favour of legalizing cannabis increased from
one person in eight to one person in three; young people show the most
change whereas the over-45s the least. According to Gould, Shaw and
Arendt (1996), drug attitudes are part of a broader constellation of
conservative beliefs. So, for example, people with liberal attitudes towards drugs tend to be somewhat less nationalistic and less ethnically
prejudiced; they are also less likely to believe that immigrants cause
crime. Given this intermeshing of attitudes about drugs with other
deeply held beliefs, it is only to be expected that the debate about drugs
and crime is heated and acrimonious.

The history of drugs legislation is *not* simply the history of a growing
reaction against escalating drug-related crime (Bean, 1974). The pattern varies from country to country. For some countries, legislation
followed the emergence of a significant drugs problem (Howitt, 1991); in
other countries, attempts to legislate against drugs preceded growth in
drug-related crime (Berridge, 1984). Legislation against drugs was one
of the first concerted international initiatives to combat crime. The
USA, with a serious drugs problem at the time, led the way to an

international opium convention at The Hague in 1912. This resulted in anti-drugs legislation being incorporated in law in many countries, including Britain, by way of the Treaty of Versailles after the First World War. New offences were created involving the possession of drugs which had previously been commonly available in patent medicines and at pharmacies (Berridge, 1989; Berridge and Edwards, 1981). The news media were partly responsible for some early drug-control initiatives in Britain. Newspaper reports during the First World War suggested that Canadian soldiers were being sold drugs by London prostitutes. Moral outrage and action to control such activities followed (Bean, 1974).

Given the overwhelming anti-media clamour, the general lack of criticism of the media over their treatment of drugs is remarkable. Media coverage of drug issues has usually not bothered the public, politicians or pressure groups. This is despite the growing 'drugs' problem richly highlighted and reported by the media (Reeves and Campbell, 1994); 'drugs hauls' valued at millions being seized by customs officers or the police are familiar in headlines. Indeed, this may be a rare instance when the media are recognized as part of a conservative hegemony against a crime. In general, the media share much the same anti-drugs stance as the police, politicians and public alike; the media effectively serve as anti-drugs lobbyists. The extensive coverage given to issues like drugs in sport is a good example. Worries, when expressed, are more likely to cluster around the lyrics to rock music recordings, which are seen to be routinely and influentially pro-drugs, rather than mainstream media. So, apart from occasional concerns about films such as *The Man with the Golden Arm* or *Train spotting*, both of which deal with drug addiction, few complaints are directed against the mainstream media. Instead, when the media are criticized it is more likely to be by academics and usually over the media's conservative, anti-drugs editorializing and ideology.

Unlike other crime, drugs may sometimes still be regarded as minority problems which concern only a small proportion of ordinary people; as such they are seen as having little bearing on normal life. Of course, this is a travesty of the truth. The numerical facts about drugs do not determine their centrality as a social issue or how they are construed. Drugs historically have been seen as a threat because they highlight differences between mainstream society and a demonized drugs subculture. The response to AIDS is similar in that the issue is marginalized, inappropriately, to 'bad' homosexuals and drug-takers or demonized as being African or monkey in origin. Drugs have frequently been construed as 'foreign'; the Chinese coolie in the opium den is an old stereotype. In Britain, concern about the use of marijuana and related drugs by black immigrants from the West Indies in the 1950s (Teff,

1975) brought government intervention. At this time, the demographic profile of 'drug addicts' changed from middle-class women to young men (Howitt, 1991). In this way, concern about drugs became focused on exactly the same social group which was also causing concern with regard to violent crime and delinquency. Other countries have different variants of this same theme—in the USA the association of drugs and violence with urban ghettos is only superficially different.

MEDIA AND DRUG REALITIES

It is commonly held that the media distort the realities of crime, including drugs. Some researchers have argued, however, that the media present a rather accurate account of the reality of drugs. The crack-cocaine trade, they claim, has ensnared inner-city youth into a spiral of drugs-related crime (Inciardi and Pottieger, 1991) which is not overly sensationalized by the media. A sample of delinquent youngsters was surveyed in Miami, Florida. Each youngster had committed a minimum of 10 FBI index offences in a single year, or a minimum of 100 less serious offences in the same time period. Each of the interviewees had a history of multiple-drug use. Typically, their histories of drug abuse had begun with alcohol at the age of seven; the majority took alcohol at least three times weekly by age nine years. Other substance use followed. Marijuana use began at about 10 years of age—usually it was used regularly within a year. An overwhelming majority had experimented with cocaine before the age of 12 years, followed shortly afterwards by experimentation with heroin, speed and prescription depressants. A few months later, the vast majority had tried crack-cocaine and were to become regular users within a few months. Four out of five were involved, at some level, in the crack-cocaine business:

> '. . . the relationship between crack trade participation and level of other criminal involvement is quite clear. The mean number of crimes per subject during the twelve-month period ranges from 375.9 for those with no involvement in the crack business to 1419.1 offenses for those in the dealer category. Furthermore, although it did not hold for vice offenses, this pattern was apparent for major felonies, property crimes, and drug business offenses.' (Inciardi and Pottieger, 1991, p. 266)

Significantly, less than 1% of offences had led to arrest.

Despite such claims of media accuracy about drugs, Brownstein (1995) argues that the New York news media during the late 1980s created an image around the issue of drugs which failed to address the objective evidence at all well. The image was that of a spreading wave of drug-related violence which was indiscriminate in its victims; drug dealers and casual passers-by were equally at risk from random drug violence. Following a statement by the Governor of New York, the news media created an image of drugs which adopted his scenario. The governor's key charges against drugs were that crack-cocaine is an addictive, lethal substance which, like other drugs, was used endemically in the community. Crack-cocaine use constituted an epidemic which brought with it both crime and violence:

> 'For the first few months of the year, the random violence theme continued to be promoted by the media. On 23 January the *Daily News* published an article about the spread of crime into previously "safe" neighborhoods. Headlined "IT'S CALLED SPILLOVER, Silk-stocking areas share run on crime", the article quoted a "community leader" from Brooklyn who said, "There are no safe neighborhoods any more". The article gave statistics showing the level of violent crime in each of the police precincts in the city. On 2 February the *New York Post* gave an example under the dramatic heading "HUMAN SHIELD—Snatched tot wounded in Brooklyn gun battle". The story was about a three-year old boy who was "critically injured yesterday when a teenager snatched him from his mother's grasp and used him as a human shield in a gun battle".'
> (Brownstein, 1995, p. 51)

Brownstein takes issue with some of these claims, although he accepts that street crime in New York had increased during the previous few years. Violent crime, despite having increased, had not become more random. The emerging evidence indicated that the same old victims continued to be victimized—minorities, the poor, women, and the young. Not everyone had an increased risk of street violence, irrespective of whether this is the result of drugs or any other factors.

A very similar view is taken by Sanders and Lyon (1995). They describe President Reagen's 'war on drugs', which was another instance of the reciprocal relationships which can exist between media images of crime and the activities of the criminal justice system. The developing idea that drug-related crime was a key issue in American society led to increased activity from the media and law enforcement agencies. Funds became available for greater spending on street-level drugs control. At the same time, the media substantially increased coverage themes related to drugs busts. Drugs were increasingly construed as a major criminogenic force, so much so that drugs crimes began to be represented as the normal or normative crime. Crime was often ascribed to drug problems and sentencing took this factor increasingly into account.

CREATION OF DRUGS ISSUES

Some of the best evidence concerning how the drugs issue has come to be so linked with crime as a social problem comes from Beckett (1994).

This study investigated the relationship between the vicissitudes of public opinion and important determinants of public opinion. In the USA, nearly two-thirds of people claimed that drugs were the nation's most important problem. About half of prisoners in federal prisons are there for drug crimes. Beckett identified two main processes involved in the spread of ideas about drug use and street crime:

- *The Objectivist Model.* This simply suggests that events become defined as a social problem largely on the basis of the availability of knowledge about the extent of that problem. The social conditions which lead to the problem become clearly identified and can be measured. The objective changes in street crime and drug crime are available for inspection from official crime statistics. Additionally, evidence based on personal experience emerges from awareness of street-crime in the community. The objectivist model assumes that 'claims-makers'—politicians of all sorts—are merely reacting to objective evidence. They are not attempting precipitously to initiate changes in public opinion. This suggested a number of hypotheses which Beckett tested against public opinion data. *Hypothesis 1* was that there will be a close relationship between the incidence of crime/ drug statistics and public opinion. *Hypothesis 2* was that changes in public opinion lead political opinion. Thus, political opinion merely lags behind public opinion and is a response to it and the facts of the situation.

- *The Constructionist Model.* This assumes that public opinion is not created from the 'objective' facts of crime statistics. Instead the issue is created as a consequence of the claims made by key and influential 'claims-makers', including the media. Beckett's *Hypothesis 3* was that one would expect public opinion to lag behind the major 'claims-making' activities and to be essentially unrelated to 'objective' facts. This, basically, is the *elite constructionism* approach. Elites lead opinion through their capacity for good organization and access to better resources. They are also, by definition, those people who are motivated to seek to change public opinion. But there is a difficulty; there is a subdivision of constructionist thought which places far less emphasis on the idea of claims-makers. Beckett describes this type of constructionist approach as *cultural constructionism*. In other words, cultural factors create a climate in which the public become anxious about the community and focus on issues which arise from the public rather than from the 'claims-makers' in the first instance. The various social, economic and political forces which contribute to this process are complex. Nevertheless, this approach sees public opinion as initially stemming from growing public concern, itself, as opposed to the influence of key and important people. Quite clearly, cultural constructionism would predict that changes in public opinion come before political claims-making, without showing any particular relationship with 'objective' evidence.

Beckett used a number of measures: *street crime* was measured by the rate of violent crimes reported to the police; data on *the incidence of drug abuse* was based on the percentage of people over 12 surveyed who admitted to having used drugs in the previous month; *media coverage* was based on the number of crime stories in a 'national newspaper' and *drug stories* came from an index of television news stories. Stories emanating from state officials were not included in either of these last two measures—but they were used as the basis of an index of the number of *claims made about drugs and crime by political actors*. Finally, information was obtained about fluctuations in public opinion from a number of public opinion polls which had been repeated several times using the same questions. *Drugs opinion* was based on the percentages agreeing that drugs and drug use were the most important problems facing America; *crime opinion* was based on the percentages of people agreeing that crime, juvenile delinquency or the breakdown of law and order were the most important problems facing the nation.

When the trends in the data were examined using sophisticated statistical methods, it was found that the elite constructionist model fitted the data for *crime* best. That is, for crime opinion there was a relationship between the media coverage of an issue and ensuing changes in public opinion; and there was also a relationship between pronouncements by state politicians and elite others and ensuing changes in public opinion. These elite pronouncements came in advance of changes in public opinion; changes in public opinion did not feed back to state pronouncements. Much the same was found for *drugs* opinion, but with one big difference—the media seemed not to be leading public opinion on this. Politicians and other elite actors did seem to be setting the agenda, as with other issues.

There are numerous journalistic devices which are employed to create the sense of drama and concern. Orcutt and Turner (1993) provide a rich source of the sorts of misleading graphs which are employed by the media in establishing a 'solid' foundation for media-constructed drug epidemics.

LICIT DRUGS

Drug messages may concern legal drugs and as a consequence be seen as being different from messages about illicit drugs. One should not, however, ignore the extent to which many now-illicit drugs have or had medical uses. For example, the opiates were routine contents of patent medicines during the nineteenth century. Current lobbying to legalize cannabis for therapeutic reasons, as for the relief of multiple sclerosis, confuses the legitimate–illicit dichotomy. Given that the boundaries between licit and illicit drugs are ill-defined, do 'licit drug messages' spill over to illegal drugs? Licit drugs are held to help us through life's crises and problems. Such messages may be seen as relevant to the effects of mood-related drugs, irrespective of their legality. If licit drugs are promoted as relieving life's little problems, this may merely be part of the advocacy of drug dependency culture. As long ago as 1975, Stimson showed how psychotropic drugs were being promoted as 'cures' for every kind of modern 'diseases'. Such 'diseases' included such routine 'difficulties' as getting on with a new boss. At that time, women were overwhelmingly held to be eminently suitable recipients of psychotropic drug 'cures' for intolerable domestic situations. Reality followed the image, according to Stimson, and this was the start of a period during which women were dispensed psychotropic drugs for their problems no matter what their cause or nature.

There is some evidence that there is a relationship between television viewing and the amount of proprietary drugs (including psychotropic drugs) used by individuals. Although extremely limited, indications are also that television viewing was actually a negative predictor of illicit drug taking—thus, the users of illicit drugs were perhaps less involved with the mainstream media and their largely anti-drug message (Milavsky, Pekowsky and Stipp, 1976).

DRUGS AND CRIME

Content analyses of television fictional programming for drugs themes are uncommon. One exception is Fernandez-Collado et al. (1978), who found a rate of illicit drug consumption which equated to one illicit act every five hours of television. While such rates are small-fry compared to the frequency of violent acts, they confirm that drugs are a steady feature of programming. There is evidence, also, that news of drugs and crime is common. The major content analysis studies of crime news consistently find relatively high levels of drug crime. In Graber's (1980) study of a Chicago newspaper, drug offences made up about one-fifth of crime stories. Another study of news (Chermak, 1995) found that one-tenth of such crime items concerned drugs. Indeed, drugs offences are among the crimes over-represented in crime news coverage (Sacco and Fair, 1988). Thus, there is good reason for the public to associate drugs with crime.

There are two broad ways in which drugs might be involved in crime:

- Deviant individuals take to crime because of their deviance.
- Drug-taking leads to crime. The relationship may be in both directions, which then compounds the difficulties, since it is hard to say which direction of influence is the most important.

The question of the impact of illicit drugs on non-drug crime levels is more difficult to answer than might be anticipated. Alleged links between drug use and crime are important since they may transform the ways in which drugs are construed. If the only victim of drug use is the user him/herself, then this can be regarded as a 'victimless crime' or a 'private sin'. On the other hand, what if there really are innocent victims of drugs, such as bystanders killed in drug 'wars' or innocent householders subject to burglary? This would constitute a more clearcut imperative for the control of drugs. Seen in this light, just what crimes should be included when considering the drug–crime relationship? Clearly, specific drug crimes such as possession or pushing are generally difficult to classify as having an obvious, unwilling victim. In contrast, theft, burglary, assault and similar crimes involve evident harm to others and might be related to drug use.

The possession and selling of certain drugs are criminal offences. The spill-over from involvement with drugs to non-drugs offences forms part of the basis of concerns about drug influences on crime. The relationships are not necessarily simple or predictable. Drugs might, for example, influence rates of violent crime because they effect emotions or, alternatively, because dealers use violence as part of their trade.

Arrestees demonstrate high rates of illicit substances use (Hser, Longshore and Anglin, 1994). Prison populations include high numbers of illicit drug users. Maden et al. (1992) found that over 40% of the male prisoners interviewed reported pre-arrest drug use, a figure which halves when cannabis use is excluded. Cannabis was used by about one-third and opiates and amphetamines by just under 10% each. Compared with all other prisoners, the drug users were approximately 50% over-represented in burglary statistics, but only half as likely to have a violence conviction. Jacobs and Ghodse (1988) compared solvent users with non-users among male delinquent adolescents admitted to a secure unit. Solvent users were first arrested at a younger age than non-users.

In the complex equation linking drugs to crime, the income available from dealing is clearly of considerable importance. At least for a proportion of users, dealing finances some of their personal drug use. Without income from dealing, possibly the links between drugs and theft and property crimes would be stronger. Cannabis and related drugs, which attract the least punishment, tend to be the least profitable. In contrast, Bean (1992) found that crack-cocaine bought 'wholesale' could be 'retailed' at about 2.5 times its cost. The potential profitability of dealing and the substantial legitimate incomes of some users are clearly among the factors which would attenuate the causal influence of drug-taking on crime, although dealing itself is an offence, of course. The Scottish Cocaine Research Group (1993) found a relatively high prevalence of use in the professional, higher-income classes.

Crime and unemployment were endemic among crack-cocaine users but some had licit and illicit occupations (Bean, 1992). In another study, users were asked to explain how they financed their drug purchases (Bean, 1990):

> 'Very few of the users could give a clear account of how they financed their drug expenditures. Clearly some did so from crime: prostitution being the obvious example. Some prostitutes also financed the crack use of their pimps. Other respondents were known drug dealers (especially the heroin users who financed crack use in the same way as they financed other drugs, i.e. crime and dealing). A small number said they paid for it out of their legitimate income.' (Bean, 1990, p. 22).

There are numerous ways of financing drug use—getting into debt, selling possessions and working more time in a legitimate job are among some of the legal solutions.

Another study compared burglar-opioid users with non-addicted burglars (Mott, 1986), using data from the court system. The known addict burglars were compared with a control group of non-addict burglars in terms of their serious offences (that is excluding motoring, drunkenness and similar prosecutions). Mott concluded that:

> '. . . the presence of relatively large numbers of young unemployed male opioid users in a local population may well contribute to increases in the number of residential burglaries in the area.' (Mott, 1986, p. 677)

Over 90% of users of the most addictive drugs, including opiates, synthetic opiates and LSD, reported criminal convictions (Bean and Wilkinson, 1988). The most common offences were theft, handling stolen goods and forgery (49% of the sample). One-quarter had convictions for violence against the person. None had committed sexual offences. These drug-users were not only frequent victimizers of other people—nearly half had been victims themselves within their own homes.

One of the most thorough investigations of the link between drugs and crime was by Parker and Newcombe (1987). In a district where heroin use was reaching 'epidemic' proportions, crime had increased nearly 100%. This was roughly twice the national rate and well above the regional rate. Over half of burglars and one-third of thieves were known drug-users, compared with less than 1 in 50 of the general population. Not all crimes were affected in this way, since only certain types of crimes increased disproportionately. These were theft from motor vehicles and burglary. Burglary was more common and criminal damage less common than expected. Although the growth in heroin use was associated with an increase in acquisitive crime in user-offenders, no such trend emerged for other classes of crime, suggesting an economic motive for the offending.

Some researchers believe that there is a general propensity to deviancy of all sorts. Hammersley; Hammersley, Forsyth and Lavelle, (1989, 1990) are proponents of the view that general deviancy underpins the drugs–crime link. Hammersley (1988), discussing the general research evidence, may have presented the situation precisely:

> '... a more balanced, consensus view is that drug abuse and criminality are interrelated. For example, being unwilling to commit crimes for money might be one reason for ceasing to escalate an otherwise unaffordable heroin habit.' (Hammersley, 1988, p. 445).

There would seem to be no invariable relationship between drug use and crime. The available evidence supports drug effects on economic crime rather than other sorts of crime. It would seem that any media involvement in encouraging or discouraging drug use has implications for crime, but not necessarily directly nor inevitably.

MEDIA AND DRUG CRIME

There are some researchers who believe that the media make the drug situation worse by defining those who take drugs as social deviants. This is essentially a *deviancy amplification model*, in which the image of law-breakers is increasingly distanced from that of 'normal' members of society (Cohen and Young, 1973); users of disapproved drugs become labelled as social deviants. Because the mass media share a consensual view with the rest of the population, they are part of a powerful coalition against drug users and other so-called deviants. This list of deviants varies but may, at any one time, include prostitutes, illegal immigrants, strikers, paedophiles, drug-takers and drug-pushers. One might add, in this context, mothers of crack babies (Day and Richardson, 1993; Reeves and Campbell, 1994) as the antithesis of good motherhood. Usually such deviants are held to be sick or hapless victims of the cruel influence of others with power over them. Characteristically, the moral world is bifurcated into 'them and us' poles. So there are the good and the bad, the right and the wrong, the punishers and the punished, and the righteous and the evil. Such a consensus makes other views difficult to sustain because of the rigidity, comprehensiveness and power of these beliefs.

Of course, this does not explain how the media worsen the drug problem. The concept of *amplification of deviance* is needed to understand the process (Cohen and Young, 1973). Any person or group of persons who are labelled as deviant by definition suffer a degree of isolation from 'decent' society. Naturally respectable individuals are reluctant to have anything to do with deviants. The people labelled deviants are thus forced more and more to seek social contact with other, similarly labelled, individuals. This begins a spiral in which the more an individual contacts other deviants, then the more he/she is likely to be involved in further deviant activities and the more society labels and shuns him/her.

This spiral of social reactance also involves the police. Because of the nature of policing, the police are often isolated from society and know little about how normal youngsters, for example, behave, their main contacts with youngsters being in the context of arrest. This may leave the police particularly vulnerable to the influence of the media and stereotypes of drug-users. Any contact between the police and drug-users in these circumstances takes place in the context of such stereotypes and is consequently likely to confirm these stereotypes. The spiral involves a heightening in police activity to contain and control the 'drug' problem which, in turn, forces drug-users into a ghetto mentality in which they seek to resist this heightened policing by whatever means they are able. Drug-users become increasingly isolated from others in society as a result.

There is evidence that public opinion might be influenced by the media. Korzenny, McClure and Ryzttki (1990) argue that the way in which drug information will be processed depends very much on the nature of the culture involved. Consequently, they studied some of the major cultural groups in the USA—Latin-Americans living in the USA, Asians, African-Americans and European-origin people. Using samples of each of these groups with average ages in the early 20s, questions were asked about the frequency of watching different television programmes and specific types of television programmes, musical tastes, newspapers and magazines read. Data were also obtained for a drugs-attitudes scale which included the following items: 'There should be harsher penalties for drug dealers'; 'Cocaine should be legalized'; 'It's OK to try almost everything at least once'; and 'The anti-drug campaign is exaggerated.' (p. 91). The relationship between media use and drug attitudes depended on the cultural group under consideration. Media factors which are associated with more favourable attitudes to drugs in one culture were not similarly associated in another culture.

For white, European-origin individuals there were harsher attitudes towards drug dealing among viewers of family-oriented programmes such as *The Cosby Show*. Among African-Americans, greater watching of action shows, such as *Hill Street Blues* and *Miami Vice*, was associated with more liberal attitudes towards drug dealing. The amount of exposure to national and local newspapers generally showed no relation at all to beliefs about drugs. The only exception was the tendency of African-Americans with greater consumption of national newspapers to be in favour of harsher penalties for drug dealers. Given the concern about hard-rock music's pro-drugs content, it is interesting to note that, in general, there was no relationship between attitudes and exposure to such music. There were exceptions, though. These were most consistent for the African-American group, for whom it was found that listening to hard-rock music was associated with more favourable attitudes towards drugs. Perhaps even more important, exposure to such music was associated with more frequent consumption of cocaine, according to self-reports (except for the European-origin group, which demonstrated no relationship at all). One should not jump to too many conclusions or over-interpret such findings, since hard-rock listening tended to be even more strongly related to the consumption of aspirin in the African-American group! Also, exposure to television sports programmes was higher for frequent cocaine takers in the white-European and Asian groups. This would be difficult to explain in terms of the contents of sports television, even given the high levels of concern about drugs in sports (Coombs and Ryan, 1990).

MEDIA AND THE SOCIAL CONSTRUCTION OF CRIME REALITIES

Nothing illustrates the quirks of media–crime debates better than drugs and crime. Although other similar moral issues such as violence and sex have revolved around a core of arguments that the media cause violent and sexual crimes, this is not the case for drugs. Rather than being seen as the cause of drug crime, if anything, the media have been regarded as being at the vanguard of anti-drugs ideology and the associated 'war on drugs'. Thus, the role of the media in creating the 'anti-drugs' agenda is crucial. This is difficult to explain, since the media report on drugs as they do many other forms of crime, although it is the case that dramas use drugs less commonly than violence as a theme. Furthermore, kids' cartoons may be full of violent imagery, but they contain no drug themes. The potential of the media to cause drug crimes by encouraging the use of drugs is clearly a possibility; that the media are not generally held to be a problem in this respect seems to be a result of the strong hegemony against drugs (Bertram et al., 1996).

CHAPTER 13

Criminal Justice and the Media

'The publication of these preliminary examinations has a tendency to pervert the public mind and to disturb the course of justice; it is therefore illegal. What is injurious to individuals and to the community the law considers criminal.' (*Regina vs Fisher*, 1811; cited in Jones, 1982, p. 56)

It was a police chase with a difference. Pictures of O. J. Simpson, apparently trying to flee arrest along American highways, were flashed around the world and broadcast in numerous news bulletins. Surely this must potentially have influenced jurors at his trial for the murder of his wife and a male friend? A number of British newspapers have been fiercely criticized in court for their coverage of alleged violence. The male partner of a female soap-opera star from *East Enders* had been charged with assault. Nevertheless, *The Daily Mirror* reported 'Knights beat me to a pulp' (18th April, 1995). *The Sun* went even further: 'Two black eyes, bust nose and jaw like the Elephant Man: East End Gillian's driver is scarred for life, say cops'. Such reports led to the abandonment of Knight's trial.

Attempts to control the media in order to prevent miscarriages of justice are not new, although the nature of legal restraints on the media vary widely world-wide. In some countries, Britain for example, court-room news coverage is still very restricted and the use of video or microphones prohibited. Elsewhere, as in the USA, constitutional guarantees about free speech ensure a more open system. The televising of important and not so important criminal trials is commonplace; interviews with lawyers involved in a case are a familiar sight. Indeed, in particularly notorious cases, such court-room television broadcasts have been syndicated world-wide, even to countries which ban such court-room broadcasts from their own courts. Other restrictions may be imposed, such as those on reporting the identities of rape victims or children involved in court proceedings. The question of the effects of prejudicial publicity, at both the pre-trial and trial stages, has been a particular concern. Damning coverage prior to individuals being charged is usually disregarded in this context, as it would have been in the O. J. Simpson case.

Potential prejudice is just a small aspect of the news media's role in relation to criminal justice. Focusing too narrowly on prejudicial publicity may result in the neglect of other potentially important matters.

LAWYERS AND PUBLICITY

It is known that the criminal justice process is subject to inter-party agreements about appropriate pleas (Maynard, 1984). Anxiety has been expressed over the political nature of criminal justice in some countries and whether the media influence decisions to prosecute cases or not. A plea-bargain is essentially a deal between the prosecution and the defence; the defendant agrees to plead guilty to a charge which is less serious than the most serious charge possible. All sides gain. The prosecution is assured of a conviction, the defence obtains a lesser charge, and the public is spared an expensive, contested legal hearing. Plea-bargaining implies that the criminal justice system operates within a considerable margin of discretion, although what factors actually influence this are less clear. Haynie and Dover (1994) argue that prosecuting attorneys in the USA are in a powerful position to exercise discretion because they can drop or reduce charges and negotiate plea-bargaining deals. For Haynie and Dover, these negotiating and bargaining attorneys are 'rational actors' who can choose to use their powers strategically. In criminal justice systems such as the USA, in which key law officers are elected by the community, prosecuting attorneys may take advantage of their powers in an attempt to facilitate their re-election to office. Issues such as toughness on crime and criminals are part of a favourable image for a prosecuting attorney, which may lead to re-election. Election campaigns for attorneys dwell disproportionately on their conviction rates, as well as their image as tough on crime and criminals. Such images are manipulable to a degree by prosecuting attorneys; the way in which they choose to allocate resources is vital. Plea-bargains, for example, have the enormous advantage that they increase conviction rates even though at the cost of a lower-tariff category of offence. Furthermore, by choosing trials to prosecute personally, an attorney may select high-profile cases which are likely to be easy to win. In this way, an image of being a winner of important cases is created.

Haynie and Dover looked at the disposition of homicide cases in part of the USA in the 1980s. They wished to know, in particular, whether the final outcome of a case was the result of a plea-bargain rather than a trial verdict. Consequently, the researchers concentrated only on crimes which had been given media attention prior to the decision being made about its disposition. Cases in which news coverage only followed the attorney's decision could not be affecting his/her actions. The researchers measured the amount of newspaper space given to each type of crime story and its prominence in terms of whether or not it appeared on the front page. Of the relevant cases given publicity, over half were plea-bargained; the remainder were tried. Despite the researchers' expectations, the disposition of cases seemed to be unaffected by the amount or type of media coverage given. This contrasted with the more positive findings in an earlier study by Pritchard (1986).

These negative findings do not prove that prosecutors are oblivious to press coverage and its public image implications. Trials can be delayed until press interest in particularly difficult cases has declined, for example. Haynie and Dover observed that some elected attorneys actually developed strong relationships with the press, which provided them with other potential ways of manipulating media coverage. Press coverage could be influenced by the selective and timely granting of interviews to the press:

'One of the cases in our study involved the murder of a police officer, which received massive press attention and clearly outraged the community. Although the defendant was a diagnosed paranoid schizophrenic who had been in and out of mental hospitals in three states more than 10 times, the case proceeded to trial, as expected. Six weeks into the trial the prosecutor offered a plea-bargain that was accepted. However, the prosecutor granted an interview with the paper and assured the community that the plea-bargain was accepted only after approval of the family members of the slain officer and the approval of two other officers wounded in the incident.' (Haynie and Dover, 1994, p. 379)

JOURNALISTIC CONSTRUCTION OF TRIALS

News media construct accounts of trials which set up expectations in the minds of the public. The essence of the issue is the frames of reference the media choose to use in their reporting. Usually, these may not produce striking difficulties, although sometimes circumstances may produce unexpected outcomes. News coverage of trials may be compared with actual court-room transcripts in order to assess the distinctive contribution made by the journalist in selecting and writing.

Condit and Selzer (1985) studied newspaper items about the arrest and trial in the USA of Philip O. Koerner from Topeka. Koerner had shot to death a fellow office worker, Terry Pettus, but then immediately reported the crime to the police. He freely confessed to killing Pettus, so the likelihood of his conviction was a reasonable one; newspaper coverage was built on the assumption that a prison term would result. There was nothing to suggest that the killing was impulsive, which might have been used in mitigation. Indeed, Pettus' death had been carefully planned, making it a premeditated crime. When it came, the 'not guilty' verdict was something of a 'bolt from the blue' for both the newspaper and its readers. Koerner had not retracted his confession; there was no last-minute evidence against anyone else.

In court, the defence freely admitted virtually all of the factual points made by the prosecution. Most of the circumstances in the case were not matters of dispute. The key to the defence lay in the reasons or motives for Koerner's violent act:

> 'The killing, Irigonegaray [the defence lawyer] proposed, was justified by several brutal facts: that Pettus, a Sunday school superintendent, was actually a sexual predator—a "Jekyll and Hyde"; that Pettus had raped Koerner, had beaten him up, had forced him to cover up for his trips to massage parlors on company time; that Pettus had asked Koerner, the accountant, to juggle the company books; and that Pettus had threatened to have him publicly raped, mutilated, murdered, and left naked in the streets of downtown Topeka. Koerner was merely the "victim of a sick man", a victim who finally struck out in fear to protect himself. The story for the jury to understand, then, was not what Koerner had done to Pettus, but rather what Pettus had done to Koerner.' (Condit and Selzer, 1985, p. 201)

The jury's 'not guilty' verdict followed directly from the defence lawyer's arguments. In keeping with the general media emphasis on prosecution arguments (Chapter 3), little was mentioned in the newspapers of the defence's claim that the fundamental purpose of the law is to protect the rights of the individual, not the punishment of law-breakers; that the rights of the individual are more basic than the law itself. Concepts such as 'rights', 'liberty' and 'justice' to which the defence alluded are known as ideographs, 'higher-order ordinary language terms', which can be used to justify behaviour which otherwise would be seen as unacceptable.

Newspaper reports, then, were not an independent and unbiased reconstruction of the events in court. Instead of reporting both the defence and the prosecution arguments, the journalists relied unduly on the prosecuting lawyer's case and point of view. The reasons for the killing given by the defence were virtually ignored. Newspaper stories rarely mentioned the background and, when they did, overlooked the essence of the turmoil between the men: 'There apparently had been hard feelings between the two for some time and it culminated in the shooting,' he [a detective] said. 'One decided he'd had enough and shot the other.' (Condit and Selzer, 1985, p. 203). Legalistic words and phrases such as 'surrendered', 'no bond', 'suspect' and 'first degree murder' peppered the newspaper reporting. Such discourse did nothing to focus the reader on the question of rights; it led directly to the false perception that conviction was inevitable.

There are other ways in which media accounts of trials may take on special significance. Charles Lindbergh was a pioneer aviator of great public fame. The trial of the kidnapper of his baby in 1935 was something of a watershed for the US court system because of the extreme and invasive news coverage. The welter of media publicity surrounding Bruno Hauptmann's trial was so great that it led to the banning of broadcasting from American courts for several decades. In his modern analysis of this historic trial, Wilkie (1981) argued that the effects of prejudicial publicity may occur long before an accused is arrested and charged—normally the point at which prejudicial publicity is regarded as an issue. The initial construal of a crime by the media may have consequences for the eventual trial itself. This may happen when early, pre-trial, reporting is part of a 'process by which the press creates rhetorical scapegoating' (Wilkie, 1981, p. 101). In this, the media may focus on a particular crime and construe it as symptomatic of society's decline into degeneracy and failure, thus making the actual trial one of society itself. Society, through the trial, engages in an act of ritual purification which symbolically rids it of all its failings by literally scapegoating the accused.

Since we all participate in an hierarchical social order, thereby implicitly sanctioning that hierarchy, we are all subject to guilt over society's imperfections and divisions:

> 'This guilt leads to the need for redemption through a correspondingly fitting victim. To cancel this absolute guilt, as in original sin, the victim must be a perfectly fitting one. Since division is the one characteristic of the entire society, the perfect victim must be a representative of all society, and not just one segment ... When likely victims present themselves, the journalists, our modern "priests", transform them into symbolically fitting victims whose characters and trangressions represent the ills present in the hierarchy ... Society is made to feel that a vote of guilty for a ... Hauptmann is a vote for the vindication of society as a whole, for the guilty party, through his sentencing and punishment, will atone for all our sins.' (Wilkie, 1981, pp. 102–3)

Lindbergh was mythologized by the media at the time of his pioneering trans-Atlantic flight as if he were a white knight on a steed. In contrast, the news pages portrayed the accused, Hauptmann, as a villain more than capable of such a heinous crime against society. According to Wilkie, direct editorialization about Hauptmann's guilt was unnecessary since the image was constructed by a prejudicial juxtaposition of stories. Any virtues that Hauptmann possessed were tucked away at the end of the news story, whereas his failings led the item. Curiously, these virtues were more than anything responsible for turning Hauptmann into society's scapegoat:

> 'Through descriptions of Hauptmann as a man, rather than as a criminal, through accounts of his work, his personal habits and his personal preferences, the press made Hauptmann appear to be a warped and watered-down imitation of the newspaper portrait of Lindbergh following his 1927 flight.' (Wilkie, 1981, p. 106)

The media coverage rhetorically presented Lindbergh and Hauptmann as Christ and anti-Christ figures. There were quite a number of similarities between the two; both were mechanically skilled, for example. Likewise, both of them had put great effort into crossing the Atlantic. Hauptmann had stowed-away several times to emigrate into the USA. Despite being discovered several times, Hauptmann's persistence matched that of Lindbergh in his Atlantic flight.

STUDIES OF THE MEDIA AND THE VERDICT

We have seen some of the biases in newspaper coverage of crime, especially the selective neglect of certain sorts of crime (Chapter 3). This is one of the longest and best established research findings in the study of the media and crime. A very early study of the media and legal prejudice in news coverage showed that only one in five defendants were ever mentioned in newspapers (Friendly and Goldfarb, 1967). The bulk of the coverage involved the time of arrest; indictment or charging with the offence was in a distant second place. Relatively few stories covered the trial itself. There was little evidence that guilty verdicts were commoner where a case had been highly publicized. On the other hand, the most publicized cases tended to be the ones in which the defendant decided to opt for trial by jury. This sets the pattern of much of the research.

In the 1960s only about 1% of US criminal cases received any publicity at all in the *national* press (Simon and Eimermann, 1971). This general trend is confirmed at all levels by the research on the contents of the media up to the present day (Chapter 3). In other words, the effects of pre-trial publicity are limited simply because so few crimes receive much media attention at all. There is a much greater chance that a crime will receive publicity in the *local* press; the figure approached a one-in-five chance for the local news media. Furthermore, there was a disproportionate emphasis on jury-tried crimes; these were two to three times more likely to be reported (Simon and Eimermann, 1971). The potential of the news media for creating prejudice is further attenuated by the fact that most of those charged with crimes plead guilty. Since crime news is selective (Katz. 1987), certain types of crime are more likely to receive publicity. The following imperatives are largely responsible for the selection and construction of crime news—immediacy, dramatization, personalization, simplification, titillation, conventionalism, structured access and novelty (Chibnall, 1977). These further ensure that prejudicial pre-trial publicity is unlikely to be an issue in the vast majority of cases. The difficulty is that prejudice tends to become a significant issue for the sorts of crimes which dominate crime news reporting—sensational, violent cases, in particular, especially those involving a celebrity. Of course, claims of prejudicial publicity may be part of the stock-in-trade of lawyers anxious to defend their clients to the full.

In present US practice, the definition of prejudice is extremely specific:

'The Supreme Court has taught that neither mere knowledge nor mere abhorrence of the offense is sufficient to insure prejudice. The mere existence of a preconceived notion is insufficient. Prejudice must be a continuing phenomenon. Most importantly, prejudice is dependent upon the holding of a "fixed" opinion that the venire person [juror] cannot change. . . . Whether or not pretrial publicity has prejudiced a juror . . . is a judgment left to the discretion of the trial judge . . . This finding will not necessarily correspond to the social scientist's intuitive notion of a preformed bias toward an issue.' (Moran and Cutler, 1991 pp. 346–7)

This suggests that prejudice exists only where the juror has been influenced to pre-judge by media publicity and there is evidence of a disregard of pertinent aspects of court proceedings. Prejudice in this US legal definition does not even require that the jurors' views change, merely that they are unreceptive to change during the course of the trial. To a social scientist, this is a quagmire.

There has been a steady stream of researchers involved in courtroom matters, in the USA particularly. An early example was when Simon and Eimermann (1971) gathered research evidence concerning possible pre-trial prejudice. A prominent local personality had been murdered by two men, so the crime received a great deal of publicity in the local press. Although little of this coverage appeared to be prejudicial in a legal sense, the articles indicated that the accused were vagrants and that there were witnesses to the crime. So, despite a lack of irresponsibility on the part of the media, the jury may have been prejudiced in the sense of having pre-judged the issue in the social scientific meaning of the term.

A telephone survey of potential jurors was conducted a week prior to the trial. Of those who would cooperate, about 80% had heard or read about the case, and 60% were also able to provide details of the offence.

Among respondents who could remember any details concerning the case, about two-thirds favoured the prosecution's case against the men and a quarter were indifferent as to their guilt. The rest were unable to answer at all. Thus, of those exposed to the pre-trial publicity about the case, *none* believed that the men were innocent. Of the people who could not remember any details of the case, less than 5% favoured the prosecution, slightly more than 5% favoured the defence and over half were indifferent as to guilt or innocence. The remainder could not answer the question. So the trend was strong for those who knew something about the case to believe the defendants guilty.

This evidence was used by the defence as part of its argument for shifting the trial to a geographical location less hostile to its client. In the end, the court rejected this evidence and the trial was not relocated. The outcome? Well, one of the men pleaded guilty to the murder and was consequently convicted, and the other was freed by the jury verdict!

Jurors seem unrealistically confident of their freedom from the influence of media-induced bias. Moran and Cutler (1991) looked at the effect of prior knowledge in potential jurors for drug-related crimes. In one of the cases they studied, the defendants were accused of the distribution of $10 million worth of marijuana. The news media had sporadically given publicity to the case; earlier court appearances had been covered. For one of the defendants, 35 newspaper articles had been published directly related to his case, while other newspaper articles had dealt with different drug cases in the locality. One of the defendants had been a minor celebrity—a racing driver—a fact which received media attention, as did claims that he had been involved in smuggling in South America. To compound an already complex situation, the media had already reported that some defendants had pleaded guilty. This high-profile, prominent newspaper publicity continued after the arrest of the defendants.

A telephone survey conducted with the general public (i.e. potential jurors) showed a modest relationship between an individual's knowledge of the case and believing that there was a great deal of evidence of the defendants' guilt. It is of some significance that knowledge about the case was not related, in the jurors' minds, with feeling that they were biased for or against the defendant. So, irrespective of their awareness of pre-trial publicity, the jurors believed themselves to be capable of reaching an impartial verdict. They believed that they could decide solely on the basis of the evidence given at the trial, anything that they had already heard about the case being disregarded!

Another study of potential jurors examined what factors predicted the judgements of guilt made in relation to a variety of criminal and civil cases (Penrod, 1990). The jurors read descriptions of various trials, including ones for rape, murder and robbery. Generally, it was difficult to know which factors led to decisions that the defendant was guilty, since different predictors applied for the different cases. Although media use was included as a predictor variable for all of the cases, only for a robbery trial was reading the local newspaper a predictor of 'juror' decisions. Taken at face value, these findings suggest that pre-trial prejudice is usually uninfluential, yet may have a bearing in specific instances.

Of course, there are problems with such studies. For instance, it is not known whether those who knew about the crime from the newspaper coverage were particularly interested in crime issues in the first place. Such people may be somewhat 'tough on crime' anyway and more inclined to jump to conclusions about the guilt or innocence of anyone accused of a crime. For this reason, there is a tradition in research which depends on the use of 'simulated' or 'mock' juries which deliberate on cases but in the researchers' laboratories, for example, rather than the court-room. No doubt it would be better to study real juries but access to them is restricted. In an early study, Kline and Jess (1966) gave 'mock' jurors either a newspaper containing 'prejudicial' material or a non-prejudicial account of the same events and used real-life judges to direct the trial. After the presentation of the evidence, the 'prejudiced' and 'non-prejudiced' juries deliberated separately. No actual differences were found between the juries in terms of the verdicts; the prejudicial material did not alter the outcome of the trials. However, they did not ignore the prejudicial information entirely, since it was regularly brought up for discussion during the jury deliberations but generally rejected it as a source of evidence on the basis of the judge's comments about the propriety of certain sorts of evidence in law. Even juries which failed to reject the prejudicial material entirely did not differ in terms of their verdicts from the other juries.

Others have looked at the effects of newspaper sensationalism on mock-jury trials. Simon (1966) gave juries either a sensational version of the coverage of the offence, much as it would be presented in the popular press, or a rather more staid version, as in serious newspapers. Before the 'trial', the 'jurors' were asked about the guilt or innocence of the accused. They then listened to a recording of the trial evidence, including an admonition from the judge, opening statements and witness evidence, and closing instructions from the judge. Sensational pre-trial publicity did affect the views of the jurors, since those who had read the sensational version in which, for example, the accused's previous convictions were reported, were more inclined to guilty judgements. The commonest response in those who had read the more conservative news stories was to have no opinion about his guilt. Proceedings at the trial itself had a big influence on the jurors, the general belief in the accused's guilt shifting to one of innocence following hearing the simulated trial.

There are indications that jurors might actually use information they have read about in court despite its admissibility being denied in court (Sue, Smith and Gilbert, 1974). Ratings of the guilt of an accused person were affected if the jurors were aware of evidence which was not admissible in court because it was obtained by illegal means. So, 'newspaper reports' that the murder weapon had been found in the accused's home influenced the jurors despite its legal inadmissibility. This might be expected, given that otherwise the accused might have been acquitted of murder because of a legal technicality (Howitt, 1982).

Pre-trial prejudice is usually regarded as being the consequence of the media broadcasting or printing comments or information directly pertinent to a specific trial itself. A rather different sort of pre-trial publicity might affect jury deliberations (Greene, 1990). Greene termed this 'general pretrial publicity', referring to the influence of wider social debates related to a particular type of crime or trial which are not prejudicial in a legal sense. What, for example, if the media have reported that a particular police force had been proven to fabricate evidence? In these circumstances, a jury may be less willing to convict on the basis of evidence coming from that force. What of the case of a rape 'victim' who falsely accused a man of rape because she was worried about her family's response to her possible pregnancy? She did not retract her evidence until after the man had been sentenced to a very long term of imprisonment for the 'crime'. Greene suggests that such a retraction, and the consequent media publicity given to it, may serve to undermine the future prosecution of similar cases.

Greene had been investigating decision-making in mock juries in cases involving eyewitness testimony when it became clear that events outside of the research laboratory were influencing downwards the number of 'guilty' verdicts. When interviewed, some mock jurors mentioned the case of Steven Titus, who had been identified by an eyewitness as a rapist; eventually another man confessed that he had committed the crime. These events received a great deal of media attention. As a consequence, the faith of the mock jurors in the value of eyewitness testimony declined. A few months later, with the Titus case no longer hitting the headlines, business was back to normal in terms of 'guilty' verdicts in eyewitness testimony cases.

Perhaps it is unremarkable to find that prejudicial publicity of various sorts can have an influence on perceptions of the guilt of the accused (see also Tans and Chaffee, 1966). Most people who are prosecuted plead guilty anyway (Hester and Eglin, 1992), so it is not unreasonable to suspect the guilt of anyone arrested and charged. The lack of a consistent influence of media-induced prejudice on the final trial outcome is also important. Clearly, in some circumstances, prejudice can be compensated for by the trial evidence and instructions from the judge.

NON-PREJUDICIAL PREJUDICE

The things that the media print and broadcast about the criminal justice process may be prejudicial in ways which escape legal definitions of prejudice. However, many apparent instances of legally defined prejudice seem not to have the major effects on the outcomes of trials that may be feared. Juries seem capable of disregarding prejudicial information in the limited number of trials for which it is potentially a problem. On the other hand, the ways in which the media report court proceedings have been somewhat neglected, especially in terms of detailed textual analyses of court reporting, which may be subtly leading.

CHAPTER 14

The Media and Crime Prevention

' "We had a larceny on Main Street," he announces before holding up a picture of the chief suspect. "This guy's got a problem, a real serious problem. He's got a drug addiction." He appeals for info, and gives out the number of the tipline. "Everything's anonymous".' (Freedland, 1996, p. 16)

Common sense would suggest that if the media can cause crime, they can stop it. This is a little too simplistic, given what we know about the limited direct criminogenic influence of the media. It is all too easy to overlook what was the most important initiative to reduce crime, since it appears to be primarily about using the media in education. As a result of the growing urban violence and unrest which characterized many American cities in the 1960s, a task force was set up by the government to tackle the problem of violence. This led, in part, to the education intervention, Operation Headstart, designed to alleviate some of the deficits apparent in the early experience of many young-sters brought up in inner-city poverty. The idea was simple—inner city problems are associated with bad education, so improve education and some of the problems might go away. Operation Headstart was a mix-ture of home-support teaching, preparatory school lessons and the popular educational programme for pre-schoolers, *Sesame Street*. The aim was to help compensate for poor children's low basic pre-school skills, such as familiarity with numbers and letters (Ball and Bogatz, 1970; Bogatz and Ball, 1971; Howitt, 1976). Children who have never seen a book, for example, are at a disadvantage when they enter school for the first time. Within certain limits, Operation Headstart was effec-tive at increasing school-readiness in the target group (Cook et al., 1975; Liebert, 1976), although middle-class youngsters benefited more from the telecasts.

Similar laudable intentions are at the roots of other types of public service broadcasting, anti-smoking and drunk-driving campaigns, for example. As for any other crime issue, the idea that the media fire 'magic bullets' producing dramatic change is misleading. Cautious opti-mism or tentative pessimism are appropriate compromises between the media's demonstrated achievements in crime prevention and hopes and expectations.

INADVERTENT CRIME REDUCTION

Media-induced anxieties about crime levels in the community may lead to personal strategies to avoid victimization, such as not going to notorious clubs and bars in high-risk areas. But there are other strategies. The media are part of the process which has made crime into a commodity or commodities, just like any other commercial product (Tunnel, 1992). Sales of television crime programmes are merely one illustration of how private gain can be achieved legitimately from crime. There is a whole raft of consumer products and services involved in this commodification process. Intruder alarms, personal alarms, mace cans, property-marking equipment and security blinds are among the commodities on offer. Similarly, self-defence lessons, the use of the lie-detector or polygraph experts in job selection, and private security firms are some of the services for sale. Profit-maximization in this industry is dependent on *perceptions* that levels of violent and property crimes are escalating.

Tunnel argues that increases in sales of crime-related products are out of proportion to rises in crime itself, although he appreciates that official crime statistics superficially suggest otherwise. Robbery, burglary and rape reports all rose in the USA throughout the 1970s and 1980s (US Department of Commerce, Economics and Statistics Information, 1996). However, surveys of victims of crime showed the reverse trend—fewer households experienced robbery, rape, assault and burglary in 1990 than had been experienced 15 years earlier. In conjunction with other evidence, Tunnell (1992) takes the view that:

'In the light of these data on recent crime trends, these new commodities undoubtedly represent false needs, because evidence suggests that commodity production and consumption, in this case, are not related to real societal needs—the need to protect our lives and property from rapidly increasing crime. Rather, commodity production is responding to the logic of the market economy that creates and transforms items into objects for buying and selling.' (pp. 305–6)

Of course, the decline in numbers experiencing victimization may have been the result of increased use of security products. Furthermore, in market economies, reductions in real costs may expand a market by increasing the affordability and thus the desirability of manufactured products. Tunnell describes the public as having a 'fetish' for crime which encourages the consumption of even more crime-related commodities. Although the media have a role to play in this process, it is equally clear that industry has an interest in promoting anxieties about crime and then providing the solution—at a price. Rosenbaum and Heath (1988) describe evidence which suggests that crime-prevention initiatives publicized by the police and others increase the fear of crime rather than reduce it. This could be the basis of a self-reinforcing spiral.

While the adoption of anti-victimization strategies by the public may reduce crime, some victimization may merely be redirected towards others who are less well-protected. Do the media have any role in reducing crime directly by influencing potential offenders not to offend? Erroneously or not, the media are regarded by many as 'a school for crime'. However, there is a stream of mass media research which suggests that the media have prosocial effects—television, for example, encourages good and socially beneficial behaviours in children and other users (Lee, 1988; Rushton, 1979, 1982). What evidence there is seems to suggest that in laboratory-type studies, prosocial media effects can be readily achieved. Meta-analyses which involve the results of many studies confirm this or even go so far as to suggest that the prosocial effects may be stronger than antisocial ones (Hearold, 1986). Unfortunately, research on the prosocial effects of the media suffers from much the same weaknesses as any other laboratory studies. So, for the purposes of criminologically relevant media research, it too lacks obvious ecological validity.

Although relatively little media coverage of crime deals with sentencing and punishment, publicity about these matters may be one mechanism of media influence on crime rates. There are commonsensical assumptions about the relationship between the magnitude of punishments for perpetrators and their deterrent effects (Fagan, 1994). Draconian new punishments (e.g. boot camps), publicized through the media, may have a deterrent effect on some potential offenders. In recent years, longer custodial sentences and extensions of life-sentencing have been introduced, partly with the intention of increasing the deterrent effects of sentences. 'Three strikes and you're out' illustrates this thinking applied to life-sentences.

Little is known about the deterrent effect of this publicity; virtually all the relevant research concerns the effectiveness of media-publicized executions for murder. Usually no relationship has been detected between the amount of publicity given an execution and changes in homicide rates afterwards. Phillips (1980) studied old British crime data and found no relationships between media coverage of executions and murder rates. However, Stack (1987) claimed to have shown a deterrent effect in American crime statistics for the period 1950–1981. His findings have been challenged for a number of reasons (Bailey and Peterson, 1989). For example, Stack had failed to control for variations in population size over time by expressing crimes as rates per 100 000 of the relevant population. In addition to correcting such unsatisfactory features of the original data, Bailey and Peterson extended the period studied to include the 1940s and the early 1980s. Newspaper and magazine publicity given to an execution was assessed according to whether it was mentioned in the *New York Times* or *Facts on File*. This new analysis revised Stack's conclusions considerably. Homicides in general did *not* decline following highly publicized executions; except for the coding errors, Stack would have reached a similar conclusion. Any possible slight deterrent effects seemed to 'wash out' over the year. Thus, the total yearly homicides remain unchanged despite very slight and unreliable fluctuations following some well-publicized executions. A similar analysis produced much the same pattern for *television* publicity about executions during the period 1976–1987 (Bailey, 1990). Once demographic and similar variables had been allowed for, the amount of television publicity given to the 93 executions during this period seemed to have no effect on homicide levels.

Those with a knowledge of the deterrent effects of punishment may not be too surprised that publicity about punishments appears to have little effect. Research on deterrents has yielded little evidence that they do deter crime in general or extensively (Fagan, 1994; Farrington, Ohlin and Wilson, 1986).

DIRECT CRIME-PREVENTION INTERVENTIONS

So what of the more intentional and directed attempts by the media to influence crime levels? There are three different styles of media interventions relevant to this question:

- *Initiatives to reduce any actual or potential influences of media crime and violence on youngsters* (Chapters 5 and 6). Attempts to use the media *directly* in crime reduction have employed a variety of different strategies. In the main, such interventions are not based on the media alone; it is relatively common to find the techniques of media education being employed in the classroom to help youngsters understand better the nature of television and video. Dubow and Cappas (1988) review the more general field of the use of social interventions to reduce aggression in children.
- *Enhancing the public's role in crime reduction*. Crime detection programmes such as *Crime Stoppers* in the USA and *Crime Watch* in the UK recruit viewers' help in clearing-up unsolved crimes. These programmes are based on a communications model of crime prevention which encourages direct communication between the police and public.

- *Pre-emptive publicity campaigns to encourage the public to avoid victimization.* Examples of this would include teaching risk-reduction by encouraging people to lock doors and not to leave car keys in the ignition.

Sacco and Trotman (1990) present a similar list.

Breaking Media Violence Influences

Many find the argument that the media make children violent and encourage criminal violence convincing. Of course, anti-violence media education may be seen as a worthwhile activity, irrespective of whether there is a media–violence link or not. Interventions based on concepts from media education and media literacy may have positive, beneficial effects on ameliorating other, non-media, causes of violence. Teaching children, for example, about alternatives to violence may have a generally positive effect, no matter whether their aggression is the result of cycles of abuse or watching violent cartoons

A basic distinction needs to be made between (a) media programming designed to reduce aggression in the audience and (b) media-education taking place in, for example, the school classroom, which attempts to alter the viewers' beliefs about violence and media violence. Media campaigns may be unsuccessful if they are not accompanied by community-based initiatives. This is illustrated by the work of Biocca et al. (1997), who carried out a study of the influence of US anti-violence public service announcements. Examples of these include:

- Boy in school hall is deliberately bumped by another. Color turns neon as imagined fight begins and victim pulls knife. Scene returns to normal as victim decides to 'Pick up my books and walk away' (p. 450).
- Rap artist talks about violence. Shots of him alternate with fast-moving graphics, statistics on gun violence. 'Numbers don't lie'. Some segments appear shot in a jail (p. 452).

These were targeted at adolescent viewers, explicitly educational, and designed to change attitudes or norms concerning violent behaviour. The research involved (a) high-school students and, perhaps more importantly, (b) adolescents in a high-security correctional school. The latter sample included large proportions committed for violent crimes such as murder, forcible rape and armed robbery. Of course, there are numerous criteria for evaluating the effectiveness of such public service announcements. Interest, understanding and remembering are features which relate to learning the message. Different announcements were more or less effective by these criteria. Using adult celebrities to 'preach' to youngsters may be less effective than employing celebrities more similar in age to the target audience. Despite the good intentions of the makers of these public service announcements, there was no evidence that they altered attitudes to the use of violence when resolving conflicts. Even if attitudes had changed, youngsters may not feel any more able to control themselves in potentially violent situations.

The same research team also evaluated the effectiveness of an award-winning video programme, *Kids Killing Kids / Kids Saving Kids*, which had the specific aim of altering adolescents' attitudes towards the use of guns. The story-line involves the ways in which the lives of four teenagers changed for the worse following the use of a handgun. The video then replays the events to give the teenagers a 'second chance' in the situation by illustrating a non-violent strategy for dealing with interpersonal conflict. Once again there was little evidence that the message penetrated—attitudes did not change. Worse still, the youngsters found this premium anti-violence video no more interesting than a fire safety video.

While Biocca et al. (1997) regard the failure of the violence prevention programming as due to competing messages from regular broadcasts, this is to assume that media messages routinely alter attitudes and behaviour. More successful outcomes seem to be found in studies which are part of a community- or school-based education programme. While the studies by Eron et al. may have done little to clarify the link between media violence and criminal violence (Chapter 5), this does not alter the success of anti-violence initiatives consequent on this. In one study, Huesmann et al. (1983) had school children write essays on why television violence is bad and unreal. The effect was to (a) reduce aggression as rated by the children's peers, and (b) reduce the correlation between television violence viewing and aggression. Similar experiments are reported in Anderson (1983), Eron (1986), Singer, Zuckerman and Singer (1980), Sprafkin, Swift and Hess (1983), Spafkin, Gadow and Kant (1988) and Vooijs and Van der Voort (1993). The ease with which links between media-violence and aggression in the young viewer are broken is significant. Few studies have involved intensive and prolonged media-education initiatives in order to be effective. This, perhaps, suggests that links between watching media-violence and aggression are weak if they are so easily broken. Studies suggest that it is equally easy, if not easier, to break the links between pornography and its effects—certainly when these 'effects' have been generated in the psychology laboratory. Normal post-experimental 'debriefing' is sufficient to overcome any effects created. Simply telling men the purpose of the study dissipated any effects of the experiment on them (Donnerstein, Linz and Penrod, 1987).

One long-term intervention study deserves careful attention by anyone interested in using the media in crime prevention. This is an exceptionally well-researched Dutch study (Vooijs and van der Voort, 1993). The researchers developed a 'critical viewing curriculum' intended to influence how 10–12 year-old children perceive televised crime series. The basic themes were explicitly laid-out in a textbook which was illustrated with the aid of video-taped excerpts from violent films. The information was also presented using videoed interviews with people judged to be credible sources by the researchers. The curriculum:

> '... attempted to convince children of the seriousness of violence by confronting them, by means of television interviews, with (a) police officers who had actually shot suspects, and who related how deep an impression this event made on them; (b) victims of violence who told about the physical and—above all—the mental consequences they had suffered; and (c) a doctor who explained the medical consequences of various types of acts. The unrealistic character of many violent films became clear from, among other things, the commentary on excerpts from crime films given by real police officers and private detectives in which the differences between film and reality were pointed out. The questionable legitimacy of a large part of the violent actions of good guys in the films was made clear by explaining, among other things, that in reality police officers and private detectives were allowed to use violence only under extremely exceptional circumstances.' (Vooijs and van der Voort, 1993, p. 135)

After seeing violent programmes, the children were asked to *decentrate*, which means that they had to concentrate on the physical harm and damage done or the reactions of the police officers; they were to ignore the details of the plot itself.

Schools were allocated to either the curriculum group or to the control condition which did not take the media education programme. The children were tested on the following:

- *Readiness to see violence.* The children rated 25 acts of violence by good guys on a scale of *dreadful* to *not so bad*.
- *Approval of violence.* These violent acts were rated in terms of a dimension of *entirely correct* to *entirely wrong*.
- *Perceived reality of violent films.* Children rated short descriptions of unrealistic events of the sort seen in violent programmes in terms of whether they were possible in real life. An example was, 'In police programs, villains are almost always caught. Does that happen in real life too?'
- *Knowledge.* A multiple-choice test was used to measure the factual knowledge learnt from the curriculum.

In the short term, the curriculum increased readiness to see violence while increasing disapproval of violence done by good characters. Similarly, media violence became increasingly regarded as unrealistic while factual knowledge about the curriculum also increased. The more a child learnt from the curriculum the more readily he/she was to perceive violence but the less likely to rate it as realistic. These effects persisted two years after the curriculum initiative had ended. As they matured, the control group children began to catch up. The individual characteristics of children seemed largely irrelevant to the success of the curriculum intervention.

Do such changes in attitudes and beliefs actually reflect changes in behaviour in real-life situations? Research in this area is scant, but one carefully evaluated investigation provides some clarification. The study examined methods of modifying the behaviour of six-year-old boys living in a deprived area of Montreal (Tremblay et al., 1991). Each boy was selected because, in the opinion of his teachers, he was disruptive and, potentially, at risk of delinquency. The boys were then allocated to one of three groups:

- *The experimental group.* Their parents received a reading programme for the child; training in monitoring their child's behaviour, giving positive reinforcement for good (prosocial) behaviour and giving non-abusive punishments; and help in trying to manage family crises. The boys, themselves, were given some training at school (in groups together with non-problem pupils), such as on how to make contact with other children, how to ask for help and how to ask 'Why?' in ways which would not lead to conflict. In addition, the programme included fantasy play training together with guided intervention about television watching. This was provided at the child's home and could involve his siblings. Twelve training sessions were employed in which active participation and prosocial alternatives to aggression were the main features.
- *The control group.* These youngsters were assessed to see how their behaviours changed without them or their parents receiving any of the training given to the experimental group.
- *The placebo group.* These boys were observed regularly during the two years of the study (not just at the end) but did not actually receive the training programme proper.

Despite all of the effort devoted to the youngsters in the experimental group, consequent improvements in the boys' behaviour were very limited. What improvements there were in the experimental group were virtually confined to *self-reported* measures. Fighting, both at home and away from home, did seem to reduce, as did thieving according to the children's own reports. Other, possibly more objective, criteria which were *not* based on self-reports suggested a different conclusion. Most of these indicators of behaviour, such as ratings by others, showed little or no change as a consequence of the training programme.

It can be difficult to separate the media aspects of anti-crime campaigns from, say, their community-based aspects. However, if crime prevention is the objective, it can be argued that a successful programme is a successful programme and we should not be too concerned what aspects of a programme contribute most to its success. The violence prevention project developed by Hausman et al. (1992) only used the media to supplement a community-based initiative to discourage youngsters from crime. The core programme for these adolescents was based on a series of 10 classroom lessons. 'Friends for life, don't let friends fight' was the campaign's overall message. The accompanying mass media publicity was delivered through public service advertising. Several broadcasts were transmitted to support the community campaign. This media advertising was designed to achieve the following objectives: (a) raising public awareness of violence by adolescents; (b) giving graphic messages to youngsters about the consequences of their violence; (c) reinforcing the messages of the community-based programme. The community project was carried out in a white socially deprived area which had a high homicide rate, and an equivalent black area. More than 3000 youngsters participated in the community project, over 20% of the youngsters in the deprived neighbourhoods. Exposure to the media part of the campaign was relatively low; only about 44% of the target group became aware of the campaign through the media. This contrasts with typical penetration figures of 75–90% in campaigns of this sort. The low figures might have been due to any of a number of factors—the nature of the target audience, the brevity of the campaign, or the use of public service broadcast time, for instance.

Encouraging Police/Public Cooperation

Daniel Handley was nine years of age when he was strangled in just the way that Timothy Morss had fantasized during therapy in prison. Morss wanted to snatch a young blond boy and bugger him. Daniel Handley fitted the description of his ideal victim. A prison officer remembered Morss's fantasy several years later when the boy's murder featured on *Crimewatch*. He contacted the police and named Morss as a possible perpetrator (*The Guardian*, 9 May 1996, p. 4). While such dramatic successes seem to justify this type of programme, they are not without their critics. There are a number of worries about the role played by *Crime Stoppers*- and *Crimewatch*-style programmes in which the public are encouraged to divulge information relevant to the detection of crimes, which are re-staged for the benefit of the television audience (Rosenbaum, Lurigio and Lavraka, 1989):

• The television re-enactments of crimes may have a prejudicial effect on local juries, given that they represent the police case and often make assertions about what individuals with particular characteristics did.

- It is possible that witnesses confuse the details of events in real life with the television re-staging.
- Witnesses recruited following media publicity may be compromised because of the effects of payments on their credibility.
- The anonymity of confidential informants risks allegations being made which are malicious or unfounded.
- The 'sneaking' strategy may foster distrust in communities and neighbourhoods, so weakening community bonds.
- Should citizens be paid to do what might be seen as the civic duty to report crime and criminals?
- The close ties between programme makers and the police necessary to produce such broadcasts may undermine the journalists' ability to act as watch-dogs over the activities of the police.

According to Rosenbaum et al., the *Crime Stoppers* broadcasts are cost-effective. Compared with the expense of paying rewards to callers, 80 times more money was recovered from stolen property recovered and the value of narcotics seized. The size of the reward made no difference to the public's response. In an experiment, callers to the programme were offered, at random, rewards of $100, $250 or $400 for effective information. Irrespective of which random amount was involved, the level of satisfaction with the appropriateness of the reward and beliefs about its fairness were the same, neither did the amount of the reward affect the likelihood that the caller would ring again in future with information about other crimes.

Pre-emptive Media Campaigns

Crime prevention is not a priority of the media in general (Roberts and Grossman, 1990); newspaper coverage can remain sparse even when television takes an interest. Furthermore, there is no guarantee that high public awareness of a crime-prevention campaign produces high participation. Crime prevention is no different in this way from commercial advertising and other media-based campaigns. While there is a common view that advertising is effective, one has to bear in mind the many failed advertising campaigns which have cost companies dear (Cashmore, 1994; Jamieson and Campbell, 1992) and the often relatively ineffective public information campaigns such as those against smoking or drunk-driving. Dramatic changes in the public's attitudes or behaviour should not be expected following media campaigns; advertising effectiveness cannot be judged from spectacular successes alone.

The criteria by which the success of anti-crime programming can be judged vary widely; some are more likely to demonstrate success than others. Attempts to measure success using end-of-process criteria such as decreases in crime rates are likely to be discouraging (Sacco and Trotman, 1990). It is far more important, initially, to concentrate on less exacting criteria, such as whether people have heard of the campaign. Their knowledge of the aims of the campaign might be the next most appropriate criterion. Modest criteria are appropriate for some very good reasons. For example, until the message has been communicated widely it is unlikely that it can begin to influence crime levels. Even then, things may not be as straightforward as they might at first appear. A downward trend in criminal statistics may not be the immediate consequence of an effective anti-crime campaign. Publicity might raise public awareness of crime, thus encouraging more reporting:

> 'These increases in reporting could cancel out, to some unspecified extent, any real decreases in crime levels that result from the campaign.' (Sacco and Trotman, 1990, p. 96)

The media, according to Sacco and Trotman, can be effective in generating public awareness in other ways. Low-cost police crime newsletters inform the public on matters of immediate relevance to their community and lifestyle. This sort of low-key approach may achieve more than grandiose attempts to deter offenders by the use of the mass media.

There are a number of factors which will increase the impact of any media campaign:

- If large numbers of the target audience are exposed to the campaign materials.
- If the themes of the campaign are perceived as salient by the target audience.
- If the messages of the campaign are not undermined by other important information sources.
- If the goals of the campaign are planned modestly and realistically.
- The campaign materials need to concentrate on specific types of change in the target audience.
- If everything is done to encourage the support of the campaign objectives through informal social interaction.
- If the campaign effectively deals with barriers to change in the audience. So, for example, it is pointless recommending anti-burglary devices if they are difficult to find in stores.
- The lifestyles and beliefs of the target audience must be properly assessed. In relation to the media, it is pointless programming initiatives at times when the target audience is unlikely to be viewing.

These are basic features of many media advertising campaigns, they are no more applicable to crime prevention than to any other form of campaign. Anti-crime messages have to compete with the slickest advertising that industry can afford.

Does this leave us where we began? Probably not, since despite our caution, we now know a great deal about the role of the media in crime and criminal justice processes. Subtle rather than grand effects seem characteristic. We should not be seduced by the fuss and fume surrounding the media into believing in the unrelenting power of the media. Nevertheless, the media are part of a complex political and social process in which questions about the criminogenic influences of the media play a part. This story can run and run.

References

Abel, G.G., Barlow, D.H., Blanchard, E.B. and Guild, D. (1977). The components of rapists' sexual arousal. *Archives of General Psychiatry*, **34**, 895–903.

Acland, C.R. (1995). *Youth, Murder, Spectacle: The Cultural Politics of 'Youth in Crisis'*. Boulder, CO: Westview.

Ainsworth, P.B. (1995). *Psychology and Policing in a Changing World*. Chichester: Wiley.

Altheide, D.L. and Johnson, J.M. (1980). *Bureaucratic Propaganda*. Boston, MA: Allyn and Bacon.

Amoroso, D.M., Brown, M., Pruesse, M., Ware, E.E. and Pilkey, D.W. (1970). An investigation of behavioral, psychological and physiological reactions to pornographic stimuli. In *Technical Report of the Commission on Obscenity and Pornography, Vol. VIII, Erotica and Social Behavior* (pp. 1–40). Washington, DC: US Government Printing Office,

Anderson, J.A. (1983). Television literacy and the critical viewer. In J. Bryant and D.R. Anderson (Eds), *Children's Understanding of Television* (pp. 297–330). New York: Academic Press.

Andison, E.R. (1977). TV violence and viewer aggression: a cumulation of study results, 1956–1979. *Public Opinion Quarterly*, **41**(3), 314–31.

Ang, I. (1996). *Living Room Wars: Rethinking Media Audiences for a Post Modern World*. London: Routledge.

Anwar, M. and Shang, A. (1982). *Television in a Multi-racial Society*. London: Commission for Racial Equality.

Armstrong, G.B., Neuendorf, K.A. and Brentar, J.E. (1992). TV entertainment, news, and racial perceptions of college students. *Journal of Communications*, **42**(3), 153–76.

Avery-Clark, C.A. and Laws, D.R. (1984). Differential erection response patterns of sexual child abusers to stimuli describing activities with children. *Behavior Therapy*, **15**, 71–83.

Bailey, W.C. (1990). Murder, capital punishment, and television: execution publicity and homicide rates. *American Sociological Review*, **55**, 628–33.

Bailey, W.C. and Peterrson, R.D. (1989). Murder and capital punishment. *American Sociological Review*, **54**, 722–43.

Baker, R.K. and Ball, S.J. (Eds) (1969). *Violence and the Media: A Staff Report to the National Commission on the Causes and Prevention of Violence*. Washington, D.C.: US Government Printing Office.

Ball, S. and Bogatz, G.A. (1970). *The First Year of Sesame Street*. Princeton, NJ: Educational Testing Service.

Bandura, A. (1973). *Aggression: A Social Learning Analysis*. Englewood Cliffs, NJ: Prentice-Hall.

Bandura, A. (1983). Psychological mechanisms of aggression. In R.G. Green and C.I. Donnerstein (Eds), *Aggression, Theoretical and Empirical Reviews, Vol I: Theoretical and Methodological Issues* (pp. 1–40). New York: Academic Press.

Bandura, A. and Huston, A.C. (1961). Identification as a process of incidental teaming. *Journal of Abnormal and Social Psychology*, **63**, 311–8.

Bandura, A., Ross, D. and Ross, S.A. (1961). Transmission of aggression through imitation of aggressive models. *Journal of Abnormal and Social Psychology*, **63**, 575–82.

Bandura, A., Ross, D. and Ross, S.A. (1963a). Imitation of film-mediated aggressive models. *Journal of Abnormal and Social Psychology*, **66**, 3–11.

Bandura, A., Ross, D. and Ross, S.A. (1963b). Vicarious reinforcement and imitative learning. *Journal of Abnormal and Social Psychology*, **67**, 6017.

Baptista-Fernandez, P. and Greenberg, B. (1980). The context, characteristics and communication behaviors of Blacks on television. In B.S. Greenberg (Ed.), *Life on Television* (pp. 13–21). Norwood, NJ: Ablex Publishing.

Barak, G. (1994). Media, crime and justice: a case for constitutive criminology. In J. Ferrell and C.R. Sanders (Eds), *Cultural Criminology*. Boston: Northeastern University Press, pp. 142–66.

Barbaree, H.E., Marshall, W.L. and Lanthier, R.K. (1979). Deviant sexual arousal in rapists. *Behavior Research and Therapy*, **17**, 215–22.

Barcus, E.G. (1983). *Images of Life on Children's Television*. New York: Praetor.

Barker, M. (1981). *The New Racism: Conservatives and the Ideology of the Tribe*. London: Junction Books.

Barker, M. (1997). The Newson Report: a case study in 'common sense'. In M. Barker and J. Petley (Eds) (pp. 12–31). London: Routledge.

Barlow, G. and Hill, A. (1985). *Video Violence and Children*. London: Hodder and Stoughton.

Barlow, M.H., Barlow, D.E. and Chiricos, T.G. (1995). Economic conditions and ideologies of crime in the media: a content analysis of crime news. *Crime and Delinquency*, **41**(1), 3–19.

Baron, J.N. and Reiss, P.S. (1985). Same time, next year: aggregate analyses of the mass media and video behavior. *American Sociological Review*, **50**, 347–63.

Baron, L. and Straus, M. (1984). Sexual stratification, pornography and rape in the United States. In N.M. Malamuth and E. Donnerstein (Eds), *Pornography and Sexual Aggression* (pp. 185–209). New York: Academic Press.

Baron, L. and Straus, M. (1987). Four theories of rape: a macrosociological analysis. *Social Problems*, **34**, 467–89.

Baron, L. and Straus, M. (1989). *Four Theories of Rape: A State-level Analysis*. New Haven, CT: Yale University Press.

Bates, A. (1996). The Origins, Development and Effect on Subsequent Behaviour of Deviant Sexual Fantasies in Sexually Violent Adult Men. Unpublished Manuscript, Thames Valley Project, 17 Park Road, Didcot, OX11 8QL.

Baxter, M. (1990). Flesh and blood. *New Scientist*, 5 May, 37–41.

Bazargan, M. (1994). The effects of health, environmental, and sociopsychological variables on fear of crime and its consequences among urban black elderly individuals. *International Journal of Ageing and Human Development*, **38** (2), 99–115.

Bean, P. (1974). *The Social Control of Drugs*. London: Martin Robinson.

Bean, P. (1990). Report to the Home Office Research and Planning Unit. Unpublished Manuscript. Midlands Centre for Criminology and Criminal Justice,

Loughborough University.

Bean, P. (1992). Cocaine and Crack: Supply and Use. Unpublished manuscript, Midlands Centre for Criminology and Criminal Justice. Loughborough University.

Bean, P.T. and Wilkinson, C.K. (1988). Drug taking, crime and the illicit supply system. *British Journal of Addiction*, **83**, 533–9.

Beck, J.C. (1994). Epidemiology of mental disorder and violence: beliefs and research findings. *Harvard Review of Psychiatry*, **2**(1), 1–6.

Becker, J. and Stein, R. (1991). Does pornography play a role in the aetiology of sexual deviance in adolescent males? *International Journal of Law and Psychiatry*, **14**(1–2), 85–95.

Beckett, K. (1994). Setting the public agenda: 'street crime' and drug use in American politics. *Social Problems*, **41**(3), 425–75).

Belson, R.B. (1996). Mass media effects on violent behaviour. *Annual Review of Sociology*, **22**, 103–28.

Belson, W.A. (1967). *The Impact of Television*. London: Crosby Lockwood.

Belson, W.A. (1975). *Juvenile Theft: The Causal Factors*. London: Harper and Row.

Belson, W.A. (1978). *Television Violence and the Adolescent Boy*. London: Saxon House.

Berelson, B. (1948). What missing the newspaper means. In P. Lazarsfeld and F.N. Stauton (Eds), *Communications Research, 1948–9*. New York: Duell, Sloan and Pearce.

Berelson, B., Lazarsfeld, P.F. and McPhee, W.N. (1954). *Voting: A Study of Opinion Formation in a Presidential Campaign*. Chicago: University of Chicago Press.

Berkowitz, L. (1962). *Aggression: A Social Psychological Analysis*. New York: McGraw-Hill.

Berkowitz, L. and Geen, R.G. (1966). Female violence and the cue properties of available targets. *Journal of Personality and Social Psychology*, **3**, 525–30.

Berkowitz, L. and Geen, R.G. (1967). Stimulus qualities of the target of aggression. *Journal of Personality and Social Psychology*, **5**, 364–8.

Berkowitz, L. and Rawlings, E. (1963). Effects of film violence on inhibitions against subsequent aggression. *Journal of Abnormal and Social Psychology*, **66**, 405–12.

Berkowitz, L., Corwin, R. and Heironimus, M. (1963). Film violence and subsequent aggressive tendencies. *Public Opinion Quarterly*, **27**, 217–29.

Berman, A. L. (1988). Fictional depiction of suicide in television films and imitation effects. *American Journal of Psychiatry*, **145**(10), 982–6.

Berridge, V. (1984). Drugs and social control: the establishment of drug control in Britain 1900–1930. *British Journal of Addictions*, **79**, 17–28.

Berridge, V. (1989). Historical Issues. In S. McGregor (Ed.), *Drugs and British Society* (pp. 20–35). London: Routledge.

Berridge, V. and Edwards, G. (1981). *Opium and the People*. London: Allen Lane/St Martin's Press.

Bertram, E., Blackman, M., Sharpe, K. and Andreas, P. (1996). *Drug War Politics: The Price of Denial*. Berkeley, CA: University of California.

Biocca, F., Brown, J., Shen, F., Bernhardt, J.M., Bastista, L., Kemp, K., Makris, G., West, M., Lee, J., Straker, H., Hsiao, H. and Carbone, E. (1997). Assessment of television's anti-violence messages: University of North Carolina at Chapel Hill study. In *National Television Violence Study: Vol. 1* (pp. 413–530). Newbury Park, CA: Sage.

Blackburn, R. (1993). *The Psychology of Criminal Conduct: Theory, Research and Practice.* Chichester: Wiley.

Blumer, H. (1933). *Movies and Conduct.* New York: Macmillan.

Blumer, H. (1995). Private monograph on movies and sex. In G.S. Jowett, I.C. Jarvie and K.H. Fuller. (Eds), *Children and the Movies: Media Influence and the Payne Fund Controversy* (pp. 281–301). Cambridge University Press.

Blumer, H. and Hauser, P.M. (1933). *Movies, Delinquency, and Crime.* New York: Macmillan.

Blumler, J.G. and Katz, E. (Eds) (1974). The uses of mass communications: current perspectives on gratifications research. *Sage Annual Reviews of Communications Research,* Vol. 3. Beverly Hills, CA: Sage.

Blumler, J.G., Brown, J.R. and McQuail, D. (1970). *The Social Origins of the Gratifications Associated with Television Viewing.* Mimeo, University of Leeds.

Bogatz, G.A. and Ball, S. (1971). *The Second Year of Sesame Street: A Continuing Evaluation.* Princeton, NJ: Educational Testing Service.

Boyce, G., Curran, J. and Wingate, P. (Eds) (1978). *Newspaper History from the Seventeenth Century to the Present Day.* London: Constable.

Bradshaw, J. and Millar, J. (1991). *Lone-parent Families in the UK: DSS Report No. 6.* London: HMSO.

Brannigan, A. (1987). Pornography and behaviour: alternative explanations. *Journal of Communication,* **37**(3), 185–9.

Brannigan, A. (1991). Obscenity and social harm: a contested terrain. *International Journal of Law and Psychiatry,* **14**(1–2), 1–12.

Branthwaite, A. and Peirce, L. (1990). The portrayal of black people in British television advertisements. *Social Behaviour,* **5**(5), 327–34.

Brigham, J.C. and Giesbrecht, L.W. (1976). 'All in the Family'—racial attitudes. *Journal of Communication,* **26**(4), 69–74.

Brinson, S.L. (1992). The use and opposition of rape myths in prime-time television dramas. *Sex Roles,* **27**(7–8), 359–75.

Bromberg, W. (1953). American achievements in Criminology. *Journal of Criminal Law, Criminology and Police Science,* **47**, 166–76.

Brown, J.D. and Newcomer, S.F. (1991). Television viewing and adolescents' sexual behavior. *Journal of Homosexuality,* **21**(1–2), 77–91.

Brownmiller, S. (1975). *Against Our Will: Men, Women and Rape.* New York: Simon and Schuster.

Brownstein, H.H. (1995). The media and the construction of random drug violence. In J. Ferrell and C.R. Sanders (Eds), *Cultural Criminology.* Boston: Northeastern University Press, pp. 45–65.

Bryant, J. and Zillmann, D. (Eds) (1986). *Perspectives on Media Effects.* Hillsdale, NJ: Erlbaum.

Bryant, J., Carveth, R.A. and Brown, D. (1981). Television viewing and anxiety. *Journal of Communication,* **31**, 106–19.

Bullis, R.K. (1995). From gag rules to blindfolds: the pornography victims' compensation act. *Journal of Sex Education and Therapy,* **21**(1). 11–12.

Burgess, A.W. and Holmstrom, L.L. (1979). *Rape: Crisis and Recovery.* Bowie, MD: Robert J. Brady.

Burt, M. (1980). Cultural myths and supports for rape. *Journal of Personality and Social Psychology,* **38**, 217–30.

Bushman, B.J. (1995). Moderating role of trait aggressiveness in the effects of violent media on aggresion. *Journal of Personality and Social Psychology,* **69**(5), 950–60.

Butler, D. and Stokes, D. (1969). *Political Change in Britain*. London: Macmillan.

Byrne, D. and Lamberth, J. (1970). The effect of erotic stimuli on sex arousal, evaluative responses, and subsequent behavior. In *Technical Report of the Commission on Obscenity and Pornography, Vol. VIII, Erotica and Social Behavior* (pp. 41–67). Washington, D.C: US Government Printing Office.

Calvert, C. (1997). Hate speech and its harms: a communications theory perspective. *Journal of Communication*, **47**(1), 4–19.

Cameron, D. (1996). Wanted: the female serial killer. *Trouble & Strife*, **33** (Summer), 21–8.

Campbell, C.P. (1995). *Race, Myth and the News*. Thousand Oaks, CA: Sage.

Canter, D. and Strickland, S. (1975). *TV Violence and the Child: The Evolution and Fate of the Surgeon General's Report*. New York: Russell Sage Foundation.

Cantor, R.D. (1975). *Voting Behavior and Presidential Elections*. Itasca, IL: F.E. Peacock.

Caputi, J. (1987). *The Age of Sex Crime*. London: The Women's Press.

Carey, J.W. (1989). *Communication as Culture: Essays on Media and Society*. London: Routledge.

Carter, D.L., Prentky, R.A., Knight, R.A., Vanderveer, P.L. and Boucher, R.J. (1987). Use of pornography in the criminal and developmental histories of sexual offenders. *Journal of Interpersonal Violence*, **2**(2), 196–211.

Cashmore, E. (1994). *... And There Was Telev!s!on*. London: Routledge.

Cavender, G. and Bond-Maupin, L. (1993). Fear and loathing on reality television: an analysis of *America's Most Wanted* and *Unsolved Mysteries*. *Sociological Inquiry*, **63**(3), 305–17.

Centerwall, B.S. (1989). Exposure to television as a Cause of Violence. *Public Communication and Behaviour*, **2**, 1–58.

Centerwall, B.S. (1993). Television and violent crime. *Public Interest* **111**, 56–71.

Check, J.V.P. (1991). *Review of Howitt and Cumberbatch (1990)*. Toronto: York University Department of Psychology.

Check, J.V.P. (1992). The effects of violent pornography, nonviolent dehumanizing pornography, and erotica: some legal implications from a Canadian Perspective. In C. Itzin (Ed.), *Pornography: Women, Violence and Civil Liberties* (pp. 350–8). Oxford: Oxford University Press.

Check, J.V.P. and Guloien, T.H. (1989). Reported proclivity for coercive sex following exposure to sexually violent pornography, nonviolent dehumanizing pornography, and erotica. In D. Zillmann and J. Bryant (Eds), *Pornography: Research Advances and Policy Considerations*. Hillsdale, NJ: Erlbaum.

Chermak, S.M. (1995). *Victims in the News: Crime and the American News Media*. Boulder, CO: Westview.

Chibnall, S. (1977). *Law and Order News*. London: Tavistock.

Christensen, F. (1986). Sexual callousness revisited. *Journal of Communication*, **36**(1), 174–84.

Christensen, F. (1987). Effects of pornography: the debate continues. *Journal of Communication*, **37**(1), 186–8.

Christensen, J., Schmidt, J. and Henderson, J. (1982). The selling of the police: media, ideology and crime control. *Contemporary Crises*, **6**, 227–39

Clark, D.C. and Blankenburg, W.B. (1971). Trends in violent content in selected mass media. In G.A. Comstock and E.A. Rubinstein (Eds), *Television and Social Behaviour, Vol. 1. Content and Control* (pp. 188–243). Washington,

DC: US Government Printing Office.

Clark, L.M.G. and Lewis, D.J. (1977). *Rape: the Price of Coercive Sexuality*. Toronto: The Women's Press.

Clifford, M. (1996). Criminal Justice System in the United States: General overview. In O.N.I. Ebbe (Ed.), *Comparative and International Criminal Justice Systems* (pp. 11–28). Boston: Butterworth-Heineman,

Cline, V.B. (Ed.) (1974). *Where Do You Draw the Line? An Exploration into Media Violence, Pornography, and Censorship*. Provo, UT: Brigham Young University Press.

Cloward, R.A. and Ohlin, L.E. (1961). *Delinquency and Opportunity*. Glencoe: Free Press.

Coates, B., Pusser, H.E. and Goodman, I. (1976). The influences of *Sesame Street* and *Mister Rogers' Neighborhood* on children's social behavior in preschool. *Child Development*, **47**, 138–44.

Cohen, S. (1972). *Folk Devils and Moral Panics*. London: McGibbon & Kee.

Cohen, S. (1980). *Folk Devils and Moral Panics*. Oxford: Basil Blackwell.

Cohen, S. and Young, J. (Eds)(1973). *The Manufacture of News*. London: Constable.

Coles, J. (1996). It feels better than it ever did, much more sensitive. *The Guardian*, 7 September, pp. 3–4.

Command Papers (1971). *Criminal Statistics: England and Wales, 1970*. London: Her Majesty's Stationery Office, Cmnd 4708.

Command Papers (1978). *Criminal Statistics: England and Wales, 1977*. London: Her Majesty's Stationery Office, Cmnd 7289.

Commission for Racial Equality (1987a). *Living in Terror: A Report on Racial Violence and Harassment in Housing*. London: Commission for Racial Equality.

Commission for Racial Equality (1987b). *Racial Attacks: A Survey in Eight Areas in Britain*. London: Commission for Racial Equality.

Commission on Obscenity and Pornography (1970). *The Report of the Commission on Obscenity and Pornography*. New York: Bantam.

Committee on Pornography and Prostitution (1985). *Report*. Ottawa: Supply and Services.

Condit, C.M. and Selzer, J.A. (1985). The rhetoric of objectivity in the newspaper coverage of a murder trial. *Critical Studies in Mass Communication*, **2**(3), 197–216.

Condron, M.K. and Nutter, D.E. (1988). A preliminary examination of the pornography experience of sex offenders, paraphiliac sexual dysfunction and controls. *Journal of Sex and Marital Therapy*, **14**(4), 285–98.

Conley, F. (1994). *General Elections Today*. Manchester: Manchester University Press.

Cook, R.F. and Fosen, R.H. (1970). Pornography and the Sex Offender. *Technical Reports of the Commission on Obscenity and Pornography*, Vol. 7. Washington, DC: US Government Printing Office.

Cook, T.D., Appleton, H., Conner, R.F., Shaffer, A., Tomkin, G. and Weber, S.J. (1975). *Sesame Street Revisited*. New York: Russell Sage Foundation.

Coombs, R.H, and Ryan, F.J. (1990). Drug testing effectiveness in identifying and preventing drug use. *American Journal of Drug and Alcohol Abuse*, **6**(3 & 4), 173–84.

Cooper, E. and Jahoda, M. (1947). The evasion of propaganda. *Journal of Psychology*, **23**, 15–25.

Coughlin, E.K. (1985). Is violence on TV harmful to our health? Some scholars, a vocal minority, say no. *Chronicle of Higher Education*, **March**, 65–71.

Court, J.H. (1977). Pornography and sex-crimes: a re-evaluation in the light of recent trends around the world. *International Journal of Criminality and Penology*, **5**, 129–57.

Court, J.H. (1984). Sex and violence: a ripple effect. In N.M. Malamuth and E. Donnerstein (Eds), *Pornography and Sexual Aggression* (pp. 143–72). Orlando, FL: Academic Press.

Cowan, G.L., Lee, C., Levy, D. and Snyder, D. (1988). Dominance and inequality in X-rated video cassettes. *Psychology of Women Quarterly*, **12**, 299–311.

Cressey, P.G. and Thrasher, F.M. (1933). *Boys, Movies and City Streets*. New York: Macmillan.

Cuklanz, L.M. (1996). *Rape on Trial: How the Mass Media Construct Legal Reform and Social Change*. Philadelphia, PA: University of Philadelphia Press.

Croll, P. (1974). The deviant image. Paper presented at British Sociological Association Mass Communication Study Group.

Cumberbatch, G. (1989). Violence and the mass media: the research evidence. In G. Cumberbatch and D. Howitt, *A Measure of Uncertainty: The Effects of the Mass Media* (pp. 31–59). London: Broadcasting Standards Council/John Libbey.

Cumberbatch, G. (1994). Legislating mythology: video violence and children. *Journal of Mental Health*, **3**(4), 485–94.

Cumberbatch, G. and Howitt, D. (1989). *A Measure of Uncertainty: The Effects of Mass Media*. London: Broadcasting Standards Council/John Libbey.

Cumberbatch, G., Hardy, G. and Lee, M. (1987). *The Portrayal of Violence on British Television*. London: BBC.

Davies, F.J. (1952). Crime news in Colorado newspapers. *American Journal of Sociology*, **57**, 325–30.

Davis, K. and Braucht, G.N. (1970). Reactions to viewing films of erotically realistic heterosexual behavior. In *Technical Report of the Commission on Obscenity and Pornography, Volume VIII, Erotica and Social Behavior* (pp. 68–96). Washington, DC: US Government Printing Office,

Day, D.M. and Page, S. (1986). Portrayal of mental illness in Canadian newspapers. *Canadian Journal of Psychiatry*, **31**, 813–6.

Day, N.L. and Richardson, G.A. (1993). Cocaine Use and Babies: science, the media, and miscommunication. *Neurotoxicology and Teratology*, **15**, 293–4.

Deem, M.D. (1996). From Bobbitt to SCUM: re-memberment, scatological rhetorics, and feminist strategies in the contemporary United States. *Public Culture*, **8**, 511–37.

Devine, P.G. (1989). Stereotypes and prejudice: their automatic and controlled components. *Journal of Personality and Social Psychology*, **56**(1), 5–18.

Dollard, J., Miller, N., Doob, L. Mowrer, O.H. and Sears, R.R. (1939). *Frustration and Aggression*. New Haven, CT: Yale University Press.

Domino, G. (1983). Impact of the film *One Flew over the Cuckoo's Nest* on attitudes toward mental illness. *Psychological Reports*, **53**, 179–82.

Donnerstein, E., Linz, D. and Penrod, S. (1987). *The Question of Pornography: Research Findings and Policy Implications*. New York: The Free Press.

Doppelt, J.C. and Manikas, P.M. (1990). Mass media and criminal justice decision making. In J. Surrette (Ed), *Media and Criminal Justice Policy* (pp. 129–42). Springfield, IL: Charles C. Thomas.

Dorn, N., Murji, K. and South, N. (1992). *Traffickers: Drug Markets and Law Enforcement*. London: Routledge.

Downes, D. and Morgan, R. (1994). 'Hostages to Fortune'? The politics of law and order in post-war Britain. In M. Maguire, R. Morgan and R. Reiner (Eds), *The Oxford Handbook of Criminology* (pp. 183–232). Oxford: Clarendon Press.

Downs, D.A. (1989). *The New Politics of Pornography*. Chicago, IL: University of Chicago Press.

Driscoll, M. (1997). Not quite as innocent as they look. *The Sunday Times*, 11 May, p. 6.

Dubow, E.F. and Cappas, C.L. (1988). Reducing aggression in children through social interventions. In S.P. Lab (Ed.), *Crime Prevention: Approaches, Practices and Evaluations* (pp. 197–219). Cincinnati, OH: C. J. Anderson.

Duhs, L.A. and Gunton, R.J. (1988). TV violence and childhood aggression: a curmudgeon's guide. *Australian Psychology*, **23**(2), 183–95.

Durkin, K. (1985). *Television, Sex Roles and Children*. Milton Keynes: Open University Press.

Einsiedel, E.F. (1988). The British, Canadian, and US pornography commissions and their use of social science research. *Journal of Communication*, **38**(2), 108–21.

Ellis, L. (1989). *Theories of Rape: Inquiries into the Causes of Sexual Aggression*. New York: Hemisphere.

Emery, F. and Emery, M. (1976). *A Choice of Futures*. Leiden: Martinus Nijhoff, Social Sciences Division.

Emsley, C. (1994). The history of crime and controls. In M. Maguire, R. Morgan and R. Reiner (Eds), *The Oxford Handbook of Criminology* (pp. 149–82). Oxford: Clarendon Press.

Entman, R.M. (1990). Modern racism and the images of blacks in local television news. *Critical Studies in Mass Communication*, **7**(4), 332–45.

Epstein, S.C. (1995). The New Mythic Monsters. In J. Ferrell and C.R. Sanders (Eds). *Cultural Criminology* (pp. 66–79). Boston, MA: Northeastern University Press.

Ericson, R.V., Baranek, P.M. and Chan, J.B.L. (1991). *Representing Order: Crime, Law, and Justice in the News Media*. Milton Keynes: Open University.

Eron, L. (1986). Interventions to mitigate the psychological effects of media. *Journal of Social Issues*, **42**, 155–70.

Eron, L.D. (1963). Relationship of TV viewing habits and aggressive behavior in children. *Journal of Abnormal and Social Psychology*, **67**, 193–6.

Eron, L.D., Lefkowitz, M.M., Huesmann, L.R. and Walder, L.O. (1972). Does television violence cause aggression? *American Psychologist*, **27**, 253–63.

Esser, F. and Brosius, H.B. (1996). Television as arsonist? The spread of right-wing violence in Germany. *European Journal of Communication*, **11**(2), 235–60.

Everywoman (1988). *Pornography and Sexual Violence: Evidence of the Links*. London: Everywoman.

Eysenck, H.J. (1977). *Crime and Personality*. London: Paladin.

Eysenck, H.J. and Nias, D.K. (1978). *Sex, Violence and the Media*. London: Maurice Temple Smith.

Fagan, J.A. (1994). Do criminal sanctions deter drug crimes? In D.L. MacKenzie and C.D. Uchida (Eds), *Drugs and Crime: Evaluating Public Policy Initiative* (pp. 188–214). Thousand Oaks, CA: Sage.

Farrington, D.P., Ohlin, L.E. and Wilson, J.Q. (1986). *Understanding and Controlling Crime: Toward a New Strategy of Research*. New York: Springer-

Verlag.

Fernandez-Collado, C.F., Greenberg, B.S., Korzenny, F. and Atkin, C.K. (1978). Sexual Intimacy and drug use in TV series. *Journal of Communication*, **28**(3), 30–37.

Fernando, S. (1988). *Race and Culture in Psychiatry*. London: Croom Helm.

Feshbach, S. (1955). The drive-reducing function of fantasy behavior. *Journal of Abnormal and Social Psychology*, **50**, 3–11.

Feshbach, S. (1961). The stimulating vs cathartic effects of a vicarious aggressive activity. *Journal of Abnormal and Social Psychology*, **63**, 381–6,

Feshbach, S. and Singer, J. (1971). *Television and Aggression: An Experimental Field Study*. San Francisco, CA: Jossey-Bass.

Fisher, R.D., Cook, I.J. and Shirkey, E.C. (1994). Correlates of support for censorship of sexual, sexually violent, and violent media. *Journal of Sex Research*, **31**(3), 219–40.

Fishman, M. (1981). Police news: constructing an image of crime. *Urban Life*, **9**(4), 371–94.

Franzblau, S., Sprafkin, J.N. and Rubinstein, E.A. (1977). Sex on TV: a content analysis. *Journal of Communication*, **27**(2), 164–70.

Freedland, J. (1996). TV's shame game. *The Guardian*, 8 January, p. 16.

Freedman, J.L. (1984). Effects of television violence on aggression. *Psychological Bulletin*, **96**(2), 227–46.

Freedman, J.L. (1986). Television violence and aggression: a rejoinder. *Psychological Bulletin*, **100**(3), 372–8.

Freedman, J.L. (1988). Television violence and aggression: what the evidence shows. In S. Oskamp (Ed.), Television as a Social Issue. *Applied Social Psychology Annual* No. 8 (pp. 144–62). Newbury Park, CA: Sage.

Freedman, J.L. and Sears, D.O. (1965). Selective exposure. *Advances in Experimental Social Psychology*, **2**, 58–97.

Freund, K. and Blanchard, R. (1989). Phallometric diagnosis of pedophilia. *Journal of Consulting and Clinical Psychology*, **57**, 100–105.

Freund, K., Watson, R. and Dickey, R. (1990). Does sexual abuse in childhood cause pedophilia: an exploratory study. *Archives of Sexual Behavior*, **19**(6), 557–68.

Friedlander, B.Z. (1993). Community violence, children's development, and mass media: in pursuit of new insights, new goals, and new strategies. *Psychiatry*, **56**(1), 66–81.

Friedlander, P. (1996). *Rock and Roll: A Social History*. Boulder, CO: Westview.

Friendly, A. and Goldfarb, R.L. (1967). *Crime and Publicity*. New York: The Twentieth Century Fund.

Gaertner, S.L. and Dovidio, J.F. (1986). The aversive form of racism. In J. Dovidio and S. Gaertner (Eds), *Prejudice, Discrimination, and Racism* (pp. 61–89). New York: Academic Press.

Gauntlett, D. (1997). *Video Critical: Children, the Environment and Media Power*. Luton: University of Luton Press.

Gebhard, P.H., Gagnon, J.H., Pomeroy, W.B. and Christenson, C.V. (1965). *Sex Offenders: An Analysis of Types*. New York: Harper and Row.

Gelles, R.J. (1979). *Family Violence*. Beverly Hills, CA: Sage.

Gelles, R.J. and Cornell, C.P. (1985). *Intimate Violence in Families*. Beverly Hills, CA: Sage.

Gentry, C.S. (1991). Pornography and rape: an empirical analysis. *Deviant Behaviour*, **12**(3), 277–88.

Gerbner, G. (1972). Violence in television drama: trends and symbolic functions. In G.A. Comstock and E.A. Rubenstein (Eds), *Television and Social Behavior, Vol 1: Media Content and Control* (pp. 28–187). Washington, DC: US Government Printing Office.

Gerbner, G., Gross, L., Eley, M.E., Jackson Beeck, M., Jeffries-Fox, S. and Signorielli, N. (1977). Television violence profile, No 8. *Journal of Communication*, **27**, 171–80.

Gerbner, G., Gross, L., Morgan, M. and Signorielli, N. (1980). The mainstreaming of America: violence profile, No. 11. *Journal of Communication*, **30**(3), 10–29.

Gerbner, G. and Signorielli, N. (1979). *Women and Minorities in Television Drama, 1969–1978*. University of Pennsylvania, Annenberg School of Communication.

Gilbert, D.T. and Hixon, J.G. (1991). The trouble with thinking: activation and application of stereotypic beliefs. *Journal of Personality and Social Psychology*, **60**(4), 509–17.

Goldstein, M.J., Kant, H.S., Judd, L.L., Rice, C.J. and Green, R. (1970). Exposure to pornography and sexual behavior in deviant and normal groups. In *Technical Report of the Commission on Obscenity and Pornography*, Volume 7. Washington, DC: US Government Printing Office.

Goldstein, M.M. and Kant, H.S. (1973). *Pornography and Sexual Deviance: A Report of the Legal and Behavioral Institute*. Berkeley, CA: University of California Press.

Goode, W. J. (1992). World changes in divorce patterns. In L.J. Weitzman and M. Maclean (Eds), *Economic Consequences of Divorce* (pp. 1–49). Oxford: Clarendon Press.

Gorn, E.J. (1995). The wicked world: the *National Police Gazette* and gilded-age America. In C.L. Lam May and E.E. Dennis (Eds), *The Culture of Crime* (pp. 9–21). New Brunswick: Transaction Publishers.

Gould, A., Shaw, A. and Arendt (1996). Illegal drugs: liberal and restrictive attitudes. In R. Jowelkl, J. Curtice, A. Park, L. Brook and K. Thomson. (Eds), *British Attitudes Survey*, 13th Report (pp. 93–116). Aldershot: Dartmouth Publishing.

Gould, M.S. and Shaffer, D. (1986). The impact of suicide in television movies: evidence of imitations. *New England Journal of Medicine*, **315**, 690–93.

Graber, D.A. (1980). *Crime News and the Public*. New York: Praeger.

Greenberg, B.S. (1980). *Life on Television*. Norwood, NJ: Ablex.

Greenberg, B.S. (1986). Minorities and the mass media. In J. Bryant and D. Zillmann (Eds), *Perspectives on Media Effects* (pp. 165–88). Hillsdale, NJ: Erlbaum,

Greenberg, D.M., Bradford, J.M.W. and Curry, C. (1993). A comparison of sexual victimization in the childhoods of pedophiles and hebephiles. *Journal of Forensic Sciences*, **38**(2), 432–36.

Greene, E. (1990). Media effects on juror. *Law and Human Behavior*, **14**(5), 1990.

Greenwald, A.G. and Sakumura, J.S. (1967). Attitude and selective learning: where are the phenomena of yesteryear? *Journal of Personality and Social Psychology*, **7**, 387–97.

Groth, A.N. (1979). Sexual trauma in the lives of rapists and child molesters. *Victimology*, **4**, 10–16.

Groth, A.N. and Hobson, W.F. (1983). The dynamics of sexual assault. In L.B. Schlesinger and E. Revitch (Eds). *Sexual Dynamics of Anti-social Behavior* (pp. 159–72). Springfield, IL: Charles C. Thomas.

Gunter, B. (1987). *Television and the Fear of Crime*. London: John Libbey.

Gunter, B. and Wober, M. (1982). Television viewing and public trust. *British Journal of Social Psychology*, **22**, 174–6.

Hagan, J. (1985). The assumption of natural science methods: criminological positivism. In R. Meier (Ed.), *Theoretical Methods in Criminology* (pp. 75–82). Beverly Hills, CA: Sage.

Hagell, A. and Newburn, T. (1994). *Young Offenders and the Media: Viewing Habits and Preferences*. London: Policy Studies Institute.

Hall, S., Crilcher, C., Jefferson, T., Clarke, J. and Roberts, B. (1978). *Policing the Crisis: Mugging, the State and Law and Order*. London: Macmillan.

Hall, G.C.N., Proctor, W.C. and Nelson, G.M. (1988). Validity of physiological measures of pedophilic sexual arousal in a sexual offender population. *Journal of Consulting and Clinical Psychology*, **56**(1), 118–2.

Haller, J.S. and Haller, R.M. (1974). *The Physician and Sexuality in Victorian America*. Urbana, IL: University of Illinois Press.

Halloran, J.D., Brown, R.L. and Chaney, D.C. (1970). *Television and Delinquency*. Leicester: Leicester University Press.

Halstead, M. (1988). *Education, Justice and Cultural Diversity: An Examination of the Honeyford Affair, 1984–5*. London: Falmer.

Hammersley, R. (1988). Drug addiction and crime. *British Journal of Addiction*, **83**, 445–6.

Hammersley, R., Forsyth, A. and Lavelle, T. (1990). The criminality of new drug users in Glasgow. *British Journal of Addiction*, **85**, 1583–94.

Hammersley, R., Forsyth, A., Morrison, V. and Davies, J.B. (1989). The relationship between crime and opioid use. *British Journal of Addiction*, **84**, 1029–43.

Hartmann, P. and Husband, C. (1974). *Racism and the Mass Media*. London: Davis-Poynter.

Hausman, A.J., Spivak, H., Prothrow-Stith, D. and Roberts, J. (1992). Patterns of teen exposure to a community-based violence prevention project. *Journal of Adolescent Health*, **13**, 668–75.

Hawkins, J.D. (Ed.) (1996). *Delinquency and Crime*. Cambridge: Cambridge University Press.

Hawkins, R. and Pingree, S. (1980). Some processes in the cultivation effect. *Communication Research*, **7**, 193–226.

Haynie, S.L. and Dover E.A. (1994). Prosecutorial discretion and press coverage. *American Politics Quarterly*, **22**(3), 370–81.

Healy, W. (1915). *The Individual Delinquent*. Boston, MA: Little, Brown.

Hearold, S. (1986). A synthesis of 1043 effects of television on social behaviour. In G. Comstock (Ed.), *Public Communications and Behavior*, Vol. 1. New York: Academic Press.

Heath, L. (1984). Impact of newspaper crime reports on fear of crime: multi-methodological investigation. *Journal of Personality and Social Psychology*, **47**(2), 263–76.

Heath, L. and Gilbert, K. (1996). Mass media and the fear of crime. *American Behavioral Scientist*, **39**(4), 379–86.

Heath, L. and Petraitis, J. (1987). Television viewing and fear of crime: where is the mean world? *Basic and Applied Social Psychology*, **8** (1/2), 97–123.

Henely, N.M., Miller, M. and Beazley, J.A. (1995). Syntax, semantics, and sexual violence: agency and the passive voice. *Journal of Language and Social Psychology*, **14**(1–2), 60–84.

Hennigan, K.M., Del Rosario, M.L., Heath, L., Cook, T.D., Wharton, J.D. and

Calder, B.J. (1982). Impact of the introduction of television on crime in the United States: empirical findings and theoretical implications. *Journal of Personality and Social Psychology*, **42**(3), 461–77.

Hennigan, K.M., Delrosario, M.L., Heath, L., Cook, T.D., Wharton, J.D. and Calder, B.J. (1982). Impact of the introduction of television crime in the United States. Empirical findings and theoretical implications. *Journal of Personality and Social Psychology*, **42**, 461–77.

Herck, G. and Berrill, K. (Eds) (1992). *Hate Crimes: Confronting Violence Against Lesbians and Gay Men*. London: Sage.

Herzog, H. (1944). What do we really know about daytime serial listeners? In P.F. Lazarsfeld and F.N. Stanton (Eds), *Radio Research 1942–1943* (pp. 3–33). New York: Duell, Sloan and Pearce.

Herzog, H. (1954). Motivations and gratifications of daily serial listeners. In W. Schramm (Ed.), *The Process and Effects of Mass Communication* (pp. 50–55). Urbana, IL: University of Illinois Press.

Hester, S. and Eglin, P. (1992). *A Sociology of Crime*. London: Routledge.

Hill, A. (1997). *Shocking Entertainment: Viewer Response to Violent Movies*. Luton: University of Luton Press.

Himmelweit, H.T., Oppenheim, A.N. and Vince, P. (1958). *Television and the Child: An Empirical Study of the Effect of Television on the Young*. London: Oxford University Press.

Hinton, J.W., O'Neill, M.T. and Webster, S. (1980). Psychophysiological assessment of sex offenders in a security hospital. *Archives of Sexual Behavior*, **9**(3), 208–16.

Hirsch, P. (1980). The scary world of the non-viewer and other anomalies: re-analysis of Gerbner et al.'s findings on the cultivation hypothesis. *Communication Research*, **7**, 403–56.

Hirsch, P. (1981a). On not learning from one's own mistakes: A re-analysis of Gerbner et al.'s findings on cultivation analysis. Part II. *Communication Research*, **8**, 3–37.

Hirsch, P. (1981b). Distinguishing good speculation from bad theory. *Communication Research*, **8**, 73–96.

Hodge, J. (1991). Addiction to Crime. *Issues in Criminological and Legal Psychology*, **17**(2), 92–6.

Holmes, J. (1993). *John Bowlby and Attachment Theory*. London: Routledge.

Holmes, R.M. (1991). *Sex Crimes*. Newbury Park, CA: Sage.

Home Office (1981). *Racial Attacks: Report of the Home Office Study*. London: HMSO.

Home Office (1982). *Report of the Expert Group on the Effects of Cannabis*. London: Advisory Council on the Misuse of Drugs.

Honeyford, R. (1983a). Multi-ethnic intolerance. *The Salisbury Review*, **4** (Summer), 12–13.

Honeyford, R. (1983b). When East is West. *Times Educational Supplement*, 2 September, p. 19b.

Honeyford, R. (1984). Education and race—an alternative view. *The Salisbury Review*, **6** (Winter). 30–32.

Honeyford, R. (1986). Anti-racist rhetoric. In F. Palmer (Ed.), *Anti-Racism—An Assault on Education and Value* (pp. 43–56). London: Sherwood Press.

Hoshino, K. (1976–1977). Police activities to raise the level of public safety from crime. *Research Report of the Division of Crime Prevention and Juvenile Delinquency, the National Research Institute of Police Science*, **17**(2), 145–62.

Hough, M. and Mayhew, P. (1985). Taking account of crime: key findings from the 1984 British Crime Survey. *Research Studies No. 85*. London: HMSO.

Hovland, C.D., Lumsdaine, A.A. and Sheffield, F.D. (1949). *Experiments in Mass Communication*. New Haven, CT: Yale University Press.

Hovland, C.I. (1954). Effects of the mass media of communication. In G. Lindzey (Ed.), *Handbook of Social Psychology*, Vol. 2 (pp. 1062–103). Cambridge, MA: Addison-Wesley.

Hovland, C.I. and Janis, I.L. (Eds) (1953). *Personality and Persuadability*. New Haven, CT: Yale University Press.

Howitt, D. (1976). The effects of television on children. In R. Brown (Ed.), *Children and Television* (pp. 320–42). London: Collier MacMillan.

Howitt, D. (1982). *Mass Media and Social Problems*. Oxford: Pergamon.

Howitt, D. (1991). Britain's 'substance abuse policy': realities and regulation in the United Kingdom. *International Journal of Addictions*, 3, 1087–111.

Howitt, D. (1991). *Concerning Psychology*. Milton Keynes: Open University Press.

Howitt, D. (1992). *Child Abuse Errors*. New York: Harvester Wheatsheaf.

Howitt, D. (1994). Pornography's piggy in the middle. In C. Haslam and A. Bryman (Eds), *Social Scientists Meet the Media* (pp. 93–107). London: Routledge.

Howitt, D. (1995a). *Paedophiles and Sexual Offences Against Children*. Chichester: Wiley.

Howitt, D. (1995b). Pornography and the paedophile: is it criminogenic? *British Journal of Medical Psychology*, 68(1), 15–27.

Howitt, D. and Cramer, D. (1997). *An Introduction to Statistics for Psychology*. London: Prentice Hall.

Howitt, D. and Cumberbatch, G. (1975). *Mass Media Violence and Society*. London: Elek.

Howitt, D. and Cumberbatch, G. (1990). *Pornography: Impacts and Influences*. London: Home Office Research and Planning Unit.

Howitt, D. and Dembo, R. (1974). A subcultural account of media effects. *Human Relations*, 27, 25–41.

Howitt, D. and Owusu-Bempah, J. (1994). *The Racism of Psychology*. New York: Harvester Wheatsheaf.

Hser, Y-I., Longshore, D. and Anglin, M.D. (1994). Prevalence of drug use among criminal offender populations: implications for control, treatment and policy. In D.L. MacKenzie and C.D. Uchida (Eds), *Drugs and Crime: Evaluating Public Policy Initiative* (pp. 18–41). Thousand Oaks, CA: Sage.

Hudson, B. (1993). Racism and Criminology: concepts and controversies. In D. Cook and B. Hudson (Eds). *Racism and Criminology* (pp. 1–27). London: Sage.

Huesmann, L.R. (1986). Psychological processes promoting the relation between exposure to media violence and aggressiveness in the viewer. *Journal of Social Issues*, 42(3), 125–39.

Huesmann, L.R. (1995). *Screen Violence and Real Violence: Understanding the Link*. Media Aware, PO Box 1354, Auckland, New Zealand.

Huesmann, L.R. and Eron, L.D. (1991). Modeles structurels du developpement de l'agressivité. In R.E. Tremblay (Ed.), *Les Enfants Agressifs* (pp. 156–96). Quebec: Editions Agence D'ARC.

Huesmann, L.R. and Eron, L.D. (Eds) (1986). *Television and the Aggressive Child: A Cross-national Comparison*. Hillsdale, NJ: Erlbaum.

Huesmann, L.R., Eron, L., Kleen, L., Brice, P. and Fisher, P. (1983). Mitigating the imitation of aggressive behaviours by changing children's attitudes to media violence. *Journal of Personality and Social Psychology*, **44**, 899–910.

Huesmann, L.R. and Malamuth, N.M. (Eds) (1986). Media violence and anti-social behaviour. *Journal of Social Issues*, **42**(3).

Hughes, M. (1980). The fruits of cultivation analysis. *Public Opinion Quarterly*, **44**, 287–302.

Huston-Stein, A., Fox, S., Green, D., Watkins, B.A. and Whitaker, J. (1981). The effects of TV action and violence on children's behavior. *Journal of Genetic Psychology*, **138**, 183–91.

Inciardi, J.A. and Pottieger, A.E. (1991). Kids, crack, and crime. *The Journal of Drug Issues*, **21**(2), 257–70.

Ito, K. (1993). Research on the fear of crime: perceptions and realities of crime in Japan. *Crime & Delinquency*, **29**(3), 385–92.

Itzin, C. (1992). 'Entertainment for Men': what it is and what it means. In C. Itzin (Ed.), *Pornography: Women, Violence and Civil Liberties* (pp. 27–53). Oxford: Oxford University Press,

Itzin, C. (Ed.) (1992). *Pornography: Women, Violence and Civil Liberties*. Oxford: Oxford University Press.

Itzin, C. and Sweet, C. (1989). Tackling the monsters on the top shelf. *The Independent*, 17 April.

Jackson, H. (1932). *The Fear of Books*. London: The Soncino Press.

Jacobs, A.M. and Ghodse, A.H. (1988). Delinquency and regular solvent abuse: an unfavourable combination? *British Journal of Addiction*, **83**, 965–8.

Jaffee, D. and Straus, M. (1987). Sexual climate and reported rape: a state level analysis. *Archives of Sexual Behavior*, **16**, 107–23.

Jamieson, K.H. and Campbell, K.K. (1992). *The Interplay of Influence: News, Advertising, Politics and the Mass Media*. Belmont, CA: Wadsworth.

Janis, I. (1980). Irving Janis. In R. I. Lewis (Ed.), *The Making of Social Psychology: Discussions with Creative Contributors* (pp. 97–111). New York: Halsted Press.

Janis, I.L. and Feshbach, S. (1953). Effects of fear-arousing communications. *Journal of Abnormal and Social Psychology*, **48**, 78–92.

Jeffery, C.R. (1976). Criminal behavior and physical environment: A perspective. *American Behavioral Scientist*, **20**, 149–74.

Jenkins, P. (1992). *Intimate Enemies: Moral Panics in Contemporary Great Britain*. New York: Aldine de Gruyter.

Jenkins, P. (1994). *Using Murder: The Social Construction of Serial Homicide*. New York: Aldine de Gruyter.

Johnson, W.T., Kupperstein, L.R. and Petters, J.J. (1970). Sex offenders' experience with erotica. In *Technical Report of the Commission on Obscenity and Pornography*, Vol. 7. Washington, DC: US Government Printing Office.

Jones, M. (1982). The relation between the courts and the mass media. In Crapwood Round Table Conference, *Crime, Justice and the Mass Media* (pp. 55–69). University of Cambridge, Institute of Criminology.

Joseph, G.C., Reddy, V. and Searle-Chatterjee (1990). Eurocentrism in the social sciences. *Race and Class*, **31**(4), 1–20.

Jowett, G.S., Jarvie, I.C. and Fuller, K.H. (1996). *Children and the Movies: Movie Influence and the Payne Fund Controversy*. Cambridge: Cambridge University Press.

Katz, E. and Larzarsfeld, P.F. (1964). *Personal Influence: The Part Played by People in the Flow of Communications*. New York: Free Press.

Katz, J. (1987). What makes crime 'news'? *Media, Culture and Society*, **9**, 47–75.

Kay, H. (1972). Weakness in the television-causes-aggression analysis by Eron et al. *American Psychologist*, **27**, 970–73.

Kelly, L. (1991). Unspeakable acts. *Trouble & Strife*, **21** (Summer), 13–20.

Kendall, K. (1991). The politics of premenstrual syndrome: implications for feminist justice. *Journal of Human Justice*, **2**(2), 77.

Kenny, D.A. (1984). The NBC study and television violence: a review. *Journal of Communication*, **34**, 176–82.

Kessler, R.C. and Stipp, H. (1984). The impact of fictional television suicide stories on US fatalities: a replication. *American Journal of Sociology*, **90**(1), 157–67.

Kessler, R.C., Downey, G., Milavsky, J.R. and Stipp, H. (1988). Clustering of teenage suicides after television stories about suicides: a re-consideration. *American Journal of Psychiatry*, **145**(11), 1379–83.

Killias, M. (1983). Mass medias: peur du crime et politique criminelle. *Revue Internationale de Criminologe et de Police Technique*, **36**(4), 60–71.

Kimble, G.A. (1984). Psychology's two cultures. *American Psychologist*, **39**(8), 833–9.

Kinder, D.R. (1986). The continuing American dilemma: white resistance to racial change 40 years after Myrdal. *Journal of Social Issues*, **42**(2), 151–71.

Kinsey, A.C., Pomeroy, W.B., Martin, C.E. and Gebhard, P. (1953). *Sexual Behavior in the Human Female*. Philadelphia, PA: Saunders.

Kinsey, A.C., Pomeroy, W.B. and Martin, C.E. (1948). *Sexual Behavior in the Human Male*. Philadelphia, PA: Saunders.

Kissman, K. and Allen, J.A. (1993). *Single Parent Families*. London: Sage.

Kitzinger, C. (1994). Anti-lesbian harassment. In C. Brand and Y. Too (Eds), *Rethinking Sexual Harassment* (pp. 123–47). London: Pluto.

Kiyonaga, K., Inoue, Y. and Oda, K. (1990). *Survey Report on Criminal Victimization*, JUSRI Report No. 1. Tokyo: Urban Security Research Institute.

Kiyonaga, K. and Takasugi, F. (1990). A study on anxiety arising from fear of crime: the effect of sex and age factors. Research report of the Division of Crime Prevention and Juvenile Delinquency, *National Institute of Police Science*, **31**(2), 94–104. Cited in K. Ito (1993), Research on the fear of crime: perceptions and realities of crime in Japan. *Crime and Delinquency*, **39**(3), 385–92.

Klapper, J. (1960). *The Effects of Mass Communication*. New York: Free Press.

Kleinman, M.A.R. (1989). *Marijuana: Cost of Abuse, Costs of Control*. New York: Greenwood.

Kline, F.G. and Jess, P.H. (1966). Prejudicial publicity: its effects on law school mock juries. *Journalism Quarterly*, **43**, 113–16.

Kline, P. (1988). *Psychology Exposed: or The Emperor's New Clothes*. London: Routledge.

Kniveton, B.H. and Stephenson, G.M. (1970). The effect of pre-experience on imitation of an aggressive film model. *British Journal of Social and Clinical Psychology*, **9**, 31–6.

Kniveton, B.H. and Stephenson, G.M. (1972). The effects of social class on imitation in a pre-experience situation. *British Journal of Social and Clinical Psychology*, **11**, 225–34.

Korzenny, F., McClure, J. and Ryzttki, B. (1990). Ethnicity, Communication, and Drugs. *Journal of Drug Issues*, **20**(1), 87–98.

Krugman, H.E. (1970). *Electroencephalographic Aspects of Low Involvement; Implications for the McLuhan Hypothesis*. New York: American Associates for Public Opinion Research.

Kruttschnitt, C., Heath, L. and Ward, D.A. (1986). Family violence, television viewing habits, and other adolescent experiences related to violent criminal behavior. *Criminology*, **24** (2), 235–65.

Kupperstein, L. and Wilson, W.C. (1970). An analysis of selected social indicator statistics. *Technical Reports of the Commission on Obscenity and Pornography*, Vol. 7, Washington, DC: US Government Printing Office.

Kutchinsky, B. (1970). The effect of pornography: a pilot experiment on perception, behavior and attitudes. In *Technical Report of the Commission on Obscenity and Pornography, Vol. VIII, Erotica and Social Behavior* (pp. 133–70). Washington, DC: US Government Printing Office.

Kutchinsky, B. (1973). The effect of easy availability of pornography on the incidence of sex crimes: the Danish experience. *Journal of Social Issues*, **29**(3), 163–91.

Kutchinsky, B. (1976). Deviance and criminality: the case of a voyeur in a peeper's paradise. *Diseases of the Nervous System*, **37**, 145–51.

Kutchinsky, B. (1985). Pornography and its effects in Denmark and the United States: a rejoinder and beyond. *Comparative Social Research*, **8**, 301–30.

Kutchinsky, B. (1991). Pornography and rape: theory and practice? *International Journal of Law and Psychiatry*, **14**(1/2), 145–51.

Lamar, V.V. (1985). I deserve punishment. *Time*, 6 February, p. 34.

Lande, R.G. (1993) The video violence debate. *Hospital and Community Psychiatry*, **44**(4), 347–51.

Langevin, R., Lang, R.A., Wright, P. and Hardy, L. (1988). Pornography and sexual offenses. *Annals of Sex Research*, **3**, 355–62.

Lashley, K.S. and Watson, J.B. (1922). *A Psychological Study of Motion Pictures in Relation to Venereal Disease*. Washington, DC: Interdepartmental Hygiene Board.

Lazarsfeld, P.F., Berelson, B. and Gaudet, H. (1948). *The People's Choice*. New York: Columbia University Press.

Lederer, L. (1980). *Take Back the Night: Women on Pornography*. New York: Morrow.

Lee, B. (1988). Prosocial content on prime-time television. *Applied Social Psychology Annual*, **8**, 238–46.

Lees, S. (1995). Media reporting of rape: the 1993 British 'date rape' controversy. In D. Kidd-Hewitt and R. Osborne (Eds), *Crime and the Media: the Post-Modern Spectacle* (pp. 107–30). London: Pluto.

Lefkowitz, M.M., Eron, D., Walder, L.O. and Huesmann, L.R. (1977). *Growing Up to Be Violent: A Longitudinal Study of the Development of Aggression*. New York: Pergamon.

Lemert, E.M. (1967). *Human Deviance, Social Problems and Social Control*. Englewood Cliffs, NJ: Prentice Hall.

Lesyna, K. and Phillips, D.P. (1989). Suicide and the media: research and policy implications. In R. Diekstra (Ed.), *The World Health Organization for Preventive Strategies on Suicide: A WHO State of the Art Publication*. Geneva: WHO.

Levey, S. and Howells, K. (1994). *Journal of Community and Applied Social Psychology*, **4**, 313–28.

Liebert, R.M. (1976). Evaluating the evaluators. *Journal of Communication*, **26**, 165–71.

Liebert, R.M. and Sprafkin, J.N. (1988). *The Early Window: Effects of Television on Children and Youths (3rd edn)*. New York: Pergamon.

Liebert, R.M., Neale, J.M. and Davidson, E.S. (1973). *The Early Window:*

Effects of Television on Children and Youths. New York: Pergamon.

Linne, O. (1976). The viewer's aggression as a function of a variously edited TV film. *Communications*, **1**, 101–11.

Liska, A.E. and Baccaglini, W. (1990). Feeling safe by comparison: crime in the newspapers. *Social Problems*, **37**(3), 360–74.

Lloyd, C. and Walmsley, R. (1989). *Changes in Rape Offences and Sentencing*. Home Office Study No. 105. London: HMSO.

Lombroso (1911). *Crime, Its Causes and Remedies*. Boston: Little, Brown.

Longford Committee Investigating Pornography (1972). *Pornography: The Longford Report*. London: Coronet.

Lowry, R., Sleet, D., Duncan, C., Poweel, K. and Kolbe, L. (1995). Adolescents at risk for violence. *Educational Psychology Review*, **7**(1), 7–39.

Lucal, B. (1995). The problem with 'battered husbands'. *Deviant Behavior: An Interdisciplinary Journal*, **16**, 95–112.

Lukesch, H. (1989). Video violence and aggression. *German Journal of Psychology*, **13**(4), 293–300.

Lynn, R., Hampson, S. and Agahi, E. (1989). Television violence and aggression: a genotype–environment, correlation and interaction theory. *Social Behavior and Personality*, **17**(2), 143–64.

Maden, A., Swinton, M. and Gann. J. (1992). A survey of pre-arrest drug use in sentenced prisoners. *British Journal of Addiction*, **87**(1), 27–33.

Maguire, M. (1994). Crime statistics, patterns, and trends: changing perceptions and the implications. In M. Maguire, R. Morgan, and R. Reimer (Eds), *The Oxford Handbook of Criminology* (pp. 233–91). Oxford: Clarendon Press.

Malamuth, N. and Spinner, B. (1980). A longitudinal content analysis of sexual violence in the best-selling erotica magazines. *Journal of Sex Research*, **16**, 227–37.

Marsh, H.L. (1991). A comparative analysis of crime coverage in newspapers in the United States and other countries from 1960 to 1989: a review of the literature. *Journal of Criminal Justice*, **19**, 67–79.

Marshall, W.C. (1988). The use of sexually explicit stimuli by rapists, child molesters and non-offenders. *Journal of Sex Research*, **25**(2), 267–88.

Mayer, A., and Barry, D.D. (1992). Working with the media to destigmatize mental illness. *Hospital and Community Psychiatry*, **43**(1), 77–8.

Mayhew, P. (1994). *Findings from the International Crime Survey*. Home Office Statistics Department, Research Findings No. 8. London: HMSO.

Maynard, D.W. (1984). *Inside Plea Bargaining*. New York: Plenum.

McCallion, H. (1966). The movies, me and violence. In K. French (Ed.), *Screen Violence* (pp. 205–13). London: Bloomsbury.

McCombs, M.E. and Shaw, D.E. (1972). The agenda setting function of the mass media. *Public Opinion Quarterly*, **36**, 176–87.

McDevitt, S. (1996). The impact of news media on child abuse reporting. *Child Abuse and Neglect*, **20**(4), 261–74.

McGuire, W.J. (1986). The myth of massive media impact: savagings and salvagings. *Public Communication and Behavior*, **1**, 175–257.

McIntyre, J.J. and Teevan, J.J. (1972). Television violence and deviant behavior. In *Television and Social Behavior*, Vol. 3. Washington, DC: US Government Printing Office.

McMillen, J.C. (1992). Attachment theory and clinical social work. *Clinical Social Work Journal*, **20**, 205–18.

McNeill, S. (1996). Getting away with murder. *Trouble & Strife*, **33** (Summer), 1–7.

McQuail, D. (1987). *Mass Communication Theory: An Introduction*. London: Sage

Medved, M. (1992). *Hollywood vs. America: Popular Culture and the War on Traditional Values*. New York: Harper Collins.

Merritt, B. and Stroman, C.A. (1993). Black family imagery and interaction on television. *Journal of Black Studies*, **23**(4), 492–9.

Messenger Davies, M. (1989). *Television is Good for Your Kids*. London: Hilary Shipman.

Messner, S.F. (1986). Television violence and violent crime: an aggregate analysis. *Social Problems*, **33**(3), 218–35.

Miethe, T.D. (1995). Fear and withdrawal from urban life. *Annals of the American Association of Political and Social Science*, **539**, 14–27.

Milavsky, J.R., Kessler, R.C., Stipp, H.H. and Rubens, W.S. (1982). *Television and Aggression: A Panel Study*. New York: Academic Press.

Milavsky, J.R., Pekowsky, B. and Stipp, H. (1976). TV drug advertising and proprietary and illicit drug use among teenage boys. *Public Opinion Quarterly*, **39**, 457–81.

Milgram, S. (1965). Some conditions of obedience and disobedience to authority. *Human Relations*, **18**, 57–76.

Milgram, S. (1974). *Obedience to Authority*. New York: Harper and Row.

Milgram, S. and Shotland, R.L. (1973). *Television and Antisocial Behavior: Field Experiments*. New York: Academic Press.

Miller, T.Q., Heath, L., Molcan, J.R. and Dugoni, B.L. (1991). Imitative violence in the real world: a reanalysis of homicide rates following championship prize fights. *Aggressive Behavior*, **17**, 121–34.

Miller, W.B. (1958). Lower-class culture as a generating milieu of gang delinquency. *Journal of Social Issues*, **14**, 5–19.

Mills, H. (1996). Rapists escape the judicial net. *The Guardian*, 10 November, p. 8.

Moran, G. and Cutler, B.L. (1991). The prejudicial impact of pretrial publicity. *Journal of Applied Social Psychology*, **21**(5), 345–67.

Morgan, M. (1983). Symbolic victimization and real-world fear. *Human Communication Research*, **9**(2), 146–57.

Morgan, M. and Shanahan, J. (1991). Do VCRs change the TV picture? VCRs and the cultivation process. *American Behavioral Scientist*, **35**(2), 12–35.

Mott, J. (1986). Opioid use and burglary. *British Journal of Addiction*, **81**, 671–7.

Motto, J.A. (1967). Suicide and suggestibility. *American Journal of Psychiatry*, **124**, 156–9.

Mueller, C.W., Donnerstein, E. and Hallam, J. (1983). Violent films and prosocial behaviour. *Journal of Personality and Social Psychology*, **9**, 83–9.

Murdock, G. (1997). Reservoirs of dogma: an archaeology of popular anxieties. In M. Barker and J. Petley (Eds), *Ill Effects: The Media / Violence Debate* (pp. 67–86). London: Routledge.

Murdock, G. and McCron, R. (1979). The television and delinquency debate. *Screen Education*, **30** (Spring), 51–67.

Mustonen, A. and Pulkkinen, L. (1991). Content analysis of television violence. *Aggressive Behavior*, **17**(2), 87.

Naylor, B. (1995). Women's crime and media coverage: making explanations. In R.E. Dobash, R.P. Dobash, and L.Noaks (Eds), *Gender and Crime* (pp. 49–76). Cardiff: University of Wales Press.

Negrine, R. (1989). *Politics and the Mass Media*. London: Routledge.

Newson, E. (1994a). Video violence and the protection of children. *The Psychologist*, **7**(6), 272–4.

Newson, E. (1994b). Video violence and the protection of children. *Report of the Home Affairs Committee* (pp. 45–9). London: HMSO.

NIMH (National Institute of Mental Health) (1982). *Television and Behavior: Ten Years of Scientific Progress and Implications for the Eighties*. Rockville, MO: NIMH.

Nobile, P. and Nadler, E. (1986). *United States of America vs. Sex: How the Meese Commission Lied about Pornography*. New York: Minotaur.

Noble, G. (1975). *Children in Front of the Small Screen*. London: Constable.

Nutter, D.E. and Kearns, M.E.. (1993). Patterns of exposure to sexually explicit material among sex offenders, child molesters and controls. *Journal of Sex and Marital Therapy*, **19**(1), 77–85.

Office for National Statistics (1997). *Social Trends 27*. London: HMSO.

Olweus, D. (1980). The consistency issue in personality psychology revisited—with special reference to aggression. *British Journal of Social and Clinical Psychology*, **19**, 377–90.

Orcutt, J.D. and Turner, J.B. (1993). Shocking numbers and graphic accounts: quantified images of drug problems in the print media. *Social Problems*, **40**(2), 190–206.

Owusu-Bempah, J. (1995). Information about the absent parent as a factor in the well-being of children of single-parent families. *International Social Work*, **38**, 253–75.

Owusu-Bempah, J. (1997). Self-identity and black children in care. In M. Davies (Ed.), *The Blackwell Companion to Social Work, 1997*. London: Blackwell.

Paik, H. and Comstock, G. (1994). The effects of television violence on anti-social behavior: a meta-analysis. *Communication Research*, **21**(4), 516–46.

Paletz, D.L. (1988). Pornography, politics, and the press: the US Attorney General's Commission on Pornography. *Journal of Communication*, **38**(2), 122–36.

Parker, H. and Newcombe, R. (1987). Heroin use and acquisitive crime in an English community. *British Journal of Sociology*, **38**(3), 331–50.

Parker, I. (1989). *The Crisis in Modern Social Psychology and How to End It*. London: Routledge.

Parton, N. (1985). *The Politics of Child Abuse*. London: Macmillan.

Payne, D.E. and Payne, K.P. (1970). Newspapers and crime in Detroit. *Journalism Quarterly*, **47**, 233–8.

Peffley, M., Shields, T. and Williams, B. (1996). The intersection of race and crime in television news stories: an experimental study. *Political Communication*, **13**, 309–27.

Penrod, S.D. (1990). Predictors of jury decision making in criminal and civil cases: a field experiment. *Forensic Reports*, **3**, 261–77.

Perse, E.M., Ferguson, D.A. and McCleod, D.M. (1994). Cultivation in the newer media environment. *Communication Research*, **21**(1), 79–104.

Peterson, J.L., Moore, K.A. and Furstenberg, F.F. (1991). Television viewing and early initiation of sexual intercourse: is there a link? *Journal of Homosexuality*, **21**(1–2), 93–118.

Petley, J. (1997). Us and them. In M. Barker and J. Petley (Eds), *Ill Effects* (pp. 87–101). London: Routledge.

Pfuhl, E. (1960). *The Relationship of Mass Media to Reported Delinquent Behavior*. Unpublished doctoral dissertation, Washington State University.

Ann Arbor, Michigan: University Microfilms 61–1308.

Pfuhl, E. (1970). Mass media and reported delinquent behavior: a negative case. In M. Wolfgang, L. Savitz, and N. Johnson (Eds), *The Sociology of Crime and Delinquency* (pp. 509–23). New York: Wiley.

Philip, T. (1995). Crime not a black and blue issue. *The Guardian*, 10 July, p. 10.

Phillips, D.P. (1980). The deterrent effect of capital punishment: new evidence on an old controversy. *American Journal of Sociology*, **86**, 139–48.

Phillips, D.P. (1982). The impact of fictitional television stories on US adult fatalities: new evidence on the effect of the mass media on violence. *American Journal of Sociology*, **87**(6), 1340–59.

Phillips, D.P. (1983). The impact of mass media violence on US homicides. *American Sociological Review*, **48**, 560–68.

Phillips, D.P. and Castersen, L.L. (1986). Clustering of teenage suicides after television stories about suicide. *New England Journal of Medicine*, **315**, 685–9.

Phillips, D.P. and Hensley, J.E. (1984). When violence is rewarded or punished: the impact of mass media stories on homicide. *Journal of Communication*, **34**, 101–16.

Phillips, D.P. and Paight, D.J. (1987). The impact of televised movies about suicide: a replicative study. *New England Journal of Medicine*, **317**, 809–11.

Philo, G. (1993). *Media Representations of Mental Health / Illness: Audience Reception Study*. Report for the Health Education Board for Scotland. Glasgow: Glasgow University Media Group.

Piepe, A., Crouch, J. and Emerson, M. (1977). Violence and television. *New Society*, **41**, 536–8.

Pierce, C.M., Carew, J.V., Pierce-Gonzalez, D. and Wills, D. (1977). An experiment in racism: TV commercials. *Education and Urban Society*, **10**(1), 61–87.

Pizzey, E. (1974). *Scream Quietly or the Neighbours Will Hear*. Short Hills: Ridley Enslow.

Potter, W.J. (1986). Perceived reality and the cultivation hypothesis. *Journal of Broadcasing and Electronic Media*, **30**(2), 159–74.

Potter, W.J. (1993). Cultivation Theory and Research: a conceptual critique. *Human Communication Research*, **19**(4), 564–601.

Potter, W.J. and Chang, I.C. (1990). Television exposure measures and the cultivation hypothesis. *Journal of Broadcasting and Electronic Media*, **34**(3), 313–33.

Pritchard, D. (1986). Homicide and bargained justice: the agenda-setting effect of crime news on prosecutors. *Public Opinion Quarterly*, **50**, 143–59.

Propper, M.M. (1970). Exposure to sexually oriented materials among young male prison offenders. In *Technical Reports of the Commission on Obscenity and Pornography, Volume 9*. Washington, DC: US Government Printing Office.

Pryor, D.W. and McGarrell, E.F. (1993). Public perceptions of youth gang crime: an exploratory analysis. *Youth & Society*, **24**(4), 399–418.

Quinsey, V.L., Chaplin, T.C. and Upton, D. (1984). Sexual arousal to non-sexual violence and sadomasochistic themes among rapists and non-sex offenders. *Journal of Consulting and Clinical Psychology*, **52**, 651–7.

Quinsey, V.L., Steinman, C.M., Bergersen, S.G. and Holmes, T.F. (1975). Penile circumference, skin conductance, and ranking responses of child molesters and 'normals' to sexual and nonsexual visual stimuli. *Behavior Therapy*, **6**, 213–19.

Radford, J. and Russell, D.E.H. (Eds) (1992). *Femicide: The Politics of Woman*

Killing. Buckingham: Open University Press.

Rainville, R.E., Roberts, A. and Sweet, A. (1978). Recognition of covert racial prejudice. *Journalism Quarterly*, **55**(2), 256–9.

Reason, P. and Rowan, J. (1981). *Human Enquiry: A Sourcebook of New Paradigm Research*. London: Wiley.

Reeves, J.L. and Campbell, R. (1994). *Cracked Coverage: Television News, the Anti-cocaine Crusade and the Reagan Legacy*. Durham: Duke University Press.

Reid, P. and Finchilescu, G. (1995). The disempowering effects of media violence against women on college women. *Psychology of Women Quarterly*, **19**(3), 397–410.

Revitch, E. (1983).Burglaries with sexual dynamics. In L.B. Schlesinger and E. Revitch (Eds). *Sexual Dynamics of Anti-social Behavior* (pp. 173–91). Springfield, IL: Charles C. Thomas.

Roberts, J.V. and Doob, A.N. (1990). News media influences on public views of sentencing. *Law and Human Behavior*, **14**(5), 451–68.

Roberts, J.V. and Grossman, M.G. (1990). Crime prevention and public opinion. *Canadian Journal of Criminology*, **32**(1), 75–9.

Roberts, Y. (1995). Is this modern justice? *The Guardian*, 7 October, p. 6.

Robinson, L. (1995). *Psychology for Social Workers: Black Perspectives*. London: Routledge.

Roe, K. (1995). Adolescents' use of the socially disvalued media: towards a theory of media delinquency. *Journal of Youth and Adolescence*, **24**(5), 617–31.

Rogers, R.W. and Prentice-Dunn, S. (1981). Deindividuation and anger-mediated interracial aggression: unmasking regressive racism. *Journal of Personality and Social Psychology*, **41**(1), 63–73.

Roll, J. (1992). *Lone Parent Families in the European Community: The 1992 Report to the European Commission*. London: European Family and Social Policy Unit.

Rosenbaum, D.P. and Heath, L.O. (1988). The 'psycho-logic' of fear-reduction and crime-prevention programs. In S.P. Lab (Ed.), *Crime Prevention: Approaches, practices and evaluations* (pp. 221–46). Cincinnati, OH: C.J. Anderson.

Rosenbaum, D.P., Lurigio, A.J. and Lavraka, P.J. (1989). Enhancing citizen participation and solving serious crime: a national evaluation of crime stoppers programs. *Crime and Delinquency*, **35**(5), 401–20.

Rosenberg, H. (1995). Nervous in the naked city. In C.L. LaMay and E.E. Dennis (Eds), *The Culture of Crime* (pp. 103–10). New Brunswick: Transaction.

Rosengren, K.E., Wenner, L.A. and Palmgreen, P. (Eds) (1985). *Media Gratifications: Current Perspectives*. Beverly Hills, CA: Sage.

Roshier, R.J. (1969). Crime and the Press. Unpublished PhD thesis, University of Newcastle.

Roshier, R.J. (1971). Crime and the press. *New Society*, **468**, 502–6.

Roshier, R.J. (1973). The selection of crime news by the press. In S. Cohen and J. Young (Eds). *The Manufacture of News* (pp. 28–39). London: Constable.

Rowland, W.D. (1983). *The Politics of TV Violence: Policy Uses of Communication Research*. Beverly Hills, CA: Sage.

Rowland, W.D. (1997). Television violence redux: the continuing mythology of effects. In M. Barker and J. Petley (Eds), *Ill Effects* (pp. 102–19). London: Routledge,

Runnymede Trust (1993). Policing and racial violence. *The Runnymede Bulletin*, 267, July/August, p. 3.

Rushton, J.P. (1979). Effects of prosocial television and film material on the behavior of viewers. In L. Berkowitz (Ed.), *Advances in Experimental Social Psychology*, **12**, 322–51.

Rushton, J.P. (1982). Television and prosocial behavior. In D. Pearl, L. Bouthilet and J. Lazar (Eds), *Television and Behavior: Ten years of scientific progress* (pp. 248–58). Rockville, MD: National Institute of Mental Health.

Russell, D.E.H. (1988). Pornography and rape: a causal model. *Journal of Political Psychology*, **9**(1), 41–73.

Russell, D.E.H. (1992). Pornography and rape: a causal model. In C. Itzin (Ed.), *Pornography: Women, Violence and Civil Liberties* (pp. 310–49). Oxford University Press

Sacco, V.F. (1982). The effects of mass media on perceptions of crime. *Pacific Sociological Review*, **25**(4), 475–93.

Sacco, V.F. (1995). Media constructions of crime. *Annals of the American Academy of Political and Social Science*, **539**, 141–54.

Sacco, V.F. and Fair, B.J. (1988). Images of legal control: crime news and the process of organizational legitimation. *Canadian Journal of Communication*, **3**(3–4), 114–23.

Sacco, V.F. and Trotman, M. (1990). Public information programming and family violence: lessons from the mass media crime prevention experience. *Canadian Journal of Criminology*, **32**(1), 91–105.

Sanders, C.R. and Lyon, E. (1995). Repetitive retribution: media images and the cultural construction of criminal justice. In J. Ferrell and C.R. Sanders (Eds). *Cultural Criminology* (pp. 25–44). Boston, MA: Northeastern University Press,

Sanders, W.B. (1980). *Rape and Woman's Identity*. Beverly Hills, CA: Sage.

Sanderson, T. (1995). *Mediawatch*. London: Cassell.

Sapolsky, B.S. and Tarbarlet, J.O. (1991). Sex in prime time television: 1979 vs. 1989. *Journal of Broadcasting and Electronic Media*, **35**(4), 505–16.

Sarason, S.B. (1981). *Psychology Misdirected*. New York: The Free Press.

Schell, B.H. and Bonin, L. (1988). Understanding pornographic tolerance levels of community residents regarding three media: magazines, movies and video cassettes. *Annals of Sex Research*, **1**(4), 501–21.

Schlesinger, L.B. and Revitch, E. (Eds) (1983). *Sexual Dynamics of Anti-social Behaviour*. Springfield, IL: C. C. Thomas.

Schlesinger, P., Tumber, H. and Murdock, G. (1991). The media politics of crime and criminal justice. *British Journal of Sociology*, **42**(3), 397–420.

Schramm, W., Lyle, J. and Parker, E.B. (1961). *Television in the Lives of Our Children*. Stanford, CA: Stanford University Press.

Schudson, M. (1978). *Discovering the News: A Social History of American Newspapers*. New York: Basic Books.

Scott, J.E. (1986). An updated longitudinal content analysis of sex references in mass circulation magazines. *Journal of Sex Research*, **22**(3), 385–92.

Scott, J.E. and Cuvelier, S.J. (1987). Sexual violence in Playboy magazine: a longitudinal content analysis. *Journal of Sex Research*, **23**, 534–9.

Scott, J.E. and Schwalm, L.A. (1988). Pornography and rape: an examination of adult theater rates and rape rates by state. In J.E. Scott and T. Hirschi (Eds), *Controversial Issues in Crime and Justice* (pp. 40–53). Beverly Hills: Sage, CA.

Scottish Cocaine Research Group (1993). 'A very greedy sort of drug': portraits of Scottish cocaine users. In P. Bean (Ed.) *Cocaine and Crack: Supply and Use* (pp. 75–98). London: MacMillan.

Searle, C. (1989). *Your Daily Dose: Racism and the Sun*. London: Campaign for Press and Broadcasting Freedom.

Sears, D.O. (1988). Symbolic racism. In A. Katz and D.A. Taylor (Eds), *Eliminating Racism: profiles in controversy* (pp. 53–84). New York: Plenum Press.

Sears, D.O. and Freedman, J.L. (1967). Selective exposure to information: a critical review. *Public Opinion Quarterly*, **31**, 194–213.

Seggar, J.F., Hafen, J.K. and Hannonen, G.H. (1981). Television's portrayals of minorities and women in drama and comedy drama 1971–80. *Journal of Broadcasting*, **25**(3), 277–88.

Sheldon, W.H. (1949). *Varieties of Delinquent Youth*. New York: Harper.

Sheley, J.F., Brody, C.J., Wright, J.D. and Williams, M.A. (1994). Women and handguns: evidence from national surveys, 1973–1991. *Social Science Research*, **23**, 219–35.

Shoemaker, D.J. (1996). *Theories of Delinquency*, 3rd ed. Oxford University Press.

Short, C. (1991). *Dear Clare...* London: Hutchinson.

Shrum, L.J. (1996). Psychological processes underlying communication effects. *Human Communication Research*, **22**(4), 482–509.

Shuttleworth, F. and May, M. (1933). *The Social Conduct and Attitudes of Movie Fans*. New York: Macmillan.

Signorielli, N. (1985). *Role Portrayal and Stereotyping on Television*. Westport, CT: Greenwood.

Signorielli, N. and Gerbner, G. (1988). *Violence and Terror in the Mass Media*. New York: Greenwood.

Silverstone, R. (1989). Let us return to the murmurings of everyday practices. *Theory Culture and Society*, **6**, 77–94.

Simon, D. (1995). Cops, killers and crispy critters. In C.L. LaMay and E.E. Dennis (Eds) *The Culture of Crime* (pp. 35–45). New Brunswick: Transaction.

Simon, R.J. (1966). Murder, juries, and the press: does sensational reporting lead to verdicts of guilty? *Transaction*, **3**, 40–42.

Simon, R.R. and Eimermann, T. (1971). The jury finds not guilty: another look at media influence on the jury. *Journalism Quarterly*, **48**, 343–4.

Singer, D.G., Zuckerman, D.M. and Singer, J.L. (1980). Helping elementary school children learn about TV. *Journal of Communication*, **30**, 84–93.

Skogan, W.G. (1996). The police and public opinion in Britain. *American Behavioral Scientist*, **39**(4), 421–32.

Slade, W. (1984). Violence in the hard-core pornography film. *Journal of Communication*, **34**(3), 148–63.

Smith, A.A. and Jamieson, B.D. (1972). Effects of attitude and ego involvement on the learning and retention of controversial material. *Journal of Personality and Social Psychology*, **22**, 303–10.

Smith, A.M. (1995). The regulation of lesbian sexuality through erasure: the case of Jennifer Saunders. In K. Jay (Ed.). *Lesbian Erotics* (pp. 164–79). New York: New York University Press.

Smith, D.D. (1976). The social content of pornography. *Journal of Communication*, **26**, 16–33.

Snyder, S. (1995). Movie portrayals of juvenile-delinquency: Part II. Sociology and Psychology. *Adolescence*, **30**(118), 325–7.

Soble, A. (1986). *Pornography, Marxism, Feminism and the Future of Sexuality*.

New Haven, CT: Yale University Press.

Soothill, K. and Walby, S. (1991). *Sex Crime in the News*. London: Routledge.

Sparks, G.G. and Ogles, R.M. (1990). The difference between fear of victimization and the probability of being victimized: implications for cultivation. *Journal of Broadcasting and Electronic Media*, **34**(3), 351–8.

Sparks, R. (1995). Entertaining the crisis: television and moral enterprise. In D. Kidd-Hewitt and R. Osborne (Eds), *Crime and the Media: the Post-Modern spectacle* (pp. 49–66). London: Pluto.

Spivack, G., Marcus, J. and Swift, M. (1986). Early classroom behaviors and later misconduct. *Developmental Psychology*, **22**(1), 124–31.

Sprafkin, J., Gadow, K.D. and Kant, G. (1988). Teaching emotionally disturbed children to discriminate reality from fantasy on television. *Journal of Special Education*, **21**(4), 99–107.

Sprafkin, J., Swift, C. and Hess, R. (1983). *Television: Enhancing the Preventative Impact of TV*. New York: Haworth.

Stack, S. (1987). Publicized Executions and Homicide, 1950–1980. *American Sociological Review*, **52**, 532–40.

Stack, S. (1992). The effect of the media on suicide: the Great Depression. *Suicide and Life Threatening Behavior*, **22**(2), 255–67.

Stalans, L.J. (1996). Family harmony or individual protection. *American Behavioral Scientist*, **39**(4), 433–48.

Stanko, E.A. (1995). Women, crime, and fear. *Annals of the American Association for Political and Social Science*, **539**, 46–58.

Stark, E. (1993). The myth of black violence. *Social Work*, **38**(4), 485–90.

Steinmetz, S. (1977). The battered husband syndrome. *Victimology*, **2**, 499–509.

Stimson, G.V. (1975). The message of psychotropic drug ads. *Journal of Communication*, **25**, 153–60.

Stipp, H. and Milavsky, J.R. (1988). US television programming's effect on aggressive behavior of children and adolescents. *Current Psychology Research and Reviews*, **7**(1), 76–92.

Straus, M. (1992). Sociological research and social policy: the case of family violence. *Sociological Forum*, **7**(2), 211–37.

Stroman, C.A. and Settger, R. (1985). Media use and perceptions of crime. *Journalism Quarterly*, **62**(2), 340–45.

Sue, S., Smith, R.E. and Gilbert, R. (1974). Biasing effects of pretrial publicity on judicial decisions. *Journal of Criminal Justice*, **2**, 163–71.

Sumner, C. (Ed.) (1990). *Censure, Politics and Criminal Justice*. Milton Keynes: Open University Press.

Surette, R. (1990). Estimating the effect of copycat crime. In R. Surette (Ed.), *The Media and Criminal Justice Policy: Recent Research and Social Effects* (pp. 87–101). Springfield, IL: Charles C. Thomas.

Surette, R. (Ed.) (1990). *The Media and Criminal Justice Policy: Recent Research and Social Effects* (pp. 129–42). Springfield, IL: Charles C. Thomas.

Surette, R. (1992). *Media, Crime and Criminal Justice*. Pacific Grove, CA: Brooks/Cole.

Surgeon General's Scientific Advisory Committee on Television and Social Behavior (1972). *Television and Growing Up: The Impact of Televised Violence*. Washington, DC: US Government Printing Office.

Surlin, S.H. and Tate, E.D. (1976). 'All in the Family': is Archie funny? *Journal of Communication*, **26**, 6108.

Szasz, T. (1986). The case against suicide prevention. *American Psychologist*, **41**(7), 806–12.

Tan, A.S. and Tan, G. (1979). Television use and self-esteem of blacks. *Journal of Communication*, **26**, 129–35.

Tans, M.D. and Chaffee, S.H. (1966). Pretrial publicity and juror prejudice. *Journalism Quarterly*, **43**, 647–54.

Tannenbaum, P. (1971). Studies of film- and television-mediated arousal and aggression: a progress report. In G.A. Comstock, E.A. Rubenstein, and J.P. Murray (Eds), *Television and Social Behavior, Vol 5: Television Effects*. Washington, DC: US Government Printing Office.

Tannenbaum, P.H. and Zillmann, D. (1975). Emotional arousal in the facilitation of aggression through communication. In L. Berkowitz (Ed.), *Advances in Experimental Social Psychology*, Vol. 8. New York: Academic Press.

Tarde, G. (1912). *Penal Philosophy*. London: Heinemann.

Tedeschi, J.T. and Felson, R.B. (1994). *Violence, Aggression and Coercive Actions*. Washington, DC: American Psychological Association.

Teff, H. (1975). *Drugs, Society and the Law*. Farnborough: Saxon House.

Thompson, B. (1994). *Soft Core: Moral Crusades Against Pornography in Britain and America*. London: Cassell.

Thurstone, L.L. (1931). Influence of Motion Pictures on Children's Attitudes. *Journal of Social Psychology*, **2**, 291–301.

Thurstone, L.L. and Chave, E.J. (1929). *The Measurement of Attitude*. Chicago: University of Chicago Press.

Torrey, E.F. (1994). Violent behavior by individuals with serious mental illness. *Hospital and Community Psychiatry*, **45**(7), 653–62.

Tremblay, R.E., McCord, J., Boileau, H., Charlesbois, Ganon, C., Le Blanc, M. and Larivee, S. (1991). Can disruptive boys be helped to become competent? *Psychiatry*, **54**, 148–61.

Tunnel, K.D. (1992). Film at eleven: recent developments in the commodification of crime. *Sociological Spectrum*, **12**, 293–313.

US Attorney General's Commission on Pornography (1986). *Final Report*. Washington, DC: US Department of Justice.

US Department of Commerce, Economics and Statistics Information (1996). *Statistical Abstract of the United States*. Washington, DC: US Government Printing Office.

Udry, R. and Ecland, B. (1984). Benefits of being attractive: differential payoffs for men and women. *Psychological Reports*, **54**, 47–56.

van Dijk, T.A. (1991). *Racism and the Press*. London: Routledge.

Viemero, V. (1996). Factors in childhood that predict later criminal behavior. *Aggressive Behavior* **22**(2), 87–97.

Vidimar, N. and Rokeach, M. (1974). Archie Bunker's bigotry: a study in Selective perception and exposure. *Journal of Communication*, **24**, 36–47.

Vine, I. (1997) The dangerous psycho-logic of media 'effects'. In M. Barker and J. Petley (Eds), *Ill Effects: The Media/Violence Debate* (pp. 125–46). London: Routledge

Vitelli, R. and Endler, N.S. (1993). Psychological determinants of fear of crime: a comparison of general and situational prediction models. *Personality and Individual Differences*, **145**(1), 77–85.

Vold, G.B. and Bernard, T.J. (1986). *Theoretical Criminology*, 3rd edn. Oxford: Oxford University Press.

Vooijs, M.W. and van der Voort, T.H.A. (1993). Learning about television violence: the impact of a critical viewing curriculum on children's attitudinal judgements of crime series. *Journal of Research and Development in Education*, **26**(3), 133–42.

Voumvakis, S.E. and Ericson, R.V. (1982). *News Accounts of Attacks on Women. A Comparison of Three Toronto Newspapers*. Toronto: University of Toronto, Centre of Criminology.

Waddington, P.A.J. (1986). Mugging as a moral panic. *The British Journal of Sociology*, **37**(2), 245–59.

Wahl, O.F. and Roth, R. (1982). Television images of mental illness: results of a metropolitan Washington media watch. *Journal of Broadcasting*, **26**, 599–605.

Wahl, O.F. and Lefkowitz, J,Y. (1989). Impact of a television film on attitudes towards mental illness. *American Journal of Community Psychology*, **17**(4), 521–8.

Walker, C.E. (1970). Erotic stimuli and the aggressive sexual offender. In *Technical Reports of the Commission on Obscenity and Pornography*, Vol. 7. Washington DC: US Government Printing Office.

Wallerstein, J. and Kelly, J. (1974). The effects of parental divorce: The adolescent experience. In E. J. Anthony and C. Koupernik (Eds), *The Child in His Family: Children at Psychiatric Risk*. New York: Wiley.

Wallerstein, J. and Kelly, J. (1980). *Surviving the Break-up: How Parents and Children Cope with Divorce*. London: Grant McIntyre.

Walmsley, R. (1986). *Personal violence*. Home Office Research Studies No. 89. London: HMSO.

Walter, N. (1996). Dead women who suit the news agenda. *The Guardian*, 18 January, p. 15.

Wanta, W. and Foote, J. (1994). The President–news media relationship: a time series analysis of agenda-setting. *Journal of Broadcasting and Electronic Media*, **38**(4), 437–48.

Warner, W.L. and Henry, W.E. (1948). The radio daytime serial: a symbolic analysis. *Genetic Psychology Monographs*, **37**, 3–71.

Wartella, E. and Reeves, B. (1985). Historical trends in research on children and the media, 1900–1960. *Journal of Communication*, **3**, 118–33.

Wasserman, I.R. and Stack, S. (1994). Communal violence and the media: lynchings and their news coverage by the *New York Times* between 1882 and 1930. In G. Barak (Ed.), *Media, Process, and the Social Construction of Crime* (pp. 69–94). New York: Garland.

Watkins, L. and Worcester, R.M. (1986). *Private Opinions, Public Polls*. London: Thames and Hudson.

Weigel, R.H. and Howes, P.W. (1982). Race relations on children's television. *Journal of Psychology*, **111**, 109–12.

Weimann, G. and Gabor, T. (1987). Placing the blame for crime in press reports. *Deviant Behavior* **8**, 283–97.

Wetherell, M. and Potter, J. (1992). *Mapping the Language of Racism*. London: Harvester Wheatsheaf.

White, G.F. (1989). Media and violence: the case of professional football championship games. *Aggressive Behavior*, **15**, 423–33.

White, G.F., Katz, J. and Scarborough, V.E. (1992). The impact of professional football games upon violent assault on women. *Violence and Victims*, **7**(2), 157–71.

Whitney, C., Wartella, E., Lasorsa, D., Danielson, W., Olivarez, A., Lopez, R. and Klijn, M. (1997). Television violence in 'reality' programming. In *National Television Violence Study*, Vol. 1 (pp. 269–359). Newbury Park, CA: Sage.

Wiegman, O., Kuttschreuter, M. and Barda, B. (1992). A longitudinal study of television viewing on aggressive and prosocial behaviours. *British Journal of*

Social Psychology, **31**, 147–64.

Wiio, O.A. (1995). Is television a killer? An international comparison. *Intermedia*, **23**(2), 26–31.

Wilcox, B.L. (1987). Pornography, social science, and politics: when research and ideology collide. *American Psychologist*, **42**(10), 941–3.

Wilhoit, G.C. and de Bock, H. (1976). 'All in the family' in Holland. *Journal of Communication*, **26**, 75–84.

Wilkie, C. (1981). The scapegoating of Bruno Richard Hauptmann: the rhetorical process in prejudicial publicity. *Central States Speech Journal*, **32**, 100–110.

Williams, B. (1979). *Report of the Committee on Pornography and Censorship*. London: HMSO, Cmd. 7772.

Williams, S. (1988). *Psychology on the Couch*. Hemel Hempstead: Harvester Wheatsheaf.

Williams, T.M., Zabrack, M.L. and Joy, L.A. (1982). The portrayal of aggression on North American television. *Journal of Applied Social Psychology*, **12**, 360–80.

Wilson, B.J., Linz, D., Donnerstein, E. and Stipp, H. (1992). The impact of social issue television programming on attitudes towards rape. *Human Communications Research*, **19**(2), 179–208.

Wilson, W. and Hunter, R. (1983). Movie-inspired violence. *Psychological Reports*, **55**, 435–44.

Winick, C. and Evans, J.T. (1996). The relationship between nonenforcement of State pornography laws and rates of sex crime arrests. *Archives of Sexual Behavior*, **25**(5), 439–53.

Winkel, F.W. (1990). Crime reporting in newspapers: an exploratory study of the effects of ethnic references in crime news. *Social Behavior*, **5**, 87–101.

Wober, M. and Gunter, B. (1982). Television and personal threat: fact or artifact? a British survey. *British Journal of Social Psychology*, **21**, 239–47.

Wober, M. and Gunter, B. (1988). *Television and Social Control*. Aldershot: Ayebury.

Wood, W., Wong, F.Y. and Chachere, J.G. (1991). Effects of media violence on viewers' aggression in unconstrained social interaction. *Psychological Bulletin*, **109**(3), 371–83.

Wormith, J.A. (1986). Assessing deviant sexual arousal: physiological and cognitive aspects. *Advances in Behaviour Research and Therapy*, **8**(3), 101–37.

Wykes, M. (1995). Passion, marriage and murder. In R.E. Dobash, R.P. Dobash, and L. Noaks (Eds), *Gender and Crime* (pp. 77–95). Cardiff: University of Wales Press.

Wyre, R. (1987). *Working with Sex Offenders*. Oxford: Perry.

Wyre, R. (1990). Why do men sexually abuse children? In T. Tate, *Child Pornography* (pp. 281–8). London: Methuen.

Wyre, R. (1992). Pornography and sex offenders: working with sex offenders. In C. Itzin (Ed.), *Pornography: Women, Violence and Civil Liberties* (pp. 236–47). Oxford: Oxford University Press,

Wyre, R. and Tate, T. (1995). *The Murder of Childhood*. Harmondsworth: Penguin.

Yeboah, S.K. (1988). *The Ideology of Racism*. London: Hansib.

Young, A. (1996a). *Imagining Crime: Textual Outlaws and Criminal Conversations*. London: Sage.

Young, A. (1996b). In the frame: crime and the limits of representation. *The Australian and New Zealand Journal of Criminology*, **29**(2), 81–101.

Zillmann, D. (1978). Attribution and misattribution of excitatory reactions. In J.H. Harvey, W.J. Ickes and R.F. Kidd (Eds), *New Directions in Attribution Research*, Vol. 2. Hillsdale, NJ: Erlbaum.

Zillmann, D. (1979). *Hostility and Aggression*. Hillsdale, NJ: Erlbaum.

Zillmann, D. (1982). Television viewing and arousal. In D. Pearl, L. Bouthilet and J. Law (Eds), *Television and Behavior. Ten years of Scientific Progress and Implications for the Eighties*. Washington, DC: US Government Printing Office.

Zillman, D. and Bryant, D. (1986a). A response. *Journal of Communication*, **36**(1), 184–8.

Zillmann, D. and Bryant, J. (1986b). Exploring the entertainment experience. In J. Bryant and D. Zillmann (Eds), *Perspectives on Media Effects* (pp. 303–24). Hillsdale, NJ: Erlbaum.

Zillman, D. and Bryant, D. (1987a). A reply. *Journal of Communication*, **37**(3), 189–92.

Zillman, D. and Bryant, D. (1987b). A response. *Journal of Communication*, **37**(3), 187–8.

Zillman, D. and Johnson, R. (1973). Motivated aggressiveness perpetrated by exposure to aggressive films and reduced by non-aggressive films. *Journal of Research in Personality*, **7**, 261–76.

Zimet, S.G. (1976). *Print and Prejudice*. London: Hodder and Stoughton.

Author Index

Subject Index

Related titles of interest...

Offender Profiling
Theory, Research and Practice
Janet L. Jackson and Debra A. Bekerian

Explores the role of offender profiling in criminal investigations and supporting a legal case.

Wiley Series in Psychology of Crime, Policing & Law
0-471-97564-8   254pp   1997   Hardback
0-471-97565-6   254pp   1997   Paperback

Making Sense with Offenders
Personal Constructs, Therapy and Change
Julia Houston

Informs about the clinical application of personal construct theory to offenders, enabling practitioners to use this approach in their assessment and treatment of a wide range of offending behaviour..

Wiley Series in Offender Rehabilitation
0-471-95415 2   288pp   1998   Hardback
0-471-96627 4   288pp   1998   Paperback

Therapeutic Communities for Offenders
Eric Cullen, Lawrence Jones and Roland Woodward

Summarises examples of 'best practice' that therapeutic communities can offer to offenders in the UK, Europe and the United States.

Wiley Series in Offender Rehabilitation
0-471-96545-6   296pp   1997   Hardback
0-471-96980-X   296pp   1997   Paperback

Changing Lives of Crime and Drugs
Intervening with Substance-Abusing Offendes
Glenn D. Walters

Provides a practical model for intervention, detailed guidelines for related work with offenders, and illustrative examples and case studies.

Wiley Series in Offender Rehabilitation
0-471-97658-X   154pp   1998   Hardback
0-471-97841-8   154pp   1998   Paperback